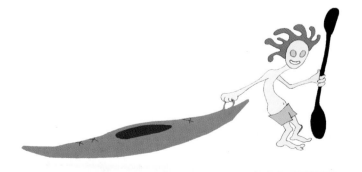

The Guide to
Baja Sea Kayaking
The Sea of Cortez and Magdalena Bay

Near Punta Colorada, Isla San José

The Guide to Baja Sea Kayaking
The Sea of Cortez and Magdalena Bay

International Standard Book Number: 978-0-9645399-1-4

Book design by Dave Eckardt and Ken Nager,
created by Ken Nager and Treehouse Creations. www.treehousecreations.net

Photography by Dave Eckardt unless otherwise noted

Town maps by Dave Eckardt, except San Felipe, by Thomas Carlin and Dave Eckardt

Wildlife stories by Lori Russell, except Coyote Camp, by Dave

Artwork by Lori and Dave

Edited by Nicolle Sloane

Printed in China through Global Interprint, Inc. Santa Rosa, California. www.globalinterprint.com

Published by David Eckardt and Paddle Publishing

Coastlines, towns, seas and oceans are dynamic mediums and are changing. Consequently, a guidebook about changing mediums is bound to have inaccuracies. You may find flaws in the mapwork, coast descriptions, or other information contained herein, and we apologize for them. If you would like to correct or inform us, please do so at:
www.paddlepublishing.com

Note: The author of this book assumes no responsibility for the well being of any user of this book. It is understood that sea kayaking involves inherent and integral risks and dangers. Users of this book are liable for their own actions. The publishers or author of *The Guide to Baja Sea Kayaking* cannot be held responsible for accidents incurred on any kayak leg, or getting to or from any kayak leg. The author does not advocate the paddling of any kayak leg, he only offers a menu of opportunities. Please read all introductory material.

5% of the profits from sales of this book will be donated to organizations that preserve wilderness shoreline in Baja Califonia.

Cover Photo: Dawn launch from Ligui

Library of Congress Cataloging-in-Pub. Data:
Eckardt, David
ISBN# 978-0-9645399-1-4
1. sea kayaking 2. Baja
3. Sea of Cortez 4. Magdalena Bay

Baja, California

Roads and Towns

Tijuana
Mexicali
Ensenada
Santo Tomas
San Felipe
San Quintin
Puertecitos
El Rosario
B. Gonzaga
Cataviña
Calamajue
Isla A. de la Guarda
P. Prieta
Isla Tiburón
B. de los Angeles
Midriff Islands
San Francisquito
Jesus Maria
Guerrero Negro
El Arco
B. Tortugas
Viscaino
San Ignacio
Santa Rosalia
Mulege
Abreojos
San Nicolás
Sea of Cortez
Pacific Ocean
Loreto
Isla Carmen
Isla Catalina
C. Insurgentes
Lopez Mateos
C. Constitución
Isla San Jose
San Evaristo
San Carlos
B. Magdalena
Chale
Isla Espiritu Santo
Isla Cerralvo
La Paz
Todos Santos
Cabo San Lucas
Cabo San José

image by SatPrints.com

Table of
Contents

Sea cave in southern Baja, Photo by: Tom Merrill

Chapter	Page

Sea of Cortez

Pacific Ocean

N
W E
S

image by SatPrints.com

Acknowledgements:

The creation of this book comes with the help and input of a number of people, and I am grateful and thankful for all who contributed knowledge, pictures, friendship, and advice. If I have forgotten anybody from this list, my apologies.

Dave Erskine, Doug Driskell, Nicolle Sloane, Stephen Bedford, Craig Miller, Rueben Daggett and sons, Alberto Walfors, John Fradess, Rito, Herb and Jenette, Diane Madsen, Tim Madsen, Debbie Karls, Ken, Woodcrafter Ben, Suzanne Clarke, Ben Gillam, Torrey Russell, Thomas Carlin, Mike Higgins, Robert Jensen, Guitar Mike, Photoshark, Tim Means, Flickr photo pals, John Granatar, Arman Eshraghi, Robin Lilly, Cap'n Ron, and all people not mentioned here that were partners on a Baja voyage with me.

A special thanks to the:
Global Land Cover Facility
Earth Science Data Interface
University of Maryland
College Park, Maryland
http://glcfapp.umiacs.umd.edu
for providing the Landsat satellite images that comprise the body of this book.

Dedication

And in extra acknowledgement for their contributions to this project and their companionship and direction on many of the voyages that were the foundation of this work, this book is dedicated to:

Tom "Cardo" Merrill—a lover of the true Baja peninsula

and Lori Russell—my confidant and life partner, and also a lover of Baja.

Introduction

Interior desert, Photo by: Lori Russell

Welcome to Baja. It is the most beautiful desert. It is the most beautiful sea. It is the most beautiful ocean. As a sea kayaker at this dry paradise of coasts, you will get to experience consistently sunny weather as your boat glides on sapphire waters past majestic headlands. You will camp under an impressive array of stars, amongst good people, with good food, and go to bed completely tired after another long day of chores, exercise, and fresh air. Your hair will be salty from the day's swim, and you will not be able to wash it because there is no fresh water to spare. And it will feel healthy. Your possessions will be all around you, close by—your tent, your supplies, and your boat: your sleek, versatile, and personal vehicle of travel through this fantastic environment. You will be on a stage of reality where decisions and strategies have immediate impact on your well-being. The desert and the sea and the air will rule your environment. Life will be uncomplicated and direct, and you will be strong and aware.

In many ways the body of this book speaks for itself. It is an annotated map showing, describing, and waypointing the eastern coast and islands of Baja California, Mexico. The book also describes and maps the primary Baja sea kayaking towns: where to shop, stay, camp, store a car, and launch. As well, there are wildlife stories scattered through the guide colorfully depicting some of the fantastic critters that roam the area. To get a taste of the Pacific, the huge Magdalena Bay area (winter home of the migratory grey whale) on the west coast of Baja is included. What an exceptional place that is! But the book's focus is on the Sea of Cortez, which because of its more protected nature and milder weather than the Pacific is the primary zone of sea kayaking for Baja.

Most general descriptions of weather and waves in the book are geared to the eastern side of the peninsula. Magdalena Bay's weather and Pacific boating in general is discussed in a final chapter. In all, including circumnavigations of some 30 islands, there are approximately 1,500 miles of shoreline covered. The guide is laid out north-to-south going down the peninsular coast and clockwise around the islands. This keeps the predominant winds at a paddler's back for a coastal run and has the inside west shore of an island protecting him from the brunt of a possible north wind as he paddles to the tip of the island.

The book is not as much of a "how to" book as it is a "where to" book. It is geared to alerting you to what places and conditions you may experience while on a sea kayaking leg. For those looking for instruction on kayaking technique, you may find useful information in anecdotes and tidbits within the leg descriptions from which may be gleamed knowledge of the sport, but that information is not directly supplied. The book will tell you how to pull off a successful Baja sea kayak adventure, but it is not intrinsically instructional. Though there is plenty of beginner terrain covered here, (Bahía Concepción and much of Bahía Magdalena, for instance), it is mainly written from a standpoint that assumes the reader has prior knowledge of the basic "how to's" of sea kayaking.

Baja California is a unique environment, with contrasts in nature unduplicated in the world:

On one hand it is desert, harsh and austere, yet enchanting in its sparse beauty. The peninsula is predominantly mountainous, arising from volcanic activity and jarring plate tectonics that pulled it apart from the mainland and allowed the sea to rush in thousands of years ago. And there are large valleys and open swaths of land between the ranges. There is something about the huge vistas of mountain and plain, of changing lights, that just speaks "freedom." Freedom to move; freedom to think.

On the other hand it is the sea, and though at times having its own desert-like appearance as a two-dimensional plain of water, at different times it is lively, with wind whipping up waves that dance and break into the air and

Islas San Diego and Santa Cruz

onto the shore. And what goes on under the surface is always amazing. The Sea of Cortez harbors the most species of marine life found in any body of water on the planet. From marlin, sailfish, manta rays, dolphin, and whales, down to small but intensely colored reef fish, and everything in between, the Sea of Cortez is abundant in life. Granted, due to over-fishing it isn't what it used to be, but it is still rich and active.

Connecting the desert and the sea are the animals that move between the two. There are pelicans flying up high or floating inches above the curl of a breaking wave, boobies, herons, gulls screeching, oyster catchers loudly peeping as they talk to each other or defend their turf, osprey hunting with that falcon eye and terrible claw, small grebes diving under water, frigates soaring high above... Sitting in camp in the morning or evening is sometimes like being in a live IMAX movie about seashore life—dolphins will pass by while gulls circle and pelicans crash into the water. There is a lot going on here.

And yet, there is a staggered timelessness to Baja. It is hard to find another place that so quietly speaks of eons—not necessarily because of the geology of the peninsula, which is relatively recent, but because of some intangible atmospheric attitude that pervades the air down here. The days talk slowly. The vast energy of the sea and barren rock becomes part of a paddler after a while. There is often a subtle sameness from one day to the next that moves a boater beyond his normal way of thinking and releases him from his civilized reality. And he grows inside himself in this slowness of dry desert and warm sea as he begins to comprehend the world around him.

But things are changing in Baja. Or rather, they are being changed. It was not too long ago that Baja Sur, the area from south of Guerrero Negro to Los Cabos, was only a sparsely populated territory, not even an official state of Mexico. The road to Los Cabos was not paved until the mid 1970's. Cabo San Lucas was a fishing village then. Now it is a bustling metropolis of high-rise hotels and streets clogged with crazy traffic. And the Cabo phenomenon is spreading to the rest of Baja. It is a disease that says one's oceanfront dreams should be realized at the side of a swimming pool, with the ocean better to be seen but not experienced. It is a disease that says the desert is ugly and should be plowed over to make room for a lush golf course. It is a disease that has people roaring up what used to be peaceful and sublime arroyos in groups of dust-crazed, helmeted ATV'ers in the name of recreation.

Baja is over-developing fast. The quaint and special towns that lend a paddling trip down here extra character are feeling resort and population pressure: La Paz now, Loreto soon, and possibly Mulegé and Bahía de los Angeles next. A number of the beautiful wilderness beaches described in this book are being plotted as future hotel sights. There are still many quiet places to go to, either because population pressure for development hasn't reached there yet, or because of resourceful action by conservation groups who have made a crusade of purchasing shorefront property to keep it out of the hands of the resort builders—but plans are in the making to develop many of the now-pristine beaches and valleys described in this book.

So the next ten to twenty years will be some of Baja's best before more coast gets plowed under. We have a wonderful sport here, sea kayaking. It is an activity, or perhaps a way of life, where you can experience a timeless place of power and splendor at a pace that puts you in synch with it. It is an activity that lets you see more by traveling slower, gracefully, and with minimal intrusion on the world around you. The Baja peninsula is a most singular area, and its adjoining sea is a star, glittering like a jewel upon the planet. Be here and experience the beauty of this place, and of yourself.

Weather

at the Sea of Cortez

If there is one word to describe the climate of Baja, it is "dry." This is a desert environment, and precipitation is seldom. On average for the whole peninsula it rains less than 10 inches per year, with more in the mountains and less at the low-lying areas. When it comes to protection from the elements, a paddler needs protection from sun more than from rain—because sun is the norm down here.

Daytime temperatures for north Baja along the Sea are (°F) 90's to low 100's in the summer and 50's to low 70's in the winter. The average daily temps for south Baja along the sea are high 90's to low 100's in the summer and 70's in the winter. Summers are brutally hot in places, with the sand sizzling on the beaches. It's a mad dash from the shade to the water in summer, forget the in between. One paddler I know who boated the coast from San Felipe to Cabo in July said he gave up paddling at daytime and switched to paddling at night to keep cool. (He only dented his boat three times!)

Winters on the other hand cool down noticeably, with pleasant days that are great for making miles in the boat. This is an especially good time to hike, as warmer months can be a real test in the desert. Though days are nice, it's necessary to have a good sweater to keep the chill off at night in winter. There can be a significant variation in temperature between day and night, often in the 25° range.

But it does rain in Baja occasionally. At the northern Sea of Cortez, most chances for rain come in the winter months, when a cyclonic storm generated in the North Pacific may be strong enough to make its way down to Baja after passing over the western United States. In the southern Sea of Cortez, most of the rain for the year comes in the fall, particularly the month of September, and originates in the tropical Eastern Pacific. This can include hurricanes. These storms usually track from southeast of the Cape near Acapulco and travel west or north, sometimes hitting Baja.

South of Santa Rosalia, looking towards Las Tres Virgenes.

Weather (Continued)

Events like hurricanes cause massive floods in the usually dry arroyos that line the peninsula, creating havoc with the roads, amongst other things. The northern winter storms are of a milder and steadier duration, possibly up to a few days, though flooding can still occur.

A seldom encountered storm system, occurring in summer and starting with a south wind, is the *torito*. This is a brief but violent event that can appear in the distance as a patch of very troubled sea, perhaps with lightning above it. I have never encountered this mysterious event, and was almost skeptical of it until talking with a gringo fisherman in Alfonsina's Restaurant at Bahía Gonzaga while looking out at the bright blue waters of the bay. He told of being out on a panga and returning from a fishing trip when they spotted a disturbance on the water not far from shore and in the direction they were heading. Paying little attention to it at first, they got closer and before they knew it the squall was upon them and they were fighting for their lives in very large and agitated seas. He recalled the violence of the water being as much as the panga could handle, that they were basically powerless while in the storm, and that it was only with luck that they got out of it or it dissipated, I can't remember which.

Despite the usual lack of rain, moisture along the seashore can come in the form of dew. When nighttime sets in, certain beaches seem prone to sweating copious amounts of it, while others stay dry. I am fond of sleeping without a tent, and often find myself paying the price of a drenched sleeping bag in the morning. The "Mulege to Loreto" leg seems particularly dew prone. But drying gear out down here under the daytime sun is never much of a problem.

Sea temperatures vary, with the mean average surface temperature being 75° F. The northern sea warms up surprisingly fast in the spring because it is quite shallow. The southern sea warms up slow because of its depth and proximity to the cool Pacific. In winter, the water temps will challenge snorkelers if they wish to stay in the water for any length of time. A good wetsuit is recommended for diving then, whereas a lesser one or none at all will do for much of the rest of the year. An exception to this is the waters of the Midriff region where the sea is pinched between Baja and the mainland causing increased tidal currents and a dredging up of cold water from the depths. Swimming can be numbing in the Midriff, even in warmer months.

Because of the lack of rain, when people refer to weather coming into Baja, they are usually talking about wind. Wind is the big issue for climate in Baja when sea kayaking. A contrary wind can slow things down considerably and dictate landing strategies because of the surf it creates. Paddling against certain winds can be like walking into a soft wall—it's a strange sensation to be out on the water a long time and hardly see the scenery along shore change while the whitecaps around you are churning with energy. In summer, the predominant wind is the southerly; in winter, it is the northerly. The northerlies can come from a winter storm system sweeping into Baja from the north (often with the wind starting from the south), but usually they are not associated with any visible signs of weather. Rather, northerlies commonly occur when clear high pressure parks itself over the Mojave Desert and Great Basin area to the north and cooler air rushes to escape it and blows south down the Sea of Cortez alley.

The other wind of note is the westerly. These are particularly unpredictable and risky because they blow away from shore, keeping paddlers out to sea if they are offshore and trying to get in. Though they might not create the surf the northerlies do, westerlies howl and can really stick it to a paddler or a tent, especially a paddler trying to set up a tent. These winds, well known in the Bahía de los Angeles area, also happen at other parts of the coast, but not as regularly. They are katabatic and generated by nighttime cooling air sweeping down mountain valleys because of its weight. These winds can blow for multiple days at a time.

Waiting for the sun, Bahía de los Ángeles,
Photo by: Lori Russell

Here are a few websites that are useful for Baja weather:

www.weatherunderground.com the tropical and marine links show developing storms and their projected tracks

www.iwindsurf.com air temperature, wind speed and wind direction a week at a time

www.buoyweather.com wind speed and direction, wave height and direction

www.wetsand.com Pacific swell size and direction

Beaches

While the Baja coasts have wondrous desert mountain geology up and down them to gaze upon, the Baja paddler much of the day is thinking ahead about where the next landing will be, and how it will be, based on the make-up of the beach and the conditions of the sea striking its shore.

Isla San José cobble beach, Photo by: Suzanne Clarke

Isla San José sandstone shield, Photo by: Suzanne (

The variety of camp terrain listed in this book varies from pure white sand beaches of vast expanse to rock shelves in minor alcoves. But basically, there are four types of beaches that categorize Baja seaside camps: sand beaches, cobble beaches, gravel beaches, and rock beaches.

Most people are familiar with sand beaches as being the beach of choice to aim for in selecting a camp. The white sand beach certainly forms the "Baja image" when people think about seaside camping here. If nothing else, these are the beaches commercial outfitters look for and camp upon most often. Sand beaches are beautiful. The landings they provide are preferred, and there is a pleasure and sensuality to walking on sand that is hard to duplicate in life's experiences. But sand beaches are not ideal camps. One of camping's worst problems is getting sand in your food. Everybody camping out looks forward to the next meal with eager anticipation both for the social experience and the nourishment factor, but sand in food ruins a dining experience, no matter how good the company or how beautiful the setting. A camp on sand can turn into a constant struggle to keep the pesky particles out of all the wrong places they finds their way into. Just crawling into a tent is harder when you have to wipe the sand off your partially wet feet multiple times a day.

Even though cobble is rock, it is its own category because it is rounded and can be walked on if it is stable and slept on if it is small enough. Cobble can also be landed on carefully without damaging a kayak if the beach is not too steep. Cobble beaches can be good camp beaches if the cobblestones are not too big. Food stays sand-free, and sleeping can be comfortable if you have a thick enough pad. One way to smooth out cobble for sleeping is to level a spot as best you can beforehand, and then fill in gaps between stones with lesser stones or gravel via collapsible bucket before setting up a tent or laying out a tarp. A little-appreciated attractiveness to cobble beaches that the gremlin in me loves is the ability to do accelerated launches from up high on the beach if you have a plastic boat. This can be a useful tool if surf has moved in overnight. You don't have to fight your sprayskirt right on the surf line and then try to break through waves with no momentum. A sliding launch means you can be combat-ready before you hit the water and when you splash in you are like a dart and can split that first wave in two before it has a chance to turn you sideways.

Rock beaches are usually poor camps made up of angular stones not conducive to landing, walking, or sleeping. However, occasionally a rock camp is a shelf of smooth rock that can be landed at and slept on. There are only a few of these mentioned here, but the ones that are make interesting camps with a certain beauty to them and if nothing else provide clean space to set up a kitchen.

Possibly the most ideal camping beach is composed of pea gravel. Soft enough not to bother your feet, yielding enough to slide a glass boat up on to, and too heavy to get into food, it also makes a good sleeping surface. It's nice to be able to spread gear out and not worry about smaller items falling in cracks between cobblestones or sand getting stuck to everything. Gravel really provides a hassle-free camp.

Aspects of Beaches

Because summer heat in Baja can be oppressive, the principal Baja boating season is fall to spring. During these late and early months of the year, the primary wind pattern in the Sea of Cortez is north to south. There are all sorts of other winds, particularly westerlies and sometimes southerlies, which are the predominant winds of summer and often linger into fall, but the north wind is main and chief and anticipation of it is central to most Baja kayaking strategies. With the predominant winds coming from the north, swell moves north to south also. A beach that is open to the north is prone to getting surf, and is often a less desirable beach to land on due to this, despite the fact that it might be just right in all other respects. Consequently, beaches that are protected from north swell are often the beaches of choice

Isla Espíritu Santo gravel camp

to a paddler worried about north wind. In this book, these beaches are given the priority descriptions, and are often referred to as "north-protected," meaning protected from a north-to-south driving sea.

With that basic Baja premise in mind, sometimes the geology of a beach can additionally determine its land-ability. Not all beaches that are exposed to surf are poor landing beaches. Whereas you probably wouldn't land on a rock beach with surf striking it, you might consider landing at a sand beach where the surf gradually breaks up before hitting the beach. Beaches like this are usually shallow offshore for a ways out into the sea, with the shallow bottom causing the swell to rise up and break before it hits land. Surfing into a soft and shallow beach is a paddling skill that opens up a lot of landing opportunities. When the term "graduated break" is used here, it refers to the likely possibility that a beach which is shallow offshore is going to be fairly user-friendly to land at because waves crest, break, and dissipate in progressively smaller rows as they approach the beach, losing most of their energy before they contact land.

The beaches to think twice about are "shore break" beaches. A shore break is likely to occur along a steep beach where the depth of the water just offshore is too significant to cause a wave to break before it crashes into the beach. Landing or launching successfully at a shore break beach during bad weather is either foolhardy or very difficult; depending on your skill level. But here is the caveat: if the weather conditions are benign and the sea flat, then exposed shore break beaches can be considered acceptable camps. Just recognize one when you're landing on it, and realize that conditions later may not be the same as when you arrived.

Medano Blanco, "Mulegé to Loreto"

Camping

Isla San Marcos, west coast

Camping Allowed Where

Mexico has a great law that allows the public to be on most beaches. Its appellation is ZOFEMAT, which is "La Zona Federal Maritime Terrestre." It states that the coast 20 meters above the general high tide line is public domain. Read literally, it means that camping is legal anywhere on the coast of Mexico. So does this mean you can set your tent anywhere in front of any private property and declare ZOFEMAT gives you the right to do so? Unfortunately, this is not the case. ZOFEMAT does not give people unlimited right be on any beach however they wish. The Mexican government has granted some landowners (usually hotels, restaurants, or campgrounds) concession rights to the beach in front of their establishments. And whereas you might land there, these people have the right to control camping if they have a commercial concession for the beach.

Personally, I try to avoid camping directly in front of developments because I do not feel comfortable in that situation, regardless of the law. I do sometimes camp where there are private property signs posted but no building or person around to enforce them. To those who wish to wave the banner of ZOFEMAT and use it for their right to camp anywhere, I am all for them. Let me know how it turns out. Continued public access to wild places is of the utmost importance if the world is going to stay sane.

But there are situations where you may think you have the right to camp, and you may (i.e.: most private seaside residences do not have concessions to the beach near their property), but you might be confronted by a landowner and told to move on. You might be confronted by a large guard that tells you to move on. Unfortunately, Mexico is ruled by money, and things are getting out of hand with rich landowners illegally shutting down access to beaches and the right to camp on them. But it's a time-consuming battle to prove who is right about where, and wandering kayakers who aren't going to stick around to fight it out with the proper authorities will probably be left kicking sand in frustration. If you are car-camping in one area for a spell, or want to but are denied, it might pay to go to the local government or even military outpost (they can be more impartial than the town government) and complain—it might get you somewhere. If in doubt about whether a beach is campable or not, a friendly conversation with whomever is taking care of the place will go a long way towards allowing you to stay without hassle.

Fish Camps

Often in the body of this book, in regards to potential camping beaches, there is mention of fish camps. Both coasts of Baja are heavily fished by contingents of local fishermen. Their boat of choice is the panga, the sturdy fiberglass open boat powered by an outboard engine. Pangas are, or can be, everywhere. There is not a cove or stretch of coast unfished by the pangueros (fishermen). Some days they will be thick, at other times non-existent, depending on the run of the fish or the season. Because there are long distances between villages, and usually no villages out on the islands, the pangueros set up remote camps on beaches throughout the sea so they can stay out at the fishing grounds for extended periods. Fish camps can be anything from just an old junked refrigerator lying on the ground (used to ice down fish till the journey back to town) with a little trash scattered about to a cluster of shacks with almost full-time residents (wives and children) staying there. It is not necessarily appropriate to camp at an inhabited fish camp, or desirable if you want privacy, but you will never be told to leave. You are a person of the sea, they are people of the sea, and even if you might seem like a gringo tourist and be kind of unwelcome, there is an unwritten law of the sea that you will not be turned away from a fish camp. But the pangueros' world is a different world than the one you are probably living in. It is simpler, harder, and more direct, and many kayakers might

not be comfortable setting themselves up amidst that different lifestyle. There's also a realistic aspect to it, and that's that there might not be enough room for everybody on the fish camp beach. Fish camps can be crowded places. Conversely, some fish camps are empty if the fish they rely on are not in season. Then it is okay to camp there, but there is no guarantee that fishermen are not going to show up. Sometimes they do, and at the weirdest hours, because sometimes they fish at night.

Punta Hornitos fish camp

Other than that, aim for wilderness beaches. There's a reasonable supply now; I hope there's plenty left for future generations.

Permits

A number of areas in the Sea of Cortez are overseen by the government and require permits in order to be able to camp there. These are: The Bahía de los Ángeles islands down to the Midriff Islands; the Loreto National Marine Park, which includes the islands and shores in the Loreto area; and Isla Espíritu Santo outside of La Paz. All are popular sea kayaking destinations and are described in this book. How to obtain permits and what regulations there are for those areas are talked about in the relevant chapters.

The government agencies that oversee these marine areas for the purposes of protection and preservation are CONANP (Comisión Nacional De Áreas Naturales Protegidas) and its subdivision SEMARNAT (Secretaría De Medio Ambiente Y Recursos Naturales). SEMARNAT is mentioned frequently throughout the book, as the islands that fall under its supervision all have signs planted on a key beach telling of the island's protected status. These signs are landmarks of sorts.

The two main offices for the government agencies are in Ensenada and La Paz. Regional offices are in Bahía de los Ángeles and Loreto.

CONANP/SEMARNAT	CONANP/SEMARNAT
Av. del Puerto No. 375-24	5 de Mayo No. 1035 Interior 1
Fracc. Playa Ensenada	e/ Primo Verdad y Marcelo Rubio
Ensenada, B.C. 22880 México	Col. Centro. CP 2300
	La Paz, B.C.S. México
Website: www.conanp.gob.mx	Email: info@conanp.gob.mx

GEAR

This section will stick to the kind of gear to take on a Baja sea kayaking trip that might be different than gear taken on a trip to other climes.

Because Baja is so dry, out in the country there is a lack of fresh running water. This means the number one item you need to pack in your boat that you might not normally concern yourself with is a large quantity of **FRESH WATER**. Certain parts of the coast have water stops at reasonable intervals; other parts of the coast (and most islands) are dry for long distances. It is not uncommon to carry 10 gallons at a time. One gallon per person per day is the general rule of thumb when considering how much fresh water will be needed on a Baja kayak trip.

Though you don't have to bring water into Baja, as you will be able to stock up at your launch town, you should come with the **CONTAINERS** necessary to carry as much fresh water as you will need for your trip. I carry a variety of containers, usually a 5-gallon collapsible in front of my feet and then multiple 2-gallon wineskin-type containers scattered around other parts of the boat. The 5-gallon container is a bear to haul up and down the beach, but you can lighten your load quickly after you land and before you drag your boat uphill if you can get that much water out fast and easy. Carrying my girlfriend's "5" at the same time helps to even the load on my arms up to camp. All boats pack differently, so the containers chosen should match the layout of the available storage space. Also, be careful where you set any soft containers down—with all the cacti around, you don't want to mistakenly spring a leak.

Something to consider bringing on a remote trip is a portable, "kayak size" **DESALINATOR**. These are beginning to change the face of long distance travel in Baja. They are not cheap and also take time pumping to produce fresh water. A fast one does about a gallon an hour, which isn't too bad.

When it comes to water purification, there is a lot of artesian well water in Baja that is safe to drink. Some water sources are shaky—if in doubt, carry **WATER PURIFICATION TABLETS** or liquid iodine to purify water. I have a water filter, but it usually just sits buried in the car and rots. If someone tells me that the water they are offering me is good and I see the source and I see the water is clear, I drink it only mildly purified—though I've also been vaccinated against hepatitis—as the Baja population grows, the water quality diminishes. There is an almost free, sure fire way to get purified fresh water before a trip, and that is to go to a "water store" and fill up before launch. This is a reverse-osmosis facility that fills up any shape and size container for pennies to the gallon. Every decent sized town in Baja has at least one of these; some of the smaller towns and outposts also have them within their grocery stores.

Baja is an extremely sun-oriented environment. It can get cloudy and foggy on the Pacific, but the Sea of Cortez is clear 90 percent of the year. So **SUN PROTECTION** is a must if you are fair-skinned. Even if you try not to get a tan, you will. **SUN CREAM** is essential. **WIDE**

BRIMMED HATS are standard boating attire down here. A BASEBALL CAP is a good backup for windy days and then a BANDANA worn under the cap can get your ears and neck covered. If you are out paddling when the wind is blowing too hard for a baseball cap, then you are having too much fun to worry about skin cancer. On the beach, a SHADE TARP is a nice thing to have. A light LONG SLEEVED SHIRT AND PANTS protect extremities from sun and also are good bug protection for those special moments in camp. In winter months, FLEECE LAYERS AND A WOOL CAP are needed for the late and early hours of the day.

You'll probably never need a dry top for paddling in the Sea of Cortez, unless you like paddling in storms in winter (some people do), but a good PADDLING JACKET that is water resistant is nice to keep the waves off on splashy days. You can double this as rain protection. Some of the dawn launches get cool, so it's nice to have an extra layer then.

Two Baja sea kayaking sub-sports are swimming and hiking. You basically live in a BATHING SUIT, so make sure it is a good one. SNORKELING GEAR comes in very handy, and a WET SUIT is needed more in the winter than other times, but is always nice to have if you swim a lot. If you want to take some long hikes, take a STOUT SET OF SHOES, as it can get rugged out there. If you're a mild hiker and alert enough to avoid cacti, a good pair of STRAP-ON SPORT SANDALS will do. These can also double as your boating shoes.

If you like to fish while you're kayaking, you probably know what to bring. Fishing of course is optional, but it is a great way to supply your group with food. The Sea of Cortez was an incredibly productive commercial and sport-fishing ground once, though the numbers have gone way down lately. Edible reef fish are found along most of the coast. Because the waters are often warm, the Cortez is ripe for spearfishing. ANGLING SETUPS vary between day kayak fishermen who carry multiple rods, a gaff hook, and a battery powered live-bait cooler to mile-making paddlers who don't want to be overburdened with equipment and carry only a HIGH TEST HANDLINE and a few LURES. There's no excitement like hooking a dorado on a trolled handline, or having a moray swim under your belly from behind when you're hovering underwater and taking aim on a grouper.

TENTS should be able to withstand a strong wind. Bring a real tent, not a K-Mart tent. Wind resistance is more important than rain resistance. Tents with a lot of mesh to let air in are preferable for fall and spring. Carry a few wide sand stakes, as they are nice to peg the tent down with (rather than spending time looking for rocks).

STOVES are the preferred method of cooking on Baja beaches. WHITE GAS (Coleman fuel) is usually available for stoves in Baja. Large department stores often carry Coleman fuel in the signature red and gray 1 gallon cans. In towns without department stores, white gas can be found in some hardware stores. Ask for *gasolina blanca*; it often comes in a glass bottle with a cork in it. Mexicans live by propane, so that is always around. There is a gas yard outside of most Baja towns where you can fill up your tank; Mulegé and Bahía de los Ángeles are two exceptions to this. Small, disposable tanks are available in larger stores, some food stores, and some hardware stores.

PORTABLE TOILETS are required for solid waste removal in some Baja locales like Loreto Marine Park and Isla Espíritu Santo. Otherwise, between the high tide and low tide lines dig a hole at least 10 inches deep and defecate in it; filling it in afterwards. Burn or pack out the TP. Poop does not degrade in the dry desert, so "going" where there will be moisture aids in breaking it down. Pee below the high tide line, not on the dry sand where the smell will linger until the next distant storm.

It is a good idea to pack a hand-held, water resistant VHF RADIO, which can aid in a possible rescue. Even though the signal might not make it to the nearest shore-based receiver, there are passing ships and yachts that you could hail. Also, some Mexican fishermen bring radios out in their pangas and can be contacted if there is an emergency. The radio is also a good way to get weather reports from passing ships or yachts, if you are not able to paddle up to one at an anchorage. Pre-set weather channels on American VHF's don't work down in Baja.

Some CELL PHONES from the States work in Baja, some don't—networking is getting better all the time. Though Baja has plenty of cell towers, reception can be spotty in the boonies; it's better to plan on not getting a signal. Other fancy electronic devices might or might not work, depending on where you are. The one thing you can count on is satellite reception for any device that feeds off the little orbiters. As far as access to the INTERNET goes, most Mexican towns have internet cafés in them.

Of Maps,
Compasses,
Mooks, and
Tide Charts

This guide is both a map and a book (...a mook), and it could be the primary and only source of navigation for a Baja paddler. However, much of the information here is derived from other maps and charts, and it is still nice to have a traditional kind of map around, particularly for inland details such as mountain heights or names and lesser roads—to unfold in camp or to tack to the front deck of your boat to keep you company while on the water. The maps in this book are created from scratch starting with raw greyscale satellite data. Up until the advent of satellite technology, all maps or charts of the Sea of Cortez had inconsistencies and mistakes caused by flaws done in the initial surveys of the sea and its coasts. These errors, when one discovers them, usually only amount to an inconvenience to a kayaker, where travel is slow and adjustments to misplaced landmarks can be made before a costly error occurs, but they do exist. So there will be inconsistencies amongst older maps. The most egregious mistake I've come across is when I found the southern light on Isla Catalina to be 2 miles away from where it was plotted on the map I was using then. Lately, INEGI, the agency responsible for the creation of Mexican topographic maps (the Mexican U.S.G.S., if you will), has come out with a new set of maps based on satellite imagery that should be accurate.

The maps here are generally made to 4 different scales. The introductory page to each chapter has a floating scale; each is different than the next chapter's intro because the opening page encompasses an area size-specific to that leg. 1:190,000 or 1 inch = 3 statute miles is the scale used for the majority of maps after the intro pages. 1:95,000 or 1 inch = 1½ statute miles is the scale used for many of the smaller islands and also for zooms to specific areas. 1:380,000 or 1 inch = 6 statute miles is used for some of the longer as well as some of the more straightforward legs. Mileage on the map scales is given in statute miles, nautical miles, and kilometers, but when mileage is referred to in the text, it is as statute miles.

A peculiar instance among maps of Baja is the variety of names or spelling of names that exist among them. There is often no consensus on what certain landmarks are called. It can happen that 3 different maps will have 3 different names for the same landmark. The maps in this book use the majority consensus amongst previous maps when choosing how to name a place. If there was no majority consensus, the Baja Almanac, a good traditional topographic map source, usually got the nod in being the basis for a place name. (So what am I saying here? "On traditional maps you might not know what it's called, but at least it's there, even if it is 2 miles farther away than it's supposed to be?" Ah, welcome to Mexico, where the spirit of adventure lives on.)

The Baja peninsula stretches northwest to southeast 800 miles from the U.S. border to the Cape. There are 9 ½ degrees of latitude change over that distance. The latitude and longitude tic lines on the maps in this book are aligned to true north. For compass adjustment, magnetic declination varies between just over 12° east in the northern Sea of Cortez to almost 10° east off East Cape above Cabo San José. The maps in this book don't show magnetic declination, so if you want compass readings for the sea along the Baja coast, settings of 12° east variation up north, 11° east variation in the central zone, 10° 30' east variation in the Loreto to La Paz region, and 10° in the East Cape region will work.

Land based navigational lights, a good reference point for paddlers even in the daytime, are sometimes referred to as lighthouses in the book, even though only a tiny minority of them actually have houses with them. Channel lights or other floating navigational lights or buoys are rarely mentioned here, and if they are it is usually just as markers for a daytime paddler to gage his progress across an open part of water. Large ships such as tankers are an infrequent sight along the east Baja coast because of a lack of big city ports, the one exception to this being the channels between Islas Cerralvo and Espíritu Santo and the peninsula, which see large ship traffic on the way to La Paz.

The eastern coast of Baja is the land of clear weather. Kayak navigation is made simpler by the fact that it is usually easy to see far into the distance to gage one's progress in a point-to-point fashion. Comparing visual notes to maps is often sufficient enough information to guide one through a large part of the day. But there are a few caveats to this. One problem that may arise in point-to-point navigation in Baja is that visibility is so good that points or islands often look closer than they are. What looks like a crossing of an hour's duration could take four hours because that island or point looks like "it's right there." I remember being on Isla San Lorenzo in the Midriff Islands and thinking as I looked across the glassy calm channel back to the Baja peninsula that I could swim the distance. In fact the width of sea I was looking at was 16 miles, a significant paddle if anything. Line of sight navigational ability deteriorates when the wind blows, even though the day is clear. Wind whips up a haze of moisture from the sea surface, diminishing long distance visibility. At horizon level, an island 12 miles away might look ridiculously close on a calm day, a long haul when the wind is developing, and then disappear from sight completely when the wind reaches a substantial, sustained velocity.

Tide Charts:

The need for a tide chart is mentioned in various chapters in the book where it is most relevant. It's always nice to have a chart for Baja paddling, but particularly when boating in the northern Sea of Cortez. Tide ranges average 5-20 feet up north, 0-2 central, and 2-4 feet in the south. (The tide change has been measured as much as 31 feet near San Felipe, one of the greatest range changes in the world.) The largest tidal change occurs twice per month: during new moon and full moon phases.

Whereas a tide chart is appreciated in the south, it is almost necessary up north. Access to northern beaches changes dramatically when the edge of the water is a quarter-mile away from the camping zone, or, as is the case on steeper beaches, when the gear carrying is over a field of rocks that at high tide is covered. The northern tides also produce significant current in the channels between islands and the peninsula, creating the necessity for a deflection strategy for some of the big crossings up there. These currents, when in opposition to the wind direction, likewise cause the formation of significant tidal races (standing waves) off certain points.

Some sources of tide charts are:
http://math.ucr.edu/~ftm/bajaPages/Tides.html
http://bajaquest.com/bajasports/tides.htm
http://oceanografia.cicese.mx/predmar/

San Felipe Harbor

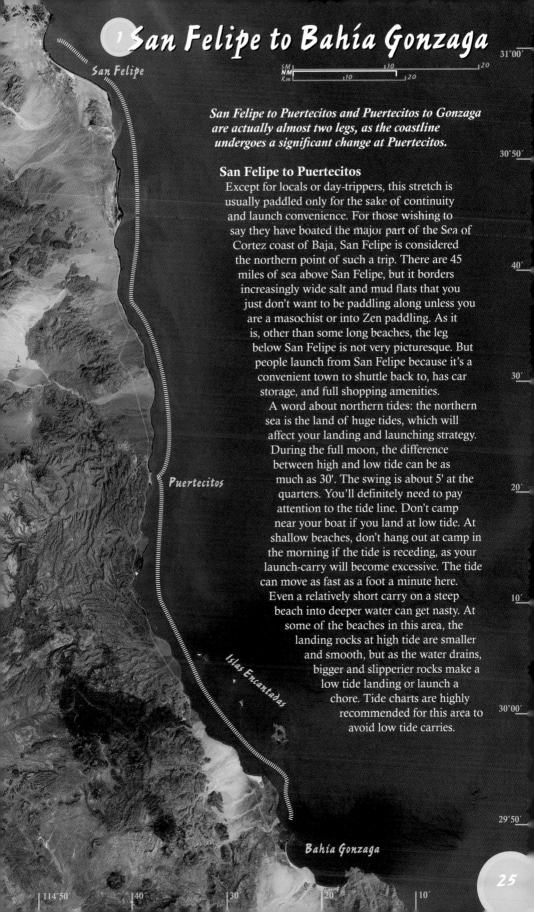

San Felipe

Puertecitos

Islas Encantadas

Bahía Gonzaga

San Felipe to Puertecitos and Puertecitos to Gonzaga are actually almost two legs, as the coastline undergoes a significant change at Puertecitos.

San Felipe to Puertecitos

Except for locals or day-trippers, this stretch is usually paddled only for the sake of continuity and launch convenience. For those wishing to say they have boated the major part of the Sea of Cortez coast of Baja, San Felipe is considered the northern point of such a trip. There are 45 miles of sea above San Felipe, but it borders increasingly wide salt and mud flats that you just don't want to be paddling along unless you are a masochist or into Zen paddling. As it is, other than some long beaches, the leg below San Felipe is not very picturesque. But people launch from San Felipe because it's a convenient town to shuttle back to, has car storage, and full shopping amenities.

A word about northern tides: the northern sea is the land of huge tides, which will affect your landing and launching strategy. During the full moon, the difference between high and low tide can be as much as 30'. The swing is about 5' at the quarters. You'll definitely need to pay attention to the tide line. Don't camp near your boat if you land at low tide. At shallow beaches, don't hang out at camp in the morning if the tide is receding, as your launch-carry will become excessive. The tide can move as fast as a foot a minute here. Even a relatively short carry on a steep beach into deeper water can get nasty. At some of the beaches in this area, the landing rocks at high tide are smaller and smooth, but as the water drains, bigger and slipperier rocks make a low tide landing or launch a chore. Tide charts are highly recommended for this area to avoid low tide carries.

31°00′
30°50′
40′
30′
20′
10′
30°00′
29°50′

114°50′   40′   30′   20′   10′

Low tide beach south of San Felipe

Decked out kayak fisherman

San Felipe is a soak-up-the-sun, drink-your-fill, anything goes sort of Mexican beach town. There are strip bars here and they are trying to put a casino in. I don't mind it too much, but it's not quaint like Mulegé or Loreto. Plus, it's getting busier by the year—in one realtor's words, "it will be the next Cancun." Its proximity to the border gives it easy access for southwestern gringos who wish to escape the north and come down south to buy some trinkets and blow some steam off. It can also be a big party town for Mexicans on holiday weekends. Avoid camping in the desert areas close by on these days: four-wheel mania rules.

San Felipe is a port town of sorts—the harbor here is a launch point for fishing trawlers. A number of private, multi-day guided fishing tours launch from here as well in converted trawlers. It's not uncommon to run into these boats and their satellite fleet of pangas off some of the more remote islands in the northern sea.

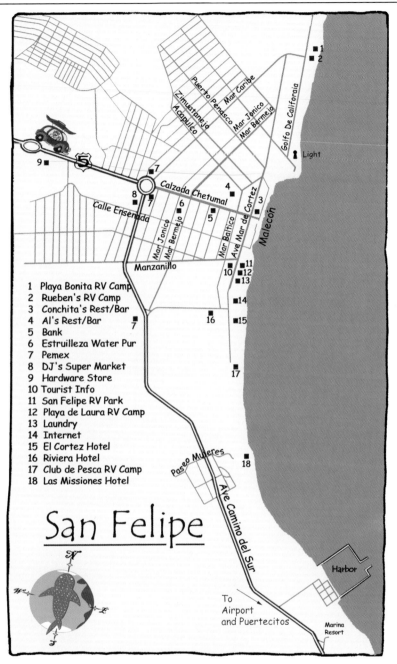

1 Playa Bonita RV Camp
2 Rueben's RV Camp
3 Conchita's Rest/Bar
4 Al's Rest/Bar
5 Bank
6 Estruilleza Water Pur
7 Pemex
8 DJ's Super Market
9 Hardware Store
10 Tourist Info
11 San Felipe RV Park
12 Playa de Laura RV Camp
13 Laundry
14 Internet
15 El Cortez Hotel
16 Riviera Hotel
17 Club de Pesca RV Camp
18 Las Missiones Hotel

San Felipe

There are many facilities here for launching a kayak trip: all the stores you need, waterfront hotels, camping, car storage, and a bus connection to southern Baja via Ensenada. The Riviera RV and Camp on the south side of town is a central place to stay and has car storage. Camping and car storage is affordable here considering this is a tourist town. Baja Buddies Storage, located on the northwestern perimeter of town on Highway 5, also offers auto storage. You could take a taxi back if you leave your car here.

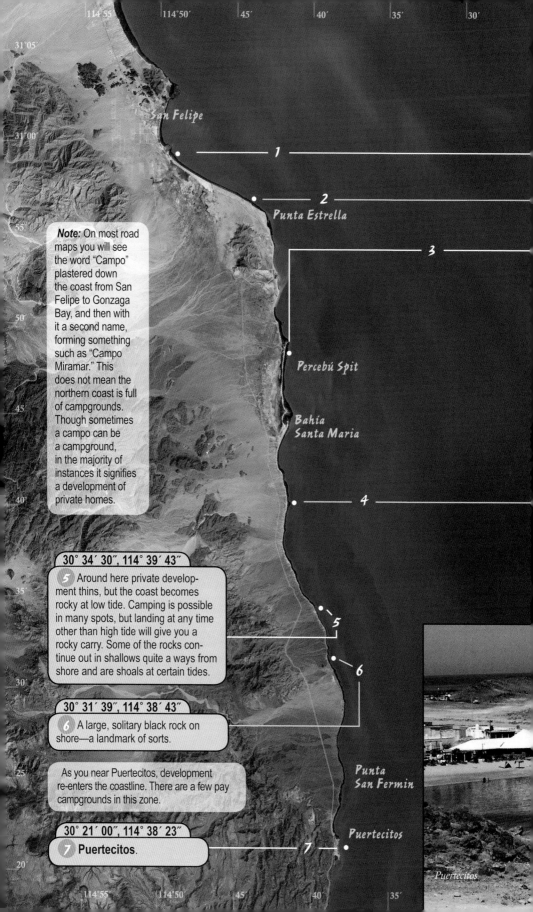

31°05′

114°55′   114°50′   45′   40′   35′   30′

San Felipe

31°00′

1

55′

Note: On most road maps you will see the word "Campo" plastered down the coast from San Felipe to Gonzaga Bay, and then with it a second name, forming something such as "Campo Miramar." This does not mean the northern coast is full of campgrounds. Though sometimes a campo can be a campground, in the majority of instances it signifies a development of private homes.

2

Punta Estrella

3

50′

45′

Percebú Spit

Bahía
Santa Maria

40′

4

30° 34′ 30″, 114° 39′ 43″

5 Around here private development thins, but the coast becomes rocky at low tide. Camping is possible in many spots, but landing at any time other than high tide will give you a rocky carry. Some of the rocks continue out in shallows quite a ways from shore and are shoals at certain tides.

35′

5

6

30′

30° 31′ 39″, 114° 38′ 43″

6 A large, solitary black rock on shore—a landmark of sorts.

As you near Puertecitos, development re-enters the coastline. There are a few pay campgrounds in this zone.

Punta
San Fermin

25′

30° 21′ 00″, 114° 38′ 23″

7 Puertecitos.

Puertecitos

7

20′

114°55′   114°50′   45′   40′   35′

Puertecitos

20′   15′   10′   05′   114°00′   113°55′

SM
NM
Km   6   12

30° 59′ 27″, 114° 49′ 25″

1 On the beach flats just outside of the **San Felipe Marina.** This is a good public launch point without the hassles of the busy Marina, though dealing with the radical tide line shift is a factor. Other recommended launch points would be at one of the seaside RV parks if you camped there or at one of the seaside hotels.

31°00′

30° 56′ 45″, 114° 44′ 09″

2 **Lighthouse.** This section has a number of pay campgrounds along it. But none charge less than $20.00.

55′

30° 48′ 29″, 114° 41′ 56″

3 **Percebú Spit** ✹✹ A great camp for a first day out from San Felipe. The body of the long spit is separated from land by Estero Percebú, which is navigable at high tide but becomes mud at low tide. The spit is too low ever to be built on, so it has more privacy than anywhere nearby. It does see four-wheel traffic, something to be aware of on any beach in this leg. From the spit, there are good sunset views of the mountains toward the interior of the peninsula. A lot of interesting bird and fish noises come from the lagoon at night. There are a few small dunes with bushes towards the middle of the spit that offer some wind protection.

50′

45′

South San Felipe lighthouse beach

40′

30° 40′ 13″, 114° 41′ 35″

35′

4 A big, duny arroyo between houses. A possible camp.

A complete whale skeleton lay underneath my boat as I snapped this shot.

Between Puertecitos and Bahía Gonzaga, a distance of 40 miles, the coast is a mixture of small gringo communities and undeveloped shoreline.

The topography below Puertecitos gets rugged in places. This leg sees the beginning of the high-relief Baja shoreline topography that will dominate much of the length of the peninsula. The native countryside here is a rocky, lava moonscape with sparse vegetation, but alluring shadow-scapes at dawn and dusk. The road parallels the coast here, sometimes very near it and sometimes removed. It looks like a somewhat major road on a map, but it is in fact a poorly maintained dirt road made of tire-biting stones (and when the stones are few the washboards are many). Also watch out for potholes and rain-created crevasses lurking on the edges of the road. (These factors are true for most of the dirt roads in Baja.) The plus feature is that traffic is minimal here. Kayakers boating the coast south of Puertecitos may not even hear one car at night if they were to choose a camp near the road.

Bahia Christina

Puertecitos is a fairly cute village nestled in a large alcove of rock that forms shallow coves north and south of town. Town has minimal amenities, but does offer the basics. In addition, Puertecitos is home to some of the nicest hot springs I've ever placed my derrière in.

Puertecitos south cove

There are camping beaches in each of the north and south coves. Both are pay beaches and cost the same. The north beach might be a touch closer to the stores, but it is farther from and not associated with the hot springs. It is also prone to being invaded by juvenile ATV terrorists. I recommend passing it by unless you've been fighting a strong southern wind on the paddle from San Felipe.

The camping in the south cove is in the back and includes shade palapas and tables and (occasionally) fresh water in pilas attached to the palapas. Use of the hot springs comes in the price of the camping. It is so worth it. The springs are hard to discern from the water as you paddle by, they come toward the south end of the distinctive headland. In any case the landing here is very rugged. It would require a calm sea to tie up anywhere nearby. The best time of day to visit the springs is between tides—high tide covers them, and at low tide the springs are too hot to sit in.

Puertecitos hot springs

The stores in Puertecitos are on the north end of town approximately 1 km from the center. They are both small and have minimal goods. The one farther north on the east side of the road to San Felipe (north of a fresh water store) is perhaps more stocked than the other.

Some car notes: Though it has a Pemex station, there is no gas in Puertecitos. Recommended restaurants: Sometimes Clara's is open right in town at the beach. The old hangout Cowpatty's ("best hot dogs in Baja") north of town is moving to a new location between Puertecitos and Gonzaga. If you are driving into Puertecitos, you can reach the campground and hot springs by driving through the blue gate in the center of the village—you can't miss it.

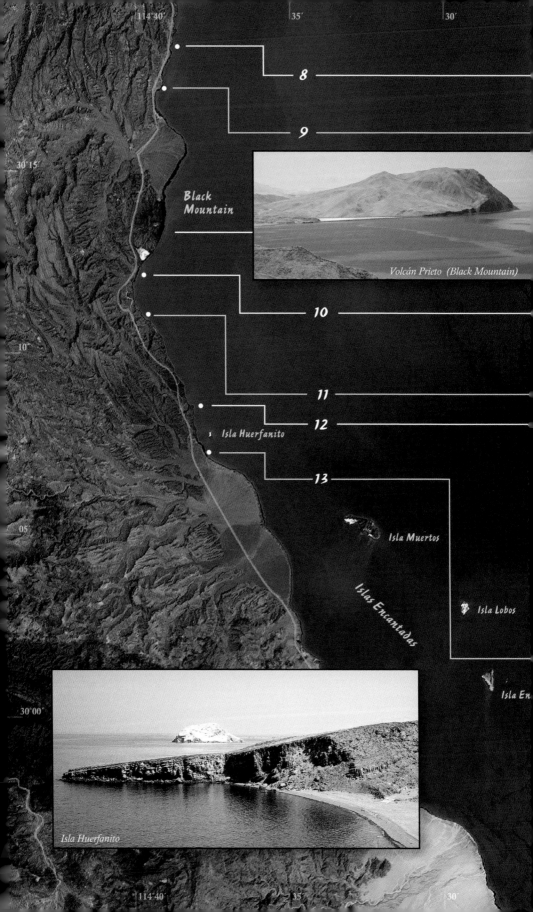

114°40'   35'   30'

8

9

30°15'

Black
Mountain

Volcán Prieto (Black Mountain)

10

10'

11

12

s *Isla Huerfanito*

13

05'

Isla Muertos

Islas Encantadas

Isla Lobos

30°00'

Isla En

Isla Huerfanito

114°40'   35'   30'

30° 18′ 29″, 114° 38′ 58″

8 An inlet with a couple of good camping spots. Both are near the road.

30° 17′ 17″, 114° 39′ 19″

9 **Bahía Christina**. A north-protected, red, grainy, sand beach. It is an affordable pay beach. It has palapas with picnic tables. There is a restaurant in back of the beach where you can pay the camping fee, or just set up camp and they will find you. This is true of almost all less formal campgrounds on the coast. There are views of the Encantada island chain in the southern distance.

Just south of Christina is Playa Costilla. It is also a pay beach with a restaurant but gets more wave-exposure from the north. It was recently sold and I'm not sure what the plans for it are.

Approaching **Volcán Prieto** (called **Black Mountain** by some), the shoreline is long and flat with a number of camping opportunities, but all are somewhat exposed and are also rocky at low tide.

Black Mountain is a large cone of dark red rock and is very pretty to see at certain lights. Some of the hills around Puertecitos were hints, but now there is no doubt that the country is becoming volcanic, with Black Mountain one of many volcanoes the coastal paddler will encounter. Baja is extremely volcanic and is thought to be a cataclysmic event waiting to happen again.

At the flank of Black Mountain, the shore becomes steep and craggy and boulders that have rolled off the sides of the volcano lie under the surface of the water, creating good snorkeling spots if the waves aren't up.

30° 12′ 10″, 114° 40′ 00″

10 Immediately south of the volcano is a large salt flat not suitable for camping and after that is a stretch of low coastline with camping zones sometimes used by car campers. It is a rocky landing at low tide along this shore. In the midst of it, there is a small camp near the road but separated from it by a short cliff. It is nestled in a walled cove. There is a little red stalagmite here.

30° 11′ 05″, 114° 39′ 51″

11 On the southern arm of the bay south of Black Mountain, the relief picks up again. Here there are a few small arroyos with beaches set in a hill of red rock. They make cute camps but are exposed to north waves and two have rocky landings at low tide. This one has more protection and a primitive boat ramp up it so you don't have to land in rocks. The camping zone is a mixture of some sand and flat cobble.

Around the corner of the next minor point is a very pretty cove with a red gravel beach. Red rock extends out into the water on the north corner of the beach and offers some protection from waves.

30° 08′ 37″, 114° 38′ 18″

12 A big, northeast-facing cove with a dark sand/cobble beach at the mouth of a wide arroyo. A good camp away from the road but car accessible. There is plenty of room to share.

Just north of El Huerfanito the coast is a pretty in-and-out array of red rock fingers amongst which is one possible camp.

30° 07′ 12″, 114° 37′ 44″

13 **El Huerfanito** (The Little Orphan) This is a gringo beach community in a pretty bay named after the white island that sits not far from shore. The island is officially the start of the Islas Encantadas chain that extends S-SE of here. However, Isla Huerfanito is more of a large rock than an island and is so removed from its sisters as to not seem part of the chain, but just an attractive landmark in the bay.

Camping is limited on this appealing beach by the row of houses that extend along it, though I have heard of small groups camping between the houses. There is more space among the houses in the southern part of the beach, and the beach's far southern arm is houseless, has fewer rocks, but is exposed to a north wind. There is no fresh water in El Huerfanito.

South of Huerfanito, the coast is low and largely campable for a ways but suffers from exposure as well as rocky landings. The alluring Encantadas will dominate the eastern view until Bahía Gonzaga.

30°15′

10′

05′

30°00′

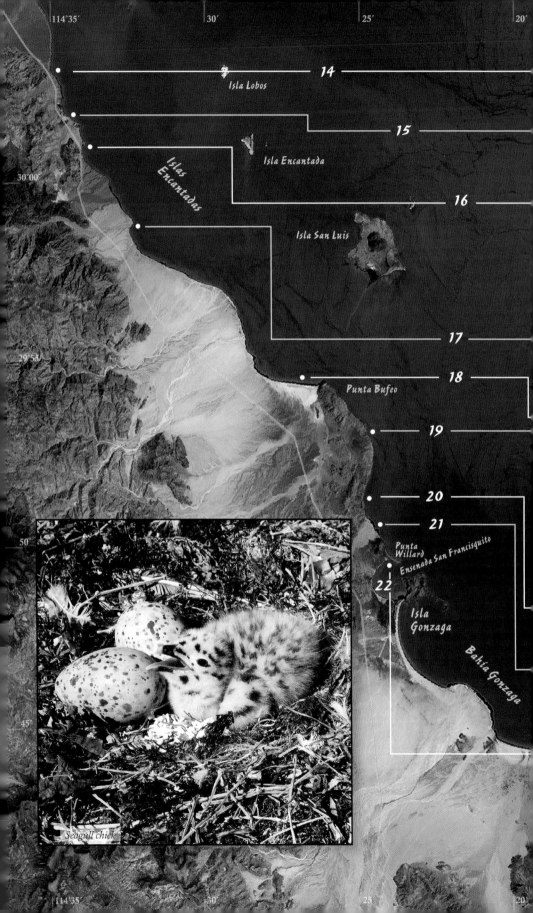

114°35'　　　　　　　　30'　　　　　　　　25'　　　　　　　20'

14
Isla Lobos

15

Isla Encantada

30°00'

Islas Encantadas

16

Isla San Luis

29°53'

17

Punta Bufeo

18

19

20

21

50

Punta
Willard
Ensenada San Francisquito

22

*Isla
Gonzaga*

Bahía Gonzaga

45

Seagull chick

114°35'　　　　　　　　30'　　　　　　　　25'　　　　　　　20'

30° 03′ 05″, 114° 35′ 00″

14 A nice, dark sand beach mixed with cobble. Near it sits an unoccupied stone house. The beach is slightly north-protected.

30° 01′ 37″, 114° 34′ 15″

15 A long beach and good camp and but not north-protected. A few pyramid-shaped hills are at the beach's south end. They turn very red at sunset. This beach is where the local fishermen launch their pangas, so it sees some traffic.

30° 00′ 59″, 114° 33′ 58″

16 **Okie Landing** is a cobble beach protectively tucked around a small point. If you don't land at high tide, you will have a carry over stones, but they are smooth and stable. There are about five small concrete pads in the camping zone. Whether they were ever built on or what, I don't know, but the pads make good kitchen/sleep spots.

Just south of Okie Landing is a beach with a cobble landing but sand camping. It is more exposed than Okie. About here, flora starts coming into the ochre-colored lavascape in the form of small bushes and intermittent cacti.

29° 58′ 48″, 114° 32′ 26″

17 A north-protected, slightly rocky cove at the mouth of an arroyo. There are no houses immediately nearby. Sleeping is on dark sand. South of here to the next reading, the coast is a mixture of low bluffs, arroyos, beaches (rocky at low tide), and houses.

29° 54′ 26″, 114° 26′ 27″

18 **Playa Bufeo** ✷✷✷ This is a huge, beautiful, white sand beach with minimal rocks to deal with at low tide, though the tide goes out a long ways. It is a pay camp with a small development nearby. The beach is exposed to the north but the break is gradual.

Behind camp is a small settlement with a rural restaurant and a bathroom. You can pay your camping fee here. The well is brackish, but there is often potable water for sale. Inland, there is a nice expanse of rolling dunes, while the south arm of the bay is a beautiful, red rock buttress. There is a pretty camp for two tents max just around Punta Bufeo. Bufeo is a preferred launch for a visit to Isla San Luis.

29° 53′ 14″, 114° 24′ 47″

19 **Hidden Camp** is a hard-to-see, narrow opening between granite rock walls. On walking in, it opens immediately onto a large savannah of rolling hills. There are rocks in the landing zone but they are smooth. The landing has protection from mild surf.

29° 51′ 29″, 114° 24′ 52″

20 Near this reading are an interesting three-eyed arch/cave and a secretive arroyo that is narrow, steep, and twisting. It looks to give a compelling hike.

29° 50′ 40″, 114° 24′ 36″

21 **El Faro Beach. Lighthouse.** This is a nice pay camp with a northeast facing aspect. The beach is sand with some cobble in the landing zone. There are dunes behind the beach and inland a few kilometers is El Pozo, a well dug and fortified in the Spanish missionary days. Its walls are constructed of hand-hewn block. The well water is salty.

29° 49′ 45″, 114° 24′ 10″

22 **Pápa Fernández** is a tidy little community that has a protected boat ramp, a mellow restaurant by shade trees, and a camping area, though this is on the outside of Punta Willard. It is a small hike over a low hill between the community and the camping area.

Ensenada San Francisquito is a very shallow bay that is loaded with clams, though some locals don't eat them as they suspect raw sewage flows into the bay. The ensenada is the best way to approach Bahía Gonzaga. Boat to the tiny channel at the southwest corner of the island. At periods of extreme low tide this channel can dry up, but even if you had to wait out such an event, it would save you time and energy over paddling around the island and entering the bay from the east. Besides, there is beer nearby.

Las Islas Encantadas, named so because of their smoky, mirage-like appearance on hot, still days, are a chain of largely barren, old volcanoes paralleling the coast south of Puertecitos. They are not far off shore and make great day trips or a possible connected route as an alternative to boating down the coast for the north-south traveler. In the spring, the islands are major nesting grounds for shore birds. Some of the birds are rare, such as the green-footed booby. If you visit in the spring, be careful with the nesting birds—adults of some species may leave their young when humans are in close vicinity. After visiting, back away from the area making sure predators have stayed out until the adults have returned.

Standing on a hill on Isla San Luis, the southernmost of the islands, and looking north-northwest, one can see the almost straight-line connectivity of the chain of volcanoes from here to other cones inland. It gives one an uncanny feeling of understanding the power of the earth, of fiery times that were, and that might possibly be again.

Islas Encantadas looking north to south with Isla Huerfanito in the foreground.

Isla Huerfanito

SM
NM
Km.

Isla Muertos

Isla Lobos

Isla Encantada

Isla San Luis

Punta Bufeo

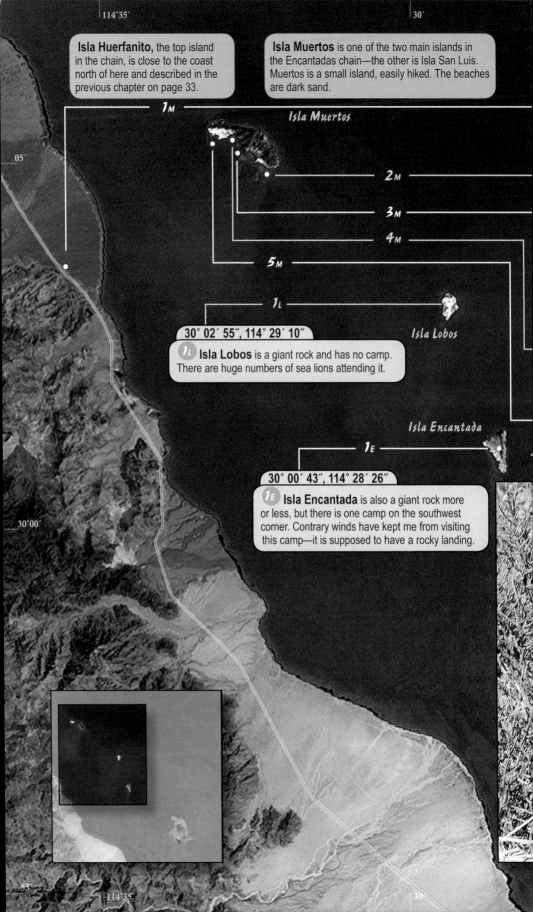

114°35′

30′

Isla Huerfanito, the top island in the chain, is close to the coast north of here and described in the previous chapter on page 33.

Isla Muertos is one of the two main islands in the Encantadas chain—the other is Isla San Luis. Muertos is a small island, easily hiked. The beaches are dark sand.

*1*M

Isla Muertos

05′

*2*M

*3*M

*4*M

*5*M

*1*L

30° 02′ 55″, 114° 29′ 10″

Isla Lobos

1L **Isla Lobos** is a giant rock and has no camp. There are huge numbers of sea lions attending it.

Isla Encantada

*1*E

30° 00′ 43″, 114° 28′ 26″

30°00′

1E **Isla Encantada** is also a giant rock more or less, but there is one camp on the southwest corner. Contrary winds have kept me from visiting this camp—it is supposed to have a rocky landing.

55′

114°35′

30′

Encantadas ~ Isla Muertos, Isla Lobos, Isla Encantada

SM
NM
Km 1.5 3 3

30° 03′ 35″, 114° 35′ 36″

1M If you want to boat out to Isla Muertos from a car, a good launch is off this turn from the road near a little white casa set in a grove of Cardón cacti. This takes you down to a reasonable camp where a trench is carved in the shallows offshore to aid in low tide launches.

30° 04′ 59″, 114° 32′ 18″

2M **Lighthouse Beach** ✲✲ This is the nicest camp on Muertos in the daytime, though I'm not sure what effect the flashing light would have on camp at night. You will have to carry gear over some rocks and some cobble bars to get to camp, but after those there is a nice sleeping area against a cliff. This camp is north-protected but not south-protected, and has excellent views of the peninsula and the rest of the Encantada chain.

30° 05′ 08″, 114° 32′ 30″

3M ✲✲ Another excellent camp. Landing is in a well-protected cove, exposed only to the west. A carry over stable cobble leads to a gravel beach and then a sandy sleep zone. It could hold a large group. Viewed from the west, this camp is in the bay below and between the two dominant hills of the island.

30° 05′ 25″, 114° 32′ 48″

4M This prominent bay could be a camp in fall, but not in spring when nesting gulls fiercely defend their turf. There is also a booby colony plastered on a wall on the bay's southern arm—but the boobies are less perturbed by visitors than the gulls.

30° 05′ 23″, 114° 33′ 08″

5M On the northwest corner of the island is a protected cove facing southwest. It has a small camp. There is a cobble landing, a sand sleeping zone, and morning shade. There is evidence of a minor fish camp in the form of a fire ring, a pile of clamshells, and a little trash. This camp attracts flies in the warmer months, especially when there is no wind.

Baby herons

114°25′

Isla San Luis. If there is one island to visit in the Encantadas, this is it. Easy enough to boat in a day but with good camping spots for an overnighter, San Luis has incredible geology, dramatic offshore reefs, and a scenic islet nearby. The easiest access point to San Luis is from Playa Bufeo, described on page 35, though it is possible to boat down to it from the north or up to it from Bahía Gonzaga.

*1*SL

30°00′

*2*SL

Isla Pomo

*3*SL

Isla San Luis

*4*SL

*5*SL

55′

Playa Bufeo

Punta Bufeo

Plaza de Toros

114°25″

SM
NM
Km
1.5

30°00´

29° 57´ 58″, 114° 25´ 08″

1sl An excellent beach of dark sand in a cove protected from every side but the south. The landing is sandy at all tides and there are large, flat sleeping areas. There is a good view of two volcanic cones on the peninsula from here, Punta Bufeo and Isla Gonzaga. Don't camp here in spring because the nesting gulls will hate you with a vengeance.

29° 58´ 01″, 114° 25´ 37″

2sl The western reef. An underwater combination of rock and kelp with mediocre visibility twenty yards from the reef and aquarium-like visibility near the reef. The current can be strong here, so be careful swimming.

29° 59´ 05″, 114° 24´ 35″

3sl ✹✹ The main camping beach on the island, though it faces north. The landing is on very firm cobble. The sleeping area is in the tundra-like terrain behind the beach but there is little-to-no shade and some gulls in the spring. You will notice a SEMARNAT sign here telling of the island's "protected" status. Across a channel to the east is Isla Pomo, a beautiful rock tower with a lunch-spot landing on the north side. Between San Luis and Pomo there extends a shallow reef that has excellent fishing.

29° 58´ 03″, 114° 23´ 46″

4sl **Plaza de Toros** ✹✹✹ Neither my pen nor my camera can describe this place as it deserves. The backdrop to the bay is the inside of an exploded volcano with half of the cone left. It is a towering semi-circle of chocolate-colored rock lined with bizarre and fascinating sand castle drip formations. And there's a thin beach here. The landing is on cobble at low tide but sand at high tide. It is possible a big tide could overtake this beach, but there is emergency retreat to slanted ground farther into the cone. There is a view of Isla Pomo, the open sea beyond, and to the south, the vague outline of Isla Ángel de la Guarda.

29° 57´ 21″, 114° 24´ 40″

5sl On the southwest tip of the island is a beach-enclosed lagoon; nearby there is a camp. There is a SEMARNAT sign there.

55´

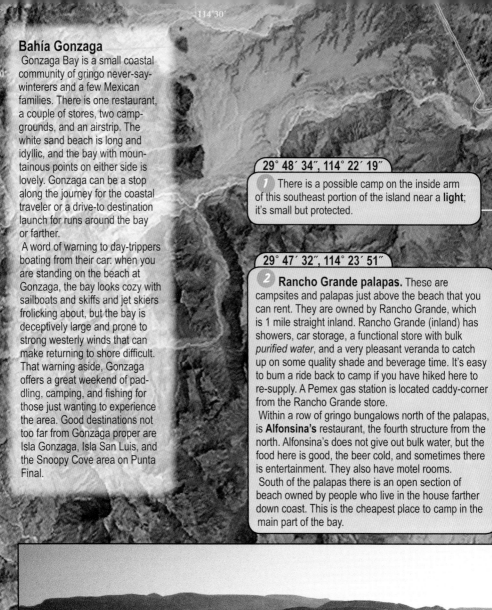

Bahía Gonzaga

Gonzaga Bay is a small coastal community of gringo never-say-winterers and a few Mexican families. There is one restaurant, a couple of stores, two campgrounds, and an airstrip. The white sand beach is long and idyllic, and the bay with mountainous points on either side is lovely. Gonzaga can be a stop along the journey for the coastal traveler or a drive-to destination launch for runs around the bay or farther.

A word of warning to day-trippers boating from their car: when you are standing on the beach at Gonzaga, the bay looks cozy with sailboats and skiffs and jet skiers frolicking about, but the bay is deceptively large and prone to strong westerly winds that can make returning to shore difficult. That warning aside, Gonzaga offers a great weekend of paddling, camping, and fishing for those just wanting to experience the area. Good destinations not too far from Gonzaga proper are Isla Gonzaga, Isla San Luis, and the Snoopy Cove area on Punta Final.

29° 48′ 34″, 114° 22′ 19″

1 There is a possible camp on the inside arm of this southeast portion of the island near a **light**; it's small but protected.

29° 47′ 32″, 114° 23′ 51″

2 **Rancho Grande palapas.** These are campsites and palapas just above the beach that you can rent. They are owned by Rancho Grande, which is 1 mile straight inland. Rancho Grande (inland) has showers, car storage, a functional store with bulk *purified water*, and a very pleasant veranda to catch up on some quality shade and beverage time. It's easy to bum a ride back to camp if you have hiked here to re-supply. A Pemex gas station is located caddy-corner from the Rancho Grande store.

Within a row of gringo bungalows north of the palapas, is **Alfonsina's** restaurant, the fourth structure from the north. Alfonsina's does not give out bulk water, but the food here is good, the beer cold, and sometimes there is entertainment. They also have motel rooms.

South of the palapas there is an open section of beach owned by people who live in the house farther down coast. This is the cheapest place to camp in the main part of the bay.

Bahía Gonzaga and Ensenada San Francisquito

Bahía Gonzaga

SM
NM
Km

20´

1.5

29°50´

Punta Willard

ndez

*Ensenada
San Francisquito*

Isla Gonzaga. The rugged Isla Gonzaga, known also as Isla Willard, makes a good day trip for kayakers hanging out at Gonzaga Bay.

There is a nice trail up the inside flank of a foothill to an airy perch overlooking the bay and the community below. It starts just at the top of the beach above Alfonsina's. If you're an industrious hiker, you could also try to summit one of the barren but rugged central peaks of the island farther inland.

1

Bahía Gonzaga

Grande

3

Punta Final

29° 46′ 31″, 114° 23′ 01″

3 **Campo Beluga.** A nice primitive campground. There is a small store here that sells bottled water, basic necessities, and some fresh produce. In ′05, the cost of camping at Campo Beluga was $15/site.

Snoopy Coves

45´

Punta Final community

20´

43

Playa Alcatraz, Photo by: Dave Erskine

3 Bahía Gonzaga to Bahía de los Ángeles

The "**Gonzaga to L.A. Bay**" run is perhaps the most serious section of sea kayaking of the inside coast. It is here that the road leaves the coast and heads inland, and the first significant wilderness paddling of a north-to-south run is encountered. Remoteness, lack of fresh water, strong currents, big tides, potentially crappy northern weather, and Punta Remedios—the long, rugged headland that is home to a large tidal race, await on this next leg.

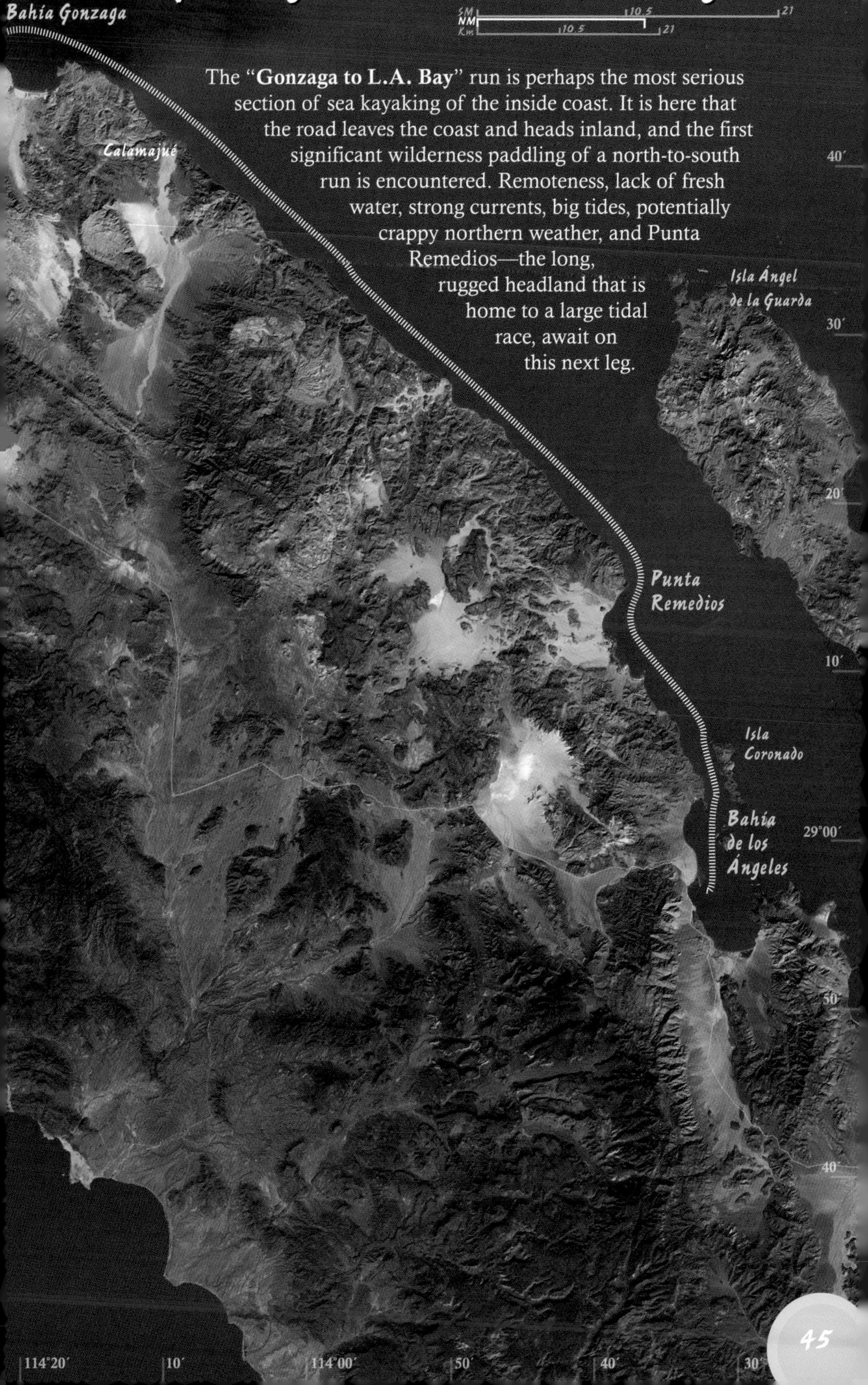

Bahía Gonzaga
SM 10.5 21
NM
Km 10.5 21
Calamajué
Isla Ángel de la Guarda
Punta Remedios
Isla Coronado
Bahía de los Ángeles
29°50′
40′
30′
20′
10′
29°00′
50′
40′
114°20′
10′
114°00′
50′
40′
30′

29° 45′ 00″, 114° 17′ 39″

5 ✱✱ A white sand beach east of the Final community. It offers some surf protection and has nice sunset views. It is a sometimes-used but clean fish camp.

Bahía Gonzaga

5

6

Punta Final

7

8

9

29°45′

4-

29° 44′ 26″, 114° 18′ 48″

4 **Punta Final houses.** There is a long section of undeveloped beach west of this community. It is more surf-exposed than Gonzaga. I am not sure if this is a pay area or free.

While the coves at the top of **Punta Final** offer good lunch spots, the camping there is only so-so. Of the two main coves, the first is an interesting one with a narrow opening that becomes almost impassable at low tide. Diving reveals this small lagoon to be a giant repository of old shells. The granite point is pretty and there is no tidal race, though there can be current.

10

Punta Calamaju

Sunrise cliffs, Photo by: Dave Erskine

29° 45′ 23″, 114° 17′ 10″

6 Snoopy Coves ✕✕✕ This is a long inlet with five or six beaches of various size and aspect. The area is named after the small island sitting in front of the Final community that looks like Snoopy in repose. Of the inlet's multiple beaches, the one farthest in could hold a large group and is totally protected, while a small one at the top outside corner is north-protected and has an intimate setting with a lot of character.

29° 45′ 50″, 114° 17′ 26″

7 A cobble/sand/pumice beach that could hold a large group. Enclosed by small hills behind it, this beach offers great sunset views in silhouetted layers of the mountains behind Gonzaga. This is a good launch point for the trip around Punta Final.

29° 45′ 38″, 114° 15′ 35″

8 A small beach with a rocky landing that could hold a medium-sized group. Though it is protected, it has a very low aspect and could be covered by a big sea. Another beach near here is okay, but not great.

The backside of Punta Final is the start of a lengthy run down coast that sees a dearth of north-protected landings. The next significant beach is at Calamajué, seven miles south, which isn't the friendliest place to camp, though you wouldn't be turned away.

29° 45′ 04″, 114° 13′ 43″

9 An area of low rock beach that has maybe one camp just north of this reading. It is unprotected and has a carry over rounded rocks at low tide.

29° 42′ 05″, 114° 10′ 10″

10 Pumice Camp. The landing is unprotected and a bit steep, yet it is the only reasonable camp in the vicinity. The beach and social areas are small cobble but the sleeping area is on a large field of pumice. Walking onto the airy field is like stepping onto a giant bed of marshmallows. The rock-filled meadow has the appearance of being unsleepable, but under the weight of a person, the pumice stones sink down amongst themselves to offer flat bedding sites.

Ensenada Blanca

29° 41′ 28″, 114° 09′ 34″

11 Calamajué. This predominantly north-facing bay is home to a large, road-accessed fish camp. It is sometimes busy, and has a petite school tucked under the cliffs of the northwestern corner of the valley. There is protected landing in this corner on a pea gravel beach, but sleeping nearby would be amongst shacks and fishermen. The east end of the beach is cleaner and quieter, and is surf-protected by rock shoals in front of its far corner.

The fish camp is dominated by a large palapa, and around it are pangas, trailers, trucks, drums of fuel and water, also a fair amount of trash. The water is trucked in, and I wouldn't bother the fishermen for any unless it was necessary. Also, there seems to be an unfriendly vibe here towards gringos.

The coast in the Calamajué area is rugged, high, and glorious. It is a rock-gazers dream. On the other hand, with a north blow, it can become foreboding and harsh due to that craggy landscape and the lack of protected landings.

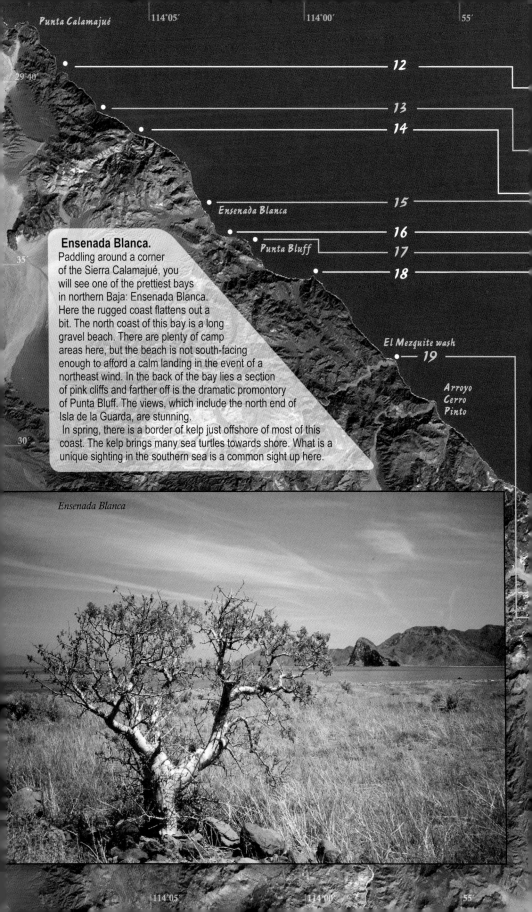

29°40′

12

13

14

Ensenada Blanca

15

35

16

Punta Bluff

17

18

El Mezquite wash

19

30

Arroyo
Cerro
Pinto

Ensenada Blanca.

Paddling around a corner
of the Sierra Calamajué, you
will see one of the prettiest bays
in northern Baja: Ensenada Blanca.
Here the rugged coast flattens out a
bit. The north coast of this bay is a long
gravel beach. There are plenty of camp
areas here, but the beach is not south-facing
enough to afford a calm landing in the event of a
northeast wind. In the back of the bay lies a section
of pink cliffs and farther off is the dramatic promontory
of Punta Bluff. The views, which include the north end of
Isla de la Guarda, are stunning.
 In spring, there is a border of kelp just offshore of most of this
coast. The kelp brings many sea turtles towards shore. What is a
unique sighting in the southern sea is a common sight up here.

Ensenada Blanca

SM
NM
Km

29° 40′ 27″, 114° 07′ 59″

29°40′

12 A tiny fair-weather camp. The beach is of large gravel and backed by cliffs with only a steep escape route up in case of a rising sea.

29° 39′ 14″, 114° 06′ 40″

13 A fair-weather gravel lunch-spot under a soaring, sheer-faced peak.

29° 38′ 35″, 114° 05′ 29″

14 A non-protected landing that leads to a camp in a valley; the sleeping area is in a wash. The berm of the wash blocks some wind for work in the kitchen. It is the first real beach since Calamajué.

29° 36′ 44″, 114° 03′ 23″

35′

15 **Pink Cliffs** ✹✹ There might be a camp on the northern edge of the pink cliffs—we stopped here for lunch but things got hectic when we spied a whale shark swimming up coast. We dropped lunch, ran to our boats, and raced out to the cruising creature. We got to study and play with the animal, and he reciprocated by doing circles around us and checking us out. When we got back to the landing our energy levels were high and there was much excited banter, and somewhere along the way my notes on this spot were…lost.

29° 35′ 44″, 114° 02′ 33″

16 A camp south of the pink cliffs and west of the pulpit rock. It is a very good but unprotected camp. The landing at low tide is on large cobble; at high tide it is on gravel. There is an arroyo behind camp. The beach is marked by a large piece of timber embedded vertically in the ground.

At many of the camps in this area, aggressive coyotes lurk in the shadows. Guard your food and loose articles.

30′

29° 35′ 26″, 114° 01′ 36″

17 Rounding **Punta Bluff** you are looking down coast at another bay and one more point. Just south of Punta Bluff is a barely sufficient beach of medium-sized cobble with a bad carry at low tide but with some north protection. There is a better beach in the southeast corner of the bay; it is south- but not north-protected.

Punta la Asamblea

29° 34′ 41″, 113° 59′ 42″

18 A point with a sea lion colony living near it. *Note:* Some maps label this as Punta Bluff.

29° 32′ 22″, 113° 57′ 15″

25′

19 **El Mezquite wash**. A sand and gravel spit at the mouth of this significant arroyo sticks out into the sea and makes a nice camp. There is a little surf protection on either side of the spit depending on which way the sea is running. The carry at low tide is a bit rocky.

Isla de la Guarda

The coast south of El Mezquite wash marks the breakup of rugged headlands and the start of a zone of large valleys that flow down to the shore. There is one more spit/camp after El Mezquite at Arroyo Cerro Pinto. One mile south of Arroyo Cerro Pinto is a north-facing beach with a valley set between glorious mountains that are lined with vanilla fudge cliffs.

20′

Canal las Ballenas

49

113°50′ 45′ 40′

20
21
22
23
24

Punta la Asamblea

Punta el Muerto

29°25′

25

Punta Candelaria

26

20

27

Elephant Rocks at high tide

28

Canal las
Ballenas

15

Punta
Remedios

10

Hauling the double, Photo by Dave Erskine

113°50′ 45′ 30

29° 29′ 06″, 113° 53′ 45″

20 There is a long, unprotected gravel beach with multiple camping opportunities north of this reading. At this reading there is a valley fringed by beautiful pink cliffs set below hills of blond and pink rock. The mountains above the hills are streaked with additional colors. This camp could hold a large group but it is exposed.

29° 28′ 22″, 113° 52′ 25″

21 **Elephant Rocks** ✱✱ A variety of attractive camps in baylets formed between outcroppings of bulbous rocks that extend into the water. From here there are pretty views up and down the coast and of the north end of Isla d.l.G. The elephant rocks protect the baylets from minor blows, but could become a hazard to anyone attempting to land in a big sea at high tide when the water is practically covering them. (I guess then they are touchy hippopotamuses.)

29° 28′ 00″, 113° 52′ 03″

22 An arroyo camp. No north protection here, but it is otherwise a good camp with plenty of sleeping space. The presence of palm trees up the arroyo indicates occasional fresh water. I found none, but perhaps there might be some after a recent rain. Farther up, the arroyo opens into a large, multi-colored valley.

29° 27′ 44″, 113° 51′ 43″

23 A major camp that offers protection from the northwest but less from the northeast. There is a steepish beach, which is evidence of a possible shore break. Introductory cobble leads up to plenty of nice sleeping areas. There are red and pink intrusions in the hillsides above.

29° 27′ 21″, 113° 49′ 58″

24 **Punta la Asamblea**

The bay south of Punta la Asamblea is large but with narrow, unprotected beaches and one mini-arroyo. The point is the beginning of Canal las Ballenas, where there are frequent whale sightings. A species commonly seen is the finback whale, a large, sleek, fast-moving beast that is the slightly smaller cousin to the giant blue whale.

29° 25′ 08″, 113° 47′ 19″

25 **Punta el Muerto.** On a clean sand beach behind the point you'll notice an infrequently used fish camp with shack. The fish camp is somewhat north-protected, and the only good camp for miles. Offshore of the point is a reef that runs perpendicular to the coast; at ebb tide water funnels water over it into a river of current, with chop. When the weather is mild, it's a fun ride in a kayak. It also makes for interesting angling: big fish congregate at the south end of the current-river waiting for little fish to be swept downstream. Casting while being shot down flow is hectic and fun, particularly if you strike a biggie and he runs one way while the current is taking you another.
If you plan on landing on the beach when the weather is poor, you should probably boat wide of the point and the race and approach the beach from the south.

29° 22′ 02″, 113° 43′ 36″

26 **Punta Candelaria.** This small point has an area of short volcanic sea stacks standing just offshore.

29° 20′ 59″, 113° 43′ 02″

27 An arroyo camp with some protection. The landing is shallow, so it probably sees a graduated break on a wave day. The beach is a mixture of cobble, gravel, and sand. Camp has a good sleeping area. There is a small spire (candle) on the northwest corner, and good views of the mountainous north end of de la Guarda.

29° 20′ 41″, 113° 42′ 34″

28 The most protected beach in this zone. An arm of lava rock enclosing a cave/arch breaks some waves. The sleeping area is scruffy but okay. Camp is lightly infested with small black beetles come night, providing a tickly-toes-during-dinner phenomenon; they can get into boats, too.

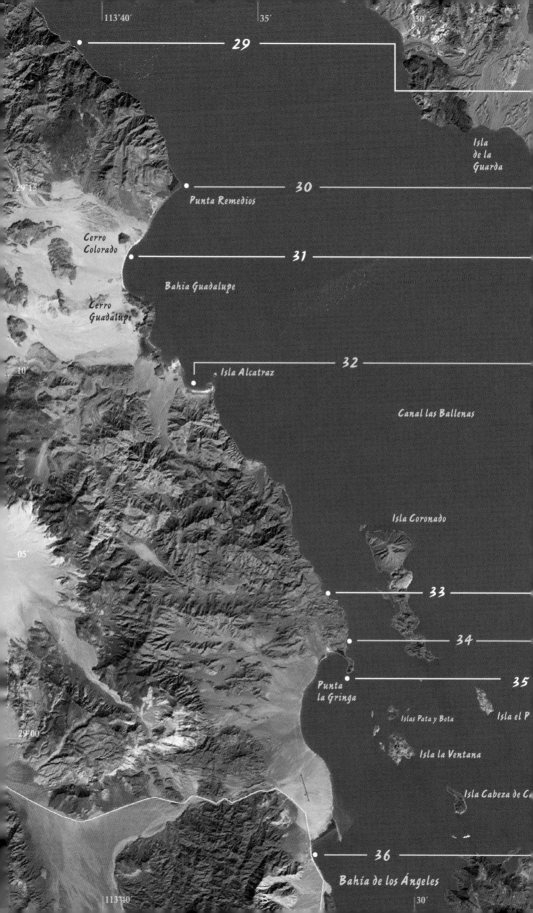

113°40′ 35′ 30′

29

Isla
de la
Guarda

29°15′

30 Punta Remedios

Cerro
Colorado

31

Bahía Guadalupe

Cerro
Guadalupe

10′

Isla Alcatraz

32

Canal las Ballenas

Isla Coronado

05′

33

34

Punta
la Gringa

35

Islas Pata y Bota   Isla el P

29°00′

Isla la Ventana

Isla Cabeza de C

113°40′ 30′

36

Bahía de los Ángeles

29° 19´ 00˝, 113° 40´ 50˝

29 When it is active, the **Remedios tidal race** starts about here; it is 5+ miles before the coast fades around the point and there is protection. The water can suddenly go from glassy to choppy, and a light breeze can quickly turn into a gusty wind. The race gets big at new and full moon tide-flow peaks, and bigger still when there is a wind contrary to the current. It is a wide race, and extends well into the channel south of the point. Waves in the middle of it are wacky, coming from multiple directions simultaneously.

29° 15´ 13˝, 113° 37´ 24˝

30 Punta Remedios is a low, oblique point. A large gravel bar with a lagoon in its center, the point lacks protection and awkward rocks on the bar make it a barren and marginal camp.

29° 13´ 23˝, 113° 39´ 14˝

31 ✸✸ Sanctuary after Remedios. A north-protected, long white sand beach distinctly marked by the small volcanic cone of **Cerro Colorado**. There is a giant plain behind the beach. Though it is lacking in shade and has no wind protection, this is a nice site, and the first totally sand camping since leaving Gonzaga. This beach has a great view of the magnificent Isla Coronado.

Bahía Guadalupe. If you have the time, this bay is worth exploring. The inside perimeter is dotted with shallow lagoons and inlets, and divided by the rocky cliffs of Cerro Guadalupe. Some of the coves are quite intimate and might offer camping potential.

29° 09´ 35˝, 113° 37´ 04˝

32 Ensenada Alcatraz ✸✸✸ Except for the east corner where there is a launch ramp dug into some rocks, this beach is not north-protected. Shallow waters precede the rest of the beach so the break will be mitigated, and the landing is soft. The beach is white sand, and there are small dunes to duck behind to avoid winds. There is a rewarding short hike up a large dune at the east end of the beach. From atop you get an airy view of Islas Alcatraz and Coronado and the next section of coast.

Isla Alcatraz. This rocky island is a major bird hangout as well as a mixing point for strong currents. At certain tides the channel between it and the land to the south becomes a river of rushing water, making paddling out difficult. If you see waves set in the channel, it might be easier to paddle around the island to continue south.

29° 04´ 02˝, 113° 32´ 48˝

33 Campo Coyote. An old RV park with road access to L.A. Bay.

29° 02´ 44˝, 113° 32´ 20˝

34 North la Gringa Beach. A car-accessible but good beach of medium-sized cobble. It is mostly north-protected. The cobble in the sleeping area is flat, and the view of Coronado is stupendous.

29° 01´ 49˝, 113° 32´ 08˝

35 Punta la Gringa. There is one camp on the very tip of the point but it is not car accessible. It has a steep landing but good camp zone on flat cobble. Around the point to the west there is a long beach and total protection, but civilization ratchets up quickly. As part of the federal government's economic development program, a new marina is planned for here. ☹

28° 56´ 50˝, 113° 33´ 28˝

36 L.A. Bay centro

Dining along the shore

South of Calamajué, Photo by: Lori Russell

Bahía de los Ángeles

To Hwy
To Daggett's 2 mi
Punta la Gringa 11 mi

1 Pemex
2 Tacos
3 Mercado las Islas/Internet
4 Mercado los Pinos
5 Motel Villa Vita
6 Octagon house
7 Permit Office
8 Camp Rosa
9 Town Square
10 Museum
11 Guillermo's Rest./Camp
12 Mercado Xitlali
13 Internet
14 Casa Diaz
15 Welder

boat ramp

boat ramp

To south end
of bay

Isla Coronado

Punta la Gringa

Islas Pata y Bota

Isla el Piojo

Isla el Borrego

Isla la Ventana

Isla Cabeza de Caballo

Pu
Don J.

Bahía de los Ángeles

A NOLS group landing at Daggett's

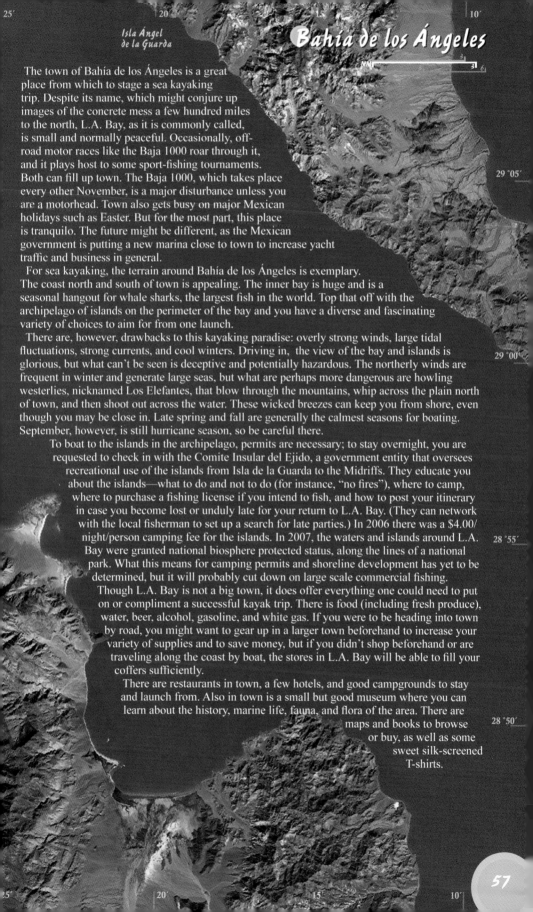

Isla Ángel
de la Guarda

Bahía de los Ángeles

25'   20'   15'   10'

29 °05'

29 °00'

28 °55'

28 °50'

The town of Bahía de los Ángeles is a great place from which to stage a sea kayaking trip. Despite its name, which might conjure up images of the concrete mess a few hundred miles to the north, L.A. Bay, as it is commonly called, is small and normally peaceful. Occasionally, off-road motor races like the Baja 1000 roar through it, and it plays host to some sport-fishing tournaments. Both can fill up town. The Baja 1000, which takes place every other November, is a major disturbance unless you are a motorhead. Town also gets busy on major Mexican holidays such as Easter. But for the most part, this place is tranquilo. The future might be different, as the Mexican government is putting a new marina close to town to increase yacht traffic and business in general.

For sea kayaking, the terrain around Bahía de los Ángeles is exemplary. The coast north and south of town is appealing. The inner bay is huge and is a seasonal hangout for whale sharks, the largest fish in the world. Top that off with the archipelago of islands on the perimeter of the bay and you have a diverse and fascinating variety of choices to aim for from one launch.

There are, however, drawbacks to this kayaking paradise: overly strong winds, large tidal fluctuations, strong currents, and cool winters. Driving in, the view of the bay and islands is glorious, but what can't be seen is deceptive and potentially hazardous. The northerly winds are frequent in winter and generate large seas, but what are perhaps more dangerous are howling westerlies, nicknamed Los Elefantes, that blow through the mountains, whip across the plain north of town, and then shoot out across the water. These wicked breezes can keep you from shore, even though you may be close in. Late spring and fall are generally the calmest seasons for boating. September, however, is still hurricane season, so be careful there.

To boat to the islands in the archipelago, permits are necessary; to stay overnight, you are requested to check in with the Comite Insular del Ejido, a government entity that oversees recreational use of the islands from Isla de la Guarda to the Midriffs. They educate you about the islands—what to do and not to do (for instance, "no fires"), where to camp, where to purchase a fishing license if you intend to fish, and how to post your itinerary in case you become lost or unduly late for your return to L.A. Bay. (They can network with the local fisherman to set up a search for late parties.) In 2006 there was a $4.00/night/person camping fee for the islands. In 2007, the waters and islands around L.A. Bay were granted national biosphere protected status, along the lines of a national park. What this means for camping permits and shoreline development has yet to be determined, but it will probably cut down on large scale commercial fishing.

Though L.A. Bay is not a big town, it does offer everything one could need to put on or compliment a successful kayak trip. There is food (including fresh produce), water, beer, alcohol, gasoline, and white gas. If you were to be heading into town by road, you might want to gear up in a larger town beforehand to increase your variety of supplies and to save money, but if you didn't shop beforehand or are traveling along the coast by boat, the stores in L.A. Bay will be able to fill your coffers sufficiently.

There are restaurants in town, a few hotels, and good campgrounds to stay and launch from. Also in town is a small but good museum where you can learn about the history, marine life, fauna, and flora of the area. There are maps and books to browse or buy, as well as some sweet silk-screened T-shirts.

There is free car camping in some areas around L.A. Bay. They are on the outskirts of town to the north and south, and in the desert to the west. If you need the conveniences of town, it is probably better to stay at one of the established campgrounds.

A word of caution about the beaches in the L.A. Bay area: this place is stingray central. Be very aware when wading. If stung by even the smallest of rays, the common cure is to soak the wound in hot water, take a painkiller, and cry for two hours.

28° 59´ 30´´, 113° 32´ 47´´

1 Daggett's Campground is located a few kilometers to the north of the center of town. It is quiet, has a boat ramp and beach, palapas for shade or wind protection, and is owned by a very area-savvy man, Rueben Daggett. Should you want information about the waters of the region, Rueben or one of his capable sons will be able to help. The Daggetts' super panga makes a great support boat. Daggett's is close to the majority of L.A. Bay islands, so it is a convenient launch point. Daggett's rents kayaks and also has car storage.

29° 00´

Isla la Ventana

Isla Cabeza de Caballo

Punta Don Juan

Bahía de los Ángeles

28° 54´ 02´´, 113° 31´ 44´´

3 Camp Gecko. This was once one of the nicer campgrounds on the bay; the owners, Sylvia and Abraham, were friendly and informative. Closed to camping since 2006, this spot more or less marks the beginning of the quiet southwest corner of the inner bay.

— 3 —

28° 54´ 51´´, 113° 28´ 16´´

4 La Mona ✳✳ This is the prettiest camp inside the bay and is accessible by boat only. Not readily apparent from a distance, this back corner of the bay holds a long strip of white sand beach that has been developed into a gringo colony called Rincon. The shore appears to be all developed until one gets closer and notices that the northern-most strip of this beach is segregated from the developed strip by a cliff. The pretty beach of La Mona is framed by this cliff and another cliff to the north. Behind the beach, the cliffs lessen into a steep hillside of fantastically shaped granite rocks. An old hulk of an abandoned vessel sticks up out of the beach.

28° 56´ 50´´, 113° 33´ 28´´

2 Guillermo's. Should you base yourself here, you are in walking distance to all that is needed in town. Guillermo's is a preferred spot for boaters without a car. The restaurant here is good, and it is a hangout for adventurers passing through town. There is a boat ramp and a small sand beach here. Guillermo's has some motel rooms, offers car storage, and also has a super panga that is available for shuttles.

Though camping here is convenient due to its town location, our overnight tent experience included bathrooms from hell, the streetlight from hell, the dog from hell, the raven from hell, the gulls from hell, the pre-dawn panga launch from hell, and, to enjoy along with morning coffee, the jet ski from hell.

The inner bay of Bahía de los Ángeles is a large body of water to the southeast of town. Sighting whale sharks is a good reason to paddle here. Known as the gentle giants of the sea, whale sharks frequent the bay because it is shallow, warms up nicely, and provides a blooming environment for plankton to feed upon. You can best find these colossal, slow-moving fish on calm days in the late summer and fall—just look for their dorsal and tail fins sticking out of the water. The dorsal is rounded and not too high. The tail fin looks like the dorsal fin of a dolphin.

The inner bay is developed along most of the shore near town and also along the far southeast corner. The only primitive spots are at the middle back of the bay where there is a large estuary good for bird watching and a nice car-camp spot, and the rugged northeast corner towards Punta Don Juan.

SM
NM
Km

05′

05′

A view of the bay from Volcán Coronado

29 °00′

28 °55′

Camping at East Bay on Isla Coronado

50′

45′

15′

10′

05′

29°05′

29° 00′ 50″, 113° 30′ 45″

1pt Pata and Bota. When speaking about either Isla Pata or Isla Bota, area locals often just say "Pata and Bota" as if it were one name. Both islands are tiny and separated by only a narrow channel. The camping is on Pata, however.

Pata is a great little place for a night's stay. There are two camps on the island, with the better one being toward the east. Both camps are in the Pata/Bota channel and provide excellent wave protection. The eastern camp, though appearing small at first, has more than a few hidden bedrooms among sandy hillocks behind the beach. There is a small cave adjacent to the beach that can comfort a few shade seeking boaters feeling the pull of that afternoon nap. Also, there is a trail up the miniature hill behind this area offering a short and painless hike with the reward of a surprisingly good vista for five minutes of effort.

Isla Coronado

1p

Punta la Gringa

Isla el Piojo

Islas Pata y Bota

1pt

Isla el Borrego

29°00′

1v

2v

3v

Isla la Ventana

28°05′

La Ventana

SM
NM
Km   1.5 3

29° 00′ 46″, 113° 27′ 44″

Isla el Piogo is a bird sanctuary and is busy with nesting shorebirds in the spring. Piogo is cliffy but has a protected landing on its south end. However, camping here is not allowed. If you were being blown out to sea by a westerly, there is a hard-luck landing at the back of the island.

Isla la Ventana. Isla la Ventana is, by location, the centerpiece of the L.A. Bay archipelago. It is not the biggest island of the group, but it is the closest to town. The island has two good camps and a wondrous arch.

28° 59′ 54″, 113° 30′ 43″

Calleta Ventana ✗✗✗ Also known as Puerto E Bonny, this cove has a pretty gravel/sand beach and protection from all wave sets. The views aren't expansive because the cove is so enclosed, but it is a pretty area. The beach can hold a large group.
There is a hiking trail that starts from behind the beach leading up into the interior. It was on this trail that I got to pat my first chuckwalla, an oversized black lizard that, as evidenced by a tail hanging out of its mouth, was digesting a meal and didn't feel like moving away from me or biting my finger. The trail splits on the interior and one branch goes to Playa Sur. It's an easy and rewarding hike with excellent flora gazing.

28° 59′ 38″, 113° 30′ 05″

La Ventana. The arch. A joyous place to visit. There is a reef off the front of the arch that has good fishing.

29°00′

28° 59′ 34″, 113° 30′ 33″

Playa Sur. Also known as Los Corralitos. This nice, north-sheltered beach is a sand/gravel mix and is best suited for a medium-sized group.

Isla Pata camp

28°55′

20′

Isla Coronado is the largest of the islands in the immediate L.A. Bay area not counting the more distant Ángel de la Guarda. The hilly Coronado is nearly five miles long. Volcán Coronado, a perfectly shaped 1,500-foot high cone that rises steeply out of the sea on the northern end of the island, dominates the topography. This mountain, besides being a key viewpoint for most of the paddling in the area, makes for a glorious hike. It can be accessed from either its southwest or southeast flank. For a rugged island, Coronado has many nice beaches. It also has a couple of small outer islands just offshore. It is easy to spend multiple days on Coronado.

Isla Coronado

Volcán Coronado

29° 04′ 03″, 113° 30′ 51″

5c ✳✳ There are two campsites on Coronado on the inside of the Mitlán channel. The northern campsite is sand and can hold a large group. It is a fairly steep beach nestled between rock walls. There is a northwest exposure here and there can be some wind/waves should the breeze blow in from the northwest.

You can paddle either on the inside or the outside of **Isla Mitlán**. The south end of the channel between Mitlán and Coronado is a ridge of rocks stretching between the two shores. The ridge is covered at high tide but exposed at low. Passage at low tide can be difficult.

Isla Mitlán

East Bay

Rada Laguna

29° 03′ 33″, 113° 30′ 40″

4c **Bahía de las Rocas.** This bay lies south of small and rocky Isla Mitlán, and harbors two good beaches. The camps, though open to the northwest, are protected from large seas by Mitlán. A big rock stands in the middle of this pretty bay.

Islas Pata y Bota

Isla la Ventana

29° 02′ 15″, 113° 29′ 45″

7c This small beach is tucked into a nook on the southwest tip of Coronado. It's a horseshoe-shaped gravel bar with a pond behind it. The landing is protected from the north but not from the west. Camp offers a direct view of the central islands of L.A. Bay.

29° 02′ 51″, 113° 30′ 25″

3c **The Lagoon, West Beach.** The island is pinched and low here. It is possible to cross the pinch with boats at a lagoon in the center. You can camp on either the west shore or the east shore of the pinch, accessing it from the opposite shore if need be. At the right time of year, sunset and moonrise can be viewed simultaneously from between the beaches.

This west beach is a minor camp, suitable for a smaller group. To its side is a narrow inlet that is a feed for the lagoon behind it. During strong tidal peaks water rushes in and out of the lagoon through this inlet with a rippling current. Eddylines develop at the respective mouths of the inlet where you can practice bracing and crosscurrent ferry moves. This is a popular landing spot for motorized day-trippers.

29° 02′ 40″, 113° 30′ 16″

2c **Rada Laguna** is a nice looking beach in the back of an inlet, but it is designated as a "No Camping" area. The island overseers request that you don't camp here in order to leave the marshy vegetation of the area to exist undisturbed.

113° 30′

SM
NM
Km
1.5 3

29° 04′ 35″, 113° 30′ 52″

6c Volcano Beach ✶✶✶ This is a nice, blonde sand beach nestled in the back of a peaceful bay at the foot of Volcán Coronado. The landing is on gravel and makes a good kitchen. Sleeping is on sand behind the beach among shrubs and small dunes. There is a small estuary at the top of the bay. Accessed from behind camp, the volcano makes an excellent day hike, though it is a bit stout. After the steep 1,500-foot climb, the summit is rolling, easy-walking terrain sparsely populated by cacti. Cool breezes and grand views await. Thoughts of the splendor of the earth and potential kayak routes to explore in the future will dance through your head from atop this airy perch. I have heard of trips spending full moon nights up here.

The north end of Coronado is extremely steep and rugged. There can be strong current here. Paddling down the east side of the island, there is a large gravel apron at water's edge below the volcano. It is a possible hard-luck camp, but is exposed.

29°05′

29° 04′ 47″, 113° 30′ 28″

7c A low saddle between the volcano and the next highland. Below it is a beach I have not checked out except by looking down on it from the flank of the volcano. It is gravel and cobble. There is a trail over the saddle connecting this beach with the beach on the west side of the island.

29° 02′ 56″, 113° 30′ 09″

8c East Bay/The Lagoon ✶✶✶ Framed by high arms of rock and set back in a little bay, this good-sized beach offers landing protection from north, south, and west swells. The landing is on gravel, but the top of the beach is sandy. It is a beautiful camp, but can get a little trashed out by motorized day traffic. This includes dog poop. For some reason it is a popular dog beach.
The lagoon behind the beach is interesting, and is home to fish and small oysters. As mentioned before, this lagoon gives access to the west side of the island. It is said that in spring, giant crabs up to one foot wide inhabit the lagoon—watch where you're wading.

29° 02′ 42″, 113° 29′ 47″

9c A mostly north-protected beach. This area below East Bay has good snorkeling.

29° 02′ 25″, 113° 29′ 39″

10c A nice but north-facing beach, with a hidden, protected entrance just around the corner. Behind a rock fin, off the outside end of the beach, is a secret landing through a narrow slot. A big cairn on shore is visible through the slot.

29°00′

Coronado calm, Photo by: Lori Russell

Cactus Comp at Isla de la Guarda

Coyote Camp

It was while I camped at La Mona on L.A. Bay that I had my first encounter with a north Baja coyote...

Photo by: [illegible]

Though the creature looked almost tame trotting around the beach and was fun to watch scampering up the incredibly steep hillsides, I still knew we had to protect our food when we went to sleep. But I didn't realize that everything else would be a target, too.

Later that night, the pillaging began. During short intervals, when the sound of the animal tugging at something woke me, I would see flickers of the ghost-like creature trotting through camp. I groggily began to realize that my loose possessions were being dragged away. I finally got up and scared the coyote into the night. I then had to gather the remnants of my gear and place them on my groundsheet near me, as I was sleeping without a tent. I had barely fallen back to sleep when I opened my eyes and the coyote's face (with one of my sandals hanging out of its mouth) was just inches from mine. We looked each other in the eyes for a couple of seconds, and then the coyote bolted. This intimate encounter happened once more later in the night.

In the morning, I took stock of what gear I had left. My partner Joe had suffered the same fate. We cursed our luck, thinking that perhaps the pilfered items were gone for good. But not giving up too easily, we went on a retrieval mission into the brush behind camp. After a little foraging, behind a bush and stacked in one pile, we found everything that had been borrowed—one of my sandals, one of Joe's sandals, Joe's snorkel, one of my fins, Joe's T-shirt...I had to laugh.

Later, recounting my story to some locals, I was told the coyotes around L.A. Bay had become so aggressive that they have been known to jump through the open window of a house and grab a pet for dinner.

Sea cave sanctuary, near Punta Rocosa

SM
NM
Km

40'

Isla Ángel de la Guarda is a large, beautiful island. Almost a world unto itself, it is as big as the island of Maui and yet nobody lives on it. Isla de la Guarda (as it is familiarly called) has all varieties of topography: beaches, mountains, plains, cactus forests, and moonscapes. It has minor points and major points to navigate. But because of its distance from the Baja peninsula, crossing to it is an earnest venture. A journey around Isla de la Guarda to the outside of the island will put you into the remotest part of the Sea of Cortez. Here, it is possible to go weeks without seeing other boats or people. More kayakers would visit Isla de la Guarda if it weren't for the long crossing, unusually strong winds that can buffet the area, and the lack of a reliable fresh water source. If you can find a way to mitigate or not be daunted by these factors, a trip to Isla de la Guarda is special.

Puerto Refugio

30'

20'

Bahía Pulpito

Punta los Machos

Punta Rocosa

Humbug Bay

Punta
Remedios

10'

Isla Coronado

Canal de Ballenas

Isla Estanque

29°00'

Punta Colorada

Punta Don Juan

Bahía de
los Ángeles

113°30'

20'

10'

Isla Ángel de la Guarda

Notable Points of an Isla de la Guarda trip

Water: Isla de la Guarda has no dependable source of fresh water. A couple of valleys on the eastern side are dotted with palm trees. You may also be able to find fresh water in the valleys but only during or after a wet spell. The walks up the valleys are long, so retrieving water in quantity would be a chore. So it's either carry a load of fresh water with you, have a desalinator, or panga-support to the island and create a water stash somewhere. The general rule of thumb is a gallon of fresh water per person per day.

Wind: Northerlies can be a problem on Isla de la Guarda and jumbo waves sometimes crash onto exposed points. Punta Rocosa on the backside is a point to be afraid of during a northerly. Yet, it is westerlies that have bothered me the most on my visits. Knowing that westerlies may kick up at any time is perhaps the number one stratagem to pulling off a successful Isla de la Guarda trip—because you have to deal with the prospect of them for the return back to the peninsula when your fresh water supply may be running low.

Currents: These run strong on Isla de la Guarda, and after three trips I am still befuddled by them. More often than not, the current running along shore is going against the ebb and flow of the channel. Tide charts are very handy, but you'll tie yourself up in knots trying to predict the current along shore unless you remain in one area for a couple of days and learn the patterns firsthand. Specifically notorious places with unusually strong currents such as Isla Estanque and Punta Rocosa are discussed in the place descriptions that follow.

Crossings: They are big so wait for a calm day, start early, paddle strong, and don't rest until at least halfway across. Though the middle of the channel (Canal de Ballenas) has a special aura about it, inviting one to linger and soak up the power of this wide-open space, the less time spent in the channel, the less time there is for something to go wrong. It is best to keep grinding out the miles, especially on the return trip, and to stay apprehensive about the arising of a westerly, because one will not make it back across on a day that sees a west wind.

Puerto Refugio layover day fishing, Photo by: Lori Russell

When looking at maps, it appears the obvious choice for a crossing is north of L.A. Bay between Punta Remedios and the point above Humbug Bay on Isla de la Guarda because this is the shortest distance between shores (eight miles). In reality, this is not always an attractive place to cross. Remedios has a huge tidal race at times, and there is a significant race north of Humbug Bay too. The center of the channel often sees whitecaps when waters north and south of the zone are calm. It may be preferable to take on a few extra miles of predictable water to the south versus the bizarre water that is periodically encountered off Remedios.

Wherever you choose to cross, have north and south backup landings in case of wind or tide deflection. Unlike along shore, the tidal currents are predictable in the channel, going north at flood and south at ebb, and at times are pronouncedly strong. If you spend enough time in the channel during either the new moon or full moon tide phases, you will encounter significant north or south pull.

Groups going to Isla de la Guarda are asked to leave an itinerary at either the Island Office in L.A. Bay or with a responsible person in town. You might be asked to buy permits, though there is no permit enforcement on Isla de la Guarda.

West coast of de la Guarda sea lions

29° 23′ 11″, 113° 33′ 25″

7 This camp is located in a sizeable bay indented into the island just enough to partially mitigate north and south wave activity at the landing. Lying north of a large arroyo descending from the interior, the beach is gray sand with a low point at the southern end. With strong westerlies, waves might overtake the narrow beach, but there is retreat to the sloping hills behind it.

29° 20′ 36″, 113° 31′ 41″

6 An unprotected, mid-sized beach with a landing on rounded stones. A sleep area up in the arroyo could offer shelter from north or south breezes.

29° 19′ 58″, 113° 31′ 40″

5 A shipwreck of an old fishing vessel. This wreck marks the narrowest part of the channel between de la Guarda and the peninsula (7.6 miles) and is a navigational landmark known to local fishermen.

29° 19′ 20″, 113° 30′ 21″

4 **Cactus Camp.** A long, steep, cobble beach. The easiest landing is at the center of the beach. It gets wave activity on a big day, but the southern end has protection from a southerly. Cactus Camp, though having an awkward landing, has a lovely interior. The ochre-colored hills highlighted with dramatic slashes of pink rock serve as a backdrop to its broad and very flat arroyo filled with widely spaced Cardón.

29° 17′ 03″, 113° 29′ 55″

3 **Punta los Machos.** Boating north of Humbug Bay involves a swing around a long headland that has a bouncy tidal race off it extending well into the channel towards Isla Coronado. Due to a strong intermingling of currents, there can be whirlpools on the edge of the race. This is an area that should be regarded with caution on windy days.

29° 15′ 35″, 113° 25′ 49″

2 **Humbug Bay.** This is a strategic landing for the central portion of the west coast of de la Guarda. From a distance, the area appears as a low point on the island. Camp is located at the southeast third of the large bay tucked into a baylet to the south of a small, steep mountain, which affords wind protection from the north. A sometimes-populated fish camp is on a flat in the lee of the mountain. Though protected from north surf, it is a trashy camp that I don't recommend. But there is a good-sized beach just south of this that is clean, however, the carry at low tide is shallow and over rocks.

There is not much scenery in the Humbug Bay area, though after hiking through a zone of Cardóns and then Ocotillo, it looks like you could crest the low saddle of hills a few miles behind camp and access a view of Bahía Pulpito on the other side of the island.

A nice but unprotected campsite can be found 1¼ mile north of Este Ton. This is a gravel beach with an arch on its southern end. A large osprey nest occupies the pinnacle of the arch.

29° 09′ 38″, 113° 19′ 59″

1 **Este Ton** ✳✳✳ is a perfect natural harbor. An enclosed bay with a narrow opening facing the southeast, it is uncommonly protected from serious seas and provides an excellent refuge for kayakers, sailboats, and other small craft. If you were to sight-navigate from L.A. Bay across the channel to Este Ton, you would aim for what looks like a road cut on the side of a hill on the island. It is actually a lighter or blondish-color rock than the surrounding rock and does a zigzag up the hillside south of Este Ton.

In Este Ton, you have your choice of campsites. The inland half of the beach is somewhat sandy, while the channel-side beach is gravel. The gravel bar is low and provides camp chair views of both the sea and the harbor. Also, a level area just below the hillside to the north of the gravel bar provides a windbreak and makes a great spot for a kitchen.

Punta
Reme

Bahía
Guadalu

Isla Ángel de la Guarda

35′   30′   25′   20′

29°25′

20′

Bahia Pulpito

7-

6

5

4

Punta los Machos

3

Humbug Bay

2

15′

Este Ton

10

Este Ton

1

Isla Coronado

35′   30′   25′   20′

113°55′   50′   45′

29°45′

40′

35′

30′

25′

Sunset from the wes[t]

29° 31′ 16″, 113° 34′ 14″

11 North of the islets and in the shadow of the minarets is a small, very north-sheltered bay with a beach. I haven't landed here, but it looked decent from the water. We spent one night on the first beach described below when we were in the area, and I remember thinking that I wished I had experienced all the beaches and that the stay was longer.

Near Minarets Area

29° 30′ 28″, 113° 34′ 02″

10 Minarets Area ✳✳✳ In this lovely stretch of the island you will see a grouping of pinnacles (I liken to minarets) rising from the shore and jutting into the sky. Nearby is a group of tiny islands. Farther out, alone in the sea, sits a huge fang of white rock. The effect of the whole scene, combined with a number of good beaches, is enchanting. The southernmost beach is rather expansive with small gravel and a big buttress at the south end. From this beach, you get a view of the fang, and there is potential for hiking in the valley that winds into the mountains. The next beach up, closer to the islands, is somewhat duny, though it has an arroyo and flat camp spots therein. It is more or less north-protected.

29° 26′ 09″, 113° 35′ 41″

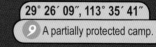

9 A partially protected camp.

From about here and continuing up to Puerto Refugio, the island gets increasingly dramatic and beautiful. A massive mountain on the interior hovers over a beautiful shoreline. Isla Coronado fades from view and groups of sea lions congregate on narrow beaches under tall red cliffs. The points of this northwest quadrant of de la Guarda see large crashing waves when contrary winds are up.

29° 25′ 03″, 113° 35′ 28″

8 This pretty beach is protected from north swell by a rock outcropping. Rock shelves extend out into the water to further break up the surf at the upper corner of the beach, but watch out for these should waves be breaking over them. Additionally, a reef extending out from the island here sometimes generates six to eight foot standing waves if a strong current and wind collide. Although it is a small beach, it does have enough room for a larger group.

SM
NM
Km

40' 35' 30' 25' 29°45'

40'

35'

30'

25'

Puerto Refugio is a beautiful area—an expansive bay bordered by the red Isla Mejia to the northwest and the lighter colored Isla Granito to the north. The center of the bay is home to a large solitary rock that rises from the water like a breaching sea creature and a colossal mountain peak looms toward the south. This is a special place to be and a most worthy destination for the adventurous sea kayaker. However, don't get lulled into a sense of ease by the bay's name—if it blows big from the north, the waves on the outside get immense and the ones on the inside get plenty big too. Also, the waters of Puerto Refugio and its satellite islands sometimes experience strong currents. Paddling against them is possible, but becomes a bit of a chore at times.

Note: This area of Isla de la Guarda can experience huge infestations of Bobo bugs. Though they don't bite, their presence will torture you if you haven't brought mosquito netting for your head. They disappear at night or if a heavy wind blows.

Isla Mejia

Isla Granito

Isla Navio

Punta Refugio

Puerto Refugio

11

10

9

8

From **West Bay**, after passing a possible camp, Puerto Refugio's East Bay can be entered south of Isla Navio at high tide over a reef that stretches between it and de la Guarda. As the tide lowers, the reef becomes a visible barrier and should be approached with caution, especially in periods of weather—then the upper route into the bay above Isla Navio is the route of choice.

The southern shoreline of Puerto Refugio's **East Bay** is divided into three sections: West Bight, Middle Bight, and East Bight.

29° 32′ 24″, 113° 33′ 48″

12 Isla Mejia is a red, mountainous island. Though its north and west coasts are very rugged, Mejia offers a tranquil lagoon and a campsite at its southeast corner. If you enter from the west, you'll see a small white shrine on a hill. Below it is a very nice red sand beach (but it's also a fish camp). Large Cardóns dot the landscape behind the beach. Farther east is another entrance to the Mejia lagoon. Here you'll find an uninhabited beach, but it's in close proximity to the fish camp and a little low for big tide comfort. There is a long reef extending north from the outside of Mejia where the fishing opportunities are ripe.

Puerto Refugio, West Bight

29° 32′ 09″, 113° 33′ 28″

13 West Bight. There are three beaches here, reading from west to east:
Beach #1: A northeast facing red sand beach in the west corner of the bight. It has very pretty views and an easy landing. However, a big north wind will cause the sea to put most of the beach under water! The only hope for a foolproof dry spot is in the dunes in the back-east corner.
Beach #2: A small, black/gray gravel beach with SEMARNAT signs and fish camp remnants strewn about. A short red cliff with an overhang and a rock floor offers a low tide shade spot.
Beach #3: A good though not ideal camp. The beach is gravel and fairly steep. The high point of the gravel stays dry during surf. Protruding out from the center of the beach is a long tongue of flat rock that is covered at high tide but acts as a nice pier to fish from and has a corner that provides a little protection for a surf launch. There are more camping spots in the small, grassy valley behind the beach. If you go back far enough you will be out of the way of the wind should it start to blow.

29° 32′ 06″, 113° 33′ 05″

14 Middle Bight. This beach is made up of dark sand and is the longest beach in the area and its waters offer a preferred anchoring zone for visiting yachts. Because of a bluff that runs along much of it, the best camping is on its western end. Behind the beach, a low valley leads into the rugged country of the island.

29°40´

35´   30´

SM
NM   1.5
km

Puerto Refugio, near East Bight, Photo by: Lori Russell

29° 32´ 06˝, 113° 33´ 05˝

15 East Bight. There are a couple of hard-luck cobble-camps in the back eastern corner of the bight. Due to surf, I wasn't able to land to check them out.

29° 33´ 47˝, 113° 32´ 08˝

16 Isla Granito. With a nice beach on the inside shoreline, this appears to be a good camping island; unfortunately, it's a busy sea lion hotel. The bellowing lions can be heard all the way across the bay at night. The island is all granite and the waters around it are very clean and clear when the sea is calm. You can find a good lunch spot on at least one sloping rock on the north side—if it's not occupied by a sea lion. On the eastern end you will find a **light** with a small beach near it, but—again—the sea lions might already be lounging there. The reef fish on the outside of Granito are huge.

35´

12

Isla Mejia

16

Isla Navio

Isla Granito

East Bay

Punta Refugio

West Bay

15

13

Isla de las Cuevas. From a slight distance it does not seem to be an actual island. At low tide it's joined to the main shore by a line of rocks. There are caves on the west side.

14

30´

30´

35´   30´   35´

Punta Refugio. This is a rugged and tricky spot to round if the waves are up, but you'll find some protection from a northerly around the corner. There is also a lot of current in this area. Except for the beaches mentioned, the coast just south of the point is rugged red cliff.

29° 32′ 18″, 113° 30′ 42″

17 A long reddish sand beach in a mid-sized bay. It is protected from northwest-to-north winds. There are low dunes and then a desert flat behind the beach. Westerlies are known to howl down on this camp from the mountains behind it. If the westerlies are blowing, consider camping a little farther south of here where you'll find an improbable looking cobble beach that doesn't get the west wind.

29° 31′ 52″, 113° 28′ 27″

18 A humpback-looking point with a camp on the outside. The beach is small and sandy with high ground, but is not north-protected. This area hosts a sea lion hangout and a booby rookery. The coast then changes from red rocks to yellow sandstone.

29° 29′ 51″, 113° 26′ 16″

19 A way-neat arroyo/camp but with an unprotected landing on bowling ball-shaped rocks at low tide. The arroyo leads into a narrow twisting sandstone canyon with a flat grassy floor. An okay stop for a small to mid-sized group, weather permitting. There are sand beaches in this vicinity but they are usually occupied by sea lions.

Puerto Refugio

17 *Punta Refugio*

18

19

20

21

22

23

24

Punta Pulpito

25

26

29° 21′ 34″, 113° 22′ 14″

26 Lagoon entrance.

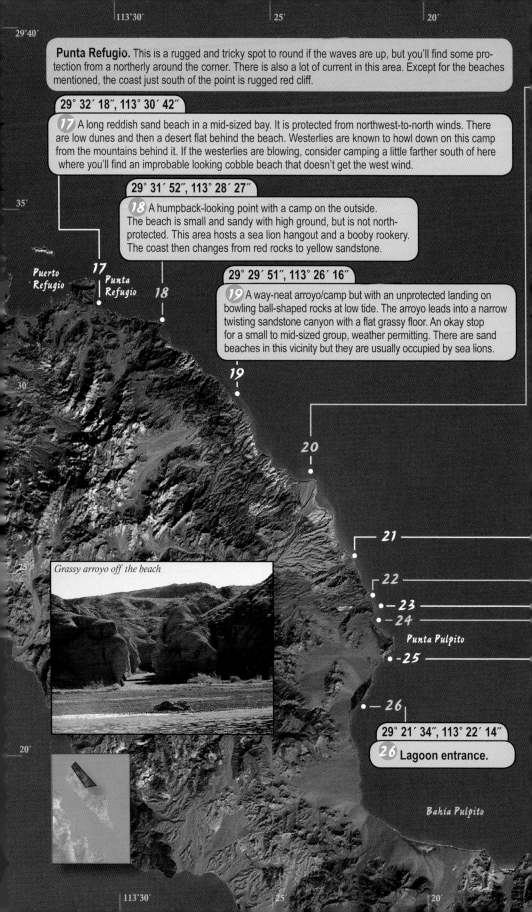
Grassy arroyo off the beach

Bahía Pulpito

29° 27′ 37″, 113° 23′ 43″

20 In the bay north of this reading are a few possible arroyo/camps. All would be mostly exposed to north swell. This beach is in front of a huge arroyo on a low point. The beach here, though prone to waves in a northerly, is low-angle permitting an easy carry of gear and boats. The big mountains recede into the interior of the island and a plain is developing behind this section of coast.

29° 25′ 24″, 113° 22′ 25″

21 A big gravel beach landmarked by a stone wind shelter set on a low hill.

29° 24′ 26″, 113° 21′ 56″

22 A small bay with a good beach protected from northwest wind.

29° 24′ 05″, 113° 21′ 45″

23 This is one of a few small coves in the immediate vicinity. Small hills behind these coves offer varying degrees of shelter from a westerly, making them good places to hole-up before tackling Pulpito. This particular camp/cove has a low dune in its southern corner. You'll find plenty of flat sleeping areas behind the gravel beach.

Playa Pulpito

29° 23′ 45″, 113° 21′ 48″

24 Playa Pulpito. A half-mile long, sand beach just north of Punta Pulpito. From here you can climb Pulpito if you so desire as a day hike. There is space here for the largest of groups; however, the low terrain behind this beach offers no protection from a strong westerly. The north end of the beach is some-what protected from north swells. But if the wind is coming in strong from the north, it might be better to head around the point and seek sanctuary on the north coast of Bahía Pulpito, perhaps even considering a crossing towards the inside of the bay if you don't mind surfing swell. If the wind is strong from the west, rounding Pulpito is like hitting a wall.

Punta Pulpito to Punta Rocosa. Punta Rocosa stands sentinel over the southeastern corner of Bahía Pulpito and is an amazing site. Gazing at Rocosa from Pulpito reminded me of Dorothy's first view of the Emerald City in *The Wizard of Oz*. It is tall, steep, and shimmering far in the distance. However, the massive water span of Bahía Pulpito lies in the interval. It is an ample crossing, upwards of 12 miles if approached directly. It is prudent to boat along shore into the northern reaches of the Bahía Pulpito before attempting to cross, as you would be in danger if a westerly caught you outside the perimeter of the bay.

29° 22′ 44″, 113° 21′ 26″

25 Pulpito South. Around the corner of Pulpito are a few gravel/cobble beaches leading to a big lagoon in the middle of the northern arm of Bahía Pulpito. I have not landed here, but the camping appears to be good and generally north-protected. Farther into the bay, the coast relief becomes low and doesn't pick up again until the southern arm. The back of the bay is a semi-continuous beach with steep gravel landings.

Punta Rocosa

South Shore, Bahía Pulpito. The next part of the island is amazing. The scenery is superb, and there is great camping and fantastic hikes. Punta Rocosa looms and is a significant navigational consideration, but if the weather is calm while you are going around the point, there are giant sea caves to explore and a wondrous mountain to gaze upon.

29° 16′ 52″, 113° 17′ 30″

27 Calleta Pulpito West ✷✷✷ Despite its lack of north pro, this beach gets the coveted five-star rating. The approach is very shallow, so even if waves were to be entering from the north, they would be knocked down in size as you got closer to the landing zone, which is soft white sand. There are small dunes rimming the beach and behind them is a lagoon.

29°20′

Bahía Pulpito

27   28   29   30

31

32

Punta Rocosa

33

34

35

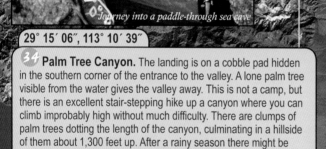
Journey into a paddle-through sea cave

29° 15′ 06″, 113° 10′ 39″

34 Palm Tree Canyon. The landing is on a cobble pad hidden in the southern corner of the entrance to the valley. A lone palm tree visible from the water gives the valley away. This is not a camp, but there is an excellent stair-stepping hike up a canyon where you can climb improbably high without much difficulty. There are clumps of palm trees dotting the length of the canyon, culminating in a hillside of them about 1,300 feet up. After a rainy season there might be pockets of water in the canyon.

29° 14′ 15″, 113° 10′ 39″

35 ✷✷ A lovely arroyo/camp with a gravel beach that is not steep but is exposed to north-east/east swell.

Calleta Pulpito West

29° 17′ 04″, 113° 16′ 24″

28 **Calleta Pulpito East.** There are landings in both the eastern and western corners, though the eastern corner has some reefs in front of it. The break is gradual leading up to a beach of small cobble. The camping spots are much smaller than Calleta West, but very pretty with the best spot being perhaps the top center of the beach.

To the east of the calleta is a cliff of great beauty where many birds congregate. There is also a pinnacle of rock out in the water with an osprey nest nearby.

29° 17′ 25″, 113° 14′ 49″

29 Offshore rocks. These protrude at low tide and can be covered with surf at times. I suspect there is good fishing here.

29° 17′ 12″, 113° 12′ 06″

30 **✷✷✸** The coastline leading up to the highlands of Punta Rocosa is a long beach of gnarly rock with a large valley behind it. For the boater heading towards Rocosa, it might appear there are no good camping spots, but this is not so. A last camp on the southern shore of Bahía Pulpito is hidden just under the western foot of the Rocosa rampart. And it is a glorious camp. A small spur of beach sticking into the bay ends in an anvil of rock with wings that protect landings on both the west and east shores of the spur. There is a fish camp built around a cave on the south side of this spit, but it is mostly clean. A towering cliff backs up the cove on the eastern side of the spur, and in the corner a spire rises from the water. Come evening the sunset views of the island's interior are superb.

29° 17′ 18″, 113° 11′ 41″

31 A giant sea cave. There are lesser, but sometimes quite deep, sea caves in the area. If the weather is calm, don't overlook exploring these. Compared to the expanse of the mountain above, some of the caves don't appear to be worth checking out but that changes when you paddle into them.

29° 17′ 22″, 113° 10′ 49″

32 **Punta Rocosa.** It has been said that in a wintertime north blow, Punta Rocosa resembles Cape Horn. The waves can get large and fierce, the currents strong and capable of generating a big tidal race, and the exposure (the "out there" factor) tremendous. It is recommended to lay back from the point if the wind is gusting. That being said, if you are not fighting surf as you round Punta Rocosa, rarely will you get the opportunity to paddle below a more majestic headland. The view is stunning.

29° 16′ 12″, 113° 10′ 26″

33 **Playa Punta Rocosa ✷✷✷** A somewhat-protected, lovely long gravel beach backed by brown sand. There are mountains on two sides of the beach, and a long view down coast to Isla Estanque.

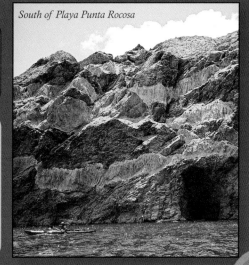

South of Playa Punta Rocosa

The terrain south of Playa Punta Rocosa is exemplary. Large cliffs of granite rise out of the water and are painted horizontally with jagged swaths of opposing colors. Above these cliffs tower high mountains

Offshore, there are rock gardens with juicy snorkeling potential. One of the larger rocks, just before the next reading, has an arch in it. Next to the arch, at the right tide level, is a barely perceptible, paddle-through sea cave—start at the southern end and believe.

In the middle part of the southeast quadrant of Isla de la Guarda the high relief fades into low plain for a number of miles until the Isla Estanque region. A couple of large arroyo mouths between the previous reading and the next make possible fair-weather camps. The hiking up the arroyos into the island's interior is good.

36

37

38

39

Isla Estanque

40

41

29° 02´ 23˝, 113° 06´ 36˝

41 A north-protected gravel bar camp south of the Estanque channel.

Punta Colorada

Isla Estanque tidal rip on a calm weather day

29° 11′ 28″, 113° 09′ 48″

36 Big Spit. This is a large gravel apron with a lagoon behind its northern half. There is some north surf protection on the southern side, but waves would probably wrap around the spit somewhat, creating a break that peels down beach. Isla Tiburón is in full view from here.

29° 06′ 30″, 113° 09′ 48″

37 There is a possible camp in the low coastal zone in this area. The shore is unprotected and the camp is in a large arroyo north of a set of bluffs, easily visible in the morning and early afternoon because of the otherwise drab nature of the coastline. But looks can be deceiving. Come late afternoon, as the light off the bluffs mellows and shadows come out, the views up and down the coast become inspirational.

Southeast coast of de la Guarda

10′

29° 03′ 25″, 113° 07′ 27″

05′

38 ✹✹ If you are paddling south it is hard to discern this camp from a distance. Wedged between dark hills, the camp is 1.25 miles in from the small volcanic cone that marks the eastern point of Isla de la Guarda. If you were dealing with a north wind you would be tempted to stay away from this part of the coast, but the best and safest camp in the area is hidden here in a cove. The surf break is very gradual with a white sand/some stone landing. In the eastern corner are low dunes where camping is possible, and above the central part of the beach is a bar of flat rocks that also makes a nice camping area. This cove appears to offer ideal swimming, but it is very crowded with stingrays. Be careful.

To the east of waypoint 38 lies a brown, gravel, mile-long beach. There is good, but unprotected camping on the western end of the beach. Here the landing terrain is not too steep, but farther east the beach gets steeper and turns to cobble. Behind it is a huge lagoon.

29° 03′ 19″, 113° 06′ 07″

29°00′

39 An interesting camp on the point. Located way out from the rest of the island, it has a very airy feeling with sweeping vistas including views of the Midriffs down south. The landing on the low bar is totally unprotected from the north but there is a southern landing around the corner. Behind the cobble bar is a recessed pocket of flat land that might be out of the brunt of north and south winds.

The Estanque Channel. The channel is very shallow in its southern half until beyond a large, white, solitary rock. It gets a rip with whitewater at numerous tide stages, but is strongest when the tide is in peak flood. Then the current flows very strongly south through the gap. Approach the channel with caution, and forget about going against the current if the rip has started.

29° 03′ 56″, 113° 05′ 45″

55′

40 Isla Estanque is a small steep hill of an island that has a very surf-sheltered cove on its western flank. The entrance to the cove is just north of the neck of the de la Guarda/Estanque channel. The rocky beach is a fish camp and has a fair amount of fish trash scattered among man-made windbreaks, and also significant quantities of human feces and used toilet paper deposited around its back half. This is a gross camp. Estanque is also called Snake Island due to a proliferation of red rattlesnakes. My personal name for the island is Isla Estinky. On my short visit I didn't see any snakes, averted my eyes as best I could when I came to the shit, and had a nice scramble up to the top of the island where the views are glorious. The current can run swift on the outside and there is the possibility of a tidal race there.

Southwest cove

In the stretch between #50 and Este Ton, there are a few unprotected arroyo camp possibilities.

29° 06′ 28″, 113° 16′ 03″

50 A stony landing to a beach with mild pro and a rocky sleeping area. The setting, however, is very attractive overall with a large white cliff rising above.

29° 05′ 57″, 113° 15′ 46″

49 A massive three-way arch. Good snorkeling abounds in this area.

29° 05′ 12″, 113° 15′ 15″

48 A south-facing beach in a pretty section of the coast.

29° 04′ 31″, 113° 14′ 56″

47 A large, fair-weather beach semi-protected at its upper end.

29° 02′ 44″, 113° 12′ 04″

46 In this large indent into the island are two or three fair-weather camps with mountainous backdrops.

29° 01′ 44″, 113° 11′ 09″

45 ✶✶✶ Sitting under a minor point, this is a mostly-protected arroyo beach with a small cobble landing. There might be some wrap effect from swell on a north wind day. There is good morning shade, the views go from Isla Coronado down to Punta San Francisquito, and the beach is clean. Should you be experiencing southerlies, there is a good camp around the next corner past the buttress of rock.

Punta Don Juan

Bahía de los Ángeles

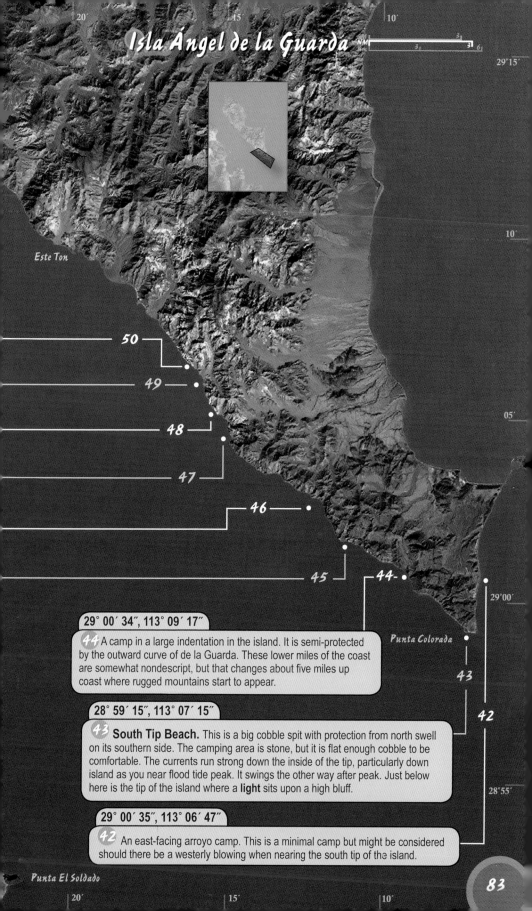

29°15′

20′

15′

10′

10″

Este Ton

05′

50

49

48

47

46

45

44

44 — •

29°00′

Punta Colorada

29° 00′ 34″, 113° 09′ 17″

44 A camp in a large indentation in the island. It is semi-protected by the outward curve of de la Guarda. These lower miles of the coast are somewhat nondescript, but that changes about five miles up coast where rugged mountains start to appear.

43

28° 59′ 15″, 113° 07′ 15″

43 **South Tip Beach.** This is a big cobble spit with protection from north swell on its southern side. The camping area is stone, but it is flat enough cobble to be comfortable. The currents run strong down the inside of the tip, particularly down island as you near flood tide peak. It swings the other way after peak. Just below here is the tip of the island where a **light** sits upon a high bluff.

42

28°55′

29° 00′ 35″, 113° 06′ 47″

42 An east-facing arroyo camp. This is a minimal camp but might be considered should there be a westerly blowing when nearing the south tip of the island.

Jellyfish

Jellyfish can pack a powerful sting, but it is rarely fatal, at least not around Baja.

Other jellyfish stings from the lion's mane (Cyanea) or sea nettle (Chrysaora) may require hospitalization. The little blue devils called Portuguese Man o' War can be common in the southern Sea of Cortez when the water gets warm in the summer. Most jellyfish stings in Baja will only cause a painful burning and welting lasting up to a few days. In some cases where there is severe allergic reaction, some medical attention may be needed. Usually, applying vinegar or meat tenderizer to a sting may alleviate some of the burning because it breaks down the proteins of the venom.

"Jellies" are a member of the class Cnidaria, related to corals and anemones because they have similar early body structures and reproduction. They have been around in the fossil record for 650 million years. All Cnidarians capture their food with stinging cells called nematocysts, used to stun or kill their prey. Jellyfish carry these nematocysts on long trailing tentacles as they float through the water. When the tentacles contact a swimmer or a fish, they release venoms that cause tissue or nerve damage. The venom is still active even if the jellyfish is dead on the beach.

Jellyfish have no heart and no brain. They breathe through their entire body surface. Jellyfish eggs, like corals, hatch into planktonic planula—tiny buds—which attach to a surface and grow into polyps with stinging cells. In coral, the baby polyps stay put and grow hard calciferous shells within colonies which form reefs. Jellyfish polyps sprout cloned buds, which float off and grow into medusa heads or jellyfish. The largest jellyfish grow to seven feet across with tentacles trailing 100 feet, but only scuba divers in deeper water see these. The larger jellies are easier to spot and avoid. The greater hazards are the small jellies because they are hard to see and their tentacles are nearly invisible. When snorkeling, give them a wide berth if you see them first. The best prevention is to wear a wet suit or shirt, even in warm water.

–Lori Russell

Photo by: Bill Schmidt

Photo by: Ron Lewis

Turtles

Occasionally as you paddle along, you will see a little dark turtle head pop above the surface for a breath of air and a curious look around. But turtles are shy and if they see you, they will dive under quickly.

There are five species of sea turtles that visit Baja and two that nest here: the Leatherback and the Olive Ridley. Turtles nest on tropical beaches all over the world, and then may spend several years traveling at sea before returning to the same beach to nest ten or fifteen years later, if they survive. They will then return to the same beach every year, sometimes twice a year, to mate and nest. The females like sandy beaches where they can bury their eggs one or two feet deep. The hatchlings take up to fifteen years to reach sexual maturity and may live up to a hundred years. Species range from one to seven feet long and up to 1,500 pounds for the Leatherback turtle.

Loggerhead turtles have been tracked with transmitters, nesting in Japan and traveling 7000 miles to Baja to feed and mature before returning to Japan. Other turtles nest in Baja and travel to distant waters to feed. Like many sea animals, they have a mechanism in their brains that can detect the magnetic field of the earth enabling them to navigate thousands of miles. Little is known of the turtles' adventures after they leave the nest. But less than one in a thousand reaches maturity to return to its nesting ground.

The plight of the turtle is another of the many sad stories of the declining animal life in Baja. All seven species of sea turtles are now endangered worldwide. A few are close to extinction; one is already extinct. Although the U.S.A. began protecting turtles in 1970, Mexico, a major nesting ground, did not forbid the killing of turtles until 1991. Consumption of turtle meat and eggs has a long cultural heritage in Mexico. It is a favorite dish at Easter time. And even though it is illegal, poaching continues. It is estimated that ten thousand may be killed each year for the black market. There are dozens of agencies and many heroic efforts to save the turtle, including turtle sanctuaries, nurseries, education programs and turtle beach-patrols to protect nesting turtles, but they are fighting a surging tide of human population and development. In Mexico, many beaches are driven on, so turtle nests are often crushed by cars.

In addition to poaching, thousands are killed unintentionally each year by the fishing industry, caught in trawling nets or long lines. Hundreds are found dead each year from eating floating plastic trash and bags which lodge in their stomachs. The plastic bags resemble the turtle's favorite food, jellyfish.

The numbers of turtles, as measured by the number of nesting sites, is declining at an alarming rate, and the last twenty years have been the worst. Some researchers think sea turtles will all be extinct in our lifetime despite huge efforts to save them, because the remaining populations are already too small to recover.

– Lori Russell

Returning from diving at the start of the leg. Photo by: Doug Drisky

Isla Ángel
de la Guarda

Isla Coronado

Bahía de los Ángeles

Bahía las
Ánimas

Punta
las Ánimas

Bahía San Rafael

Punta
Ballena

San
Francisquito

Punta
San Francisquito

SM
NM
Km

This is the first half of the L.A. Bay to Santa Rosalia leg, which, taken as a whole (140 miles), is one of the longer and wilder legs on the coast. Fresh water is unavailable for extended stretches, the points to be rounded are rugged and large (with ensuing large bays to cross), and the leg lies in the north of the sea where the waves seem to be larger during storms than down south. This stretch sees three major tidal races in its course: off Punta las Ánimas, Punta Ballena, and Punta San Francisquito.

The tidal races are a result of the Midriff, the narrow land pinch filled with islands between Baja and mainland Mexico. Strong currents from tides squeezing and accelerating through the Midriff conflict with winds to create the races.

So it is a heads-up leg, but with the above-mentioned concerns respected, it is one of the most attractive and rewarding on the peninsula.

Most trips heading south to Santa Rosalia will stop at the outpost of San Francisquito, about halfway along, to restock fresh water. It is possible to begin and end a trip at San Francisquito, but San Francisquito is a hard place to shuttle from due to a long dirt road access.

The start of the trip in L.A. Bay will give you an idea of what is in store for much of the journey—a paddle across a large bay to a wild headland. Do not launch if the westerlies are up, and if they come up when you're paddling, get ready with a right hand brace or look for safe haven if it is close. Within the bays along the way, there are more than a few long sand beaches; however, many of these are exposed to the north and require surf landings should the northerlies be kicking.

10'

29°00'

50'

40'

30'

20'

30'   20'   10'   113°00'   112°50'

87

1
Punta Don Juan
2
3
4
Punta el Pescador
5
6
Ensenada el Pescador
7
28·55
8
Punta el Soldado

28° 53′ 57″, 113° 22′ 45″

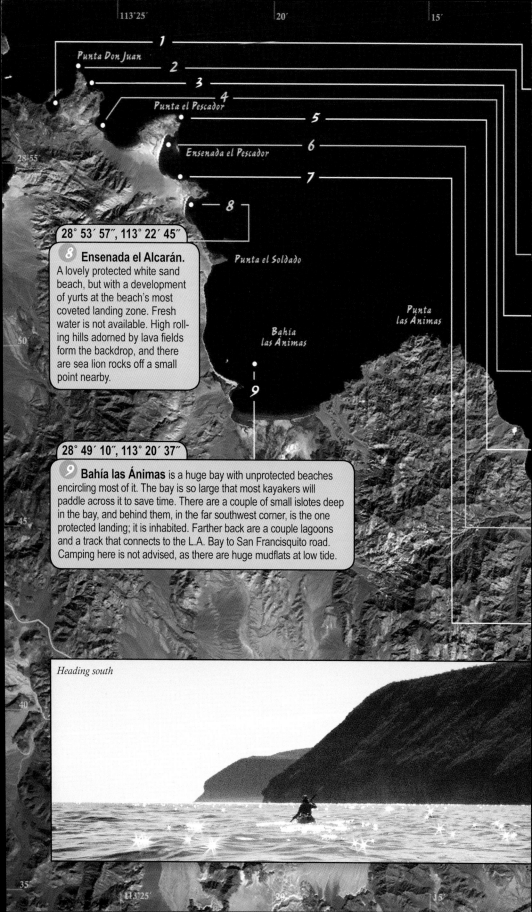

8 **Ensenada el Alcarán.**
A lovely protected white sand beach, but with a development of yurts at the beach's most coveted landing zone. Fresh water is not available. High rolling hills adorned by lava fields form the backdrop, and there are sea lion rocks off a small point nearby.

Punta
las Ánimas

Bahía
las Ánimas

50

9

28° 49′ 10″, 113° 20′ 37″

9 **Bahía las Ánimas** is a huge bay with unprotected beaches encircling most of it. The bay is so large that most kayakers will paddle across it to save time. There are a couple of small islotes deep in the bay, and behind them, in the far southwest corner, is the one protected landing; it is inhabited. Farther back are a couple lagoons and a track that connects to the L.A. Bay to San Francisquito road. Camping here is not advised, as there are huge mudflats at low tide.

45

40

Heading south

35

L.A. Bay to San Francisquito

28° 56′ 25″, 113° 26′ 45″

1 **Don Juan Cove** ✶✶ This reading is from the primary beach in the back of Don Juan Cove, also called Puerto Don Juan. It is a popular yacht anchorage. But before you get into the cove, there is a possible camp on the isthmus that forms the cove's north arm. This camp is on flat cobble and offers great views of the L.A. Bay archipelago. A gravel beach on the way into the cove, near a shipwreck, is also an acceptable camp. The cove has a totally protected landing. The main beach is rough sand and big enough for the largest group. A low saddle behind camp invites hiking. There is sometimes great phosphorescence in this cove at nighttime, though it was not that way when I was there. However, a small beach farther into the leg was amazingly rich in phosphorescence.

28°55′

Isla Partida

28° 57′ 36″, 113° 26′ 16″

2 **Punta Don Juan.**

28° 57′ 07″, 113° 25′ 57″

3 A small camp behind the point.

28° 55′ 58″, 113° 25′ 37″

50′

4 **Ensenada el Quemado.** A beautiful, partially protected white sand beach. The more protected corner is cobble. There is a fair-weather beach near red rock on the south-eastern arm of the bay.

28° 56′ 10″, 113° 23′ 07″

5 **Punta el Pescador** ✶✶ A pretty, very private white sand/small cobble beach just behind the point. It would be five-star if it were a little more protected. There is good snorkeling off the small rock outcropping to the northwest.

28° 55′ 33″, 113° 23′ 27″

45′

6 **Ensenada el Pescador.** There is a low but protected camp that is just north of this reading on the east side of the point. This northern beach is lovely and backed by red cliffs. The main beach of the ensenada is beautiful but has a development of 10 or so cabañas in the primary camp zone.

28° 54′ 33″, 113° 22′ 52″

7 An exposed beach on the south arm of the ensenada that could hold a mid-sized group. It is a pretty camp and has a shade cave that's accessible at low tide.

40′

Swimming with whale shark, Photo by: Mary Ellen Schoeman

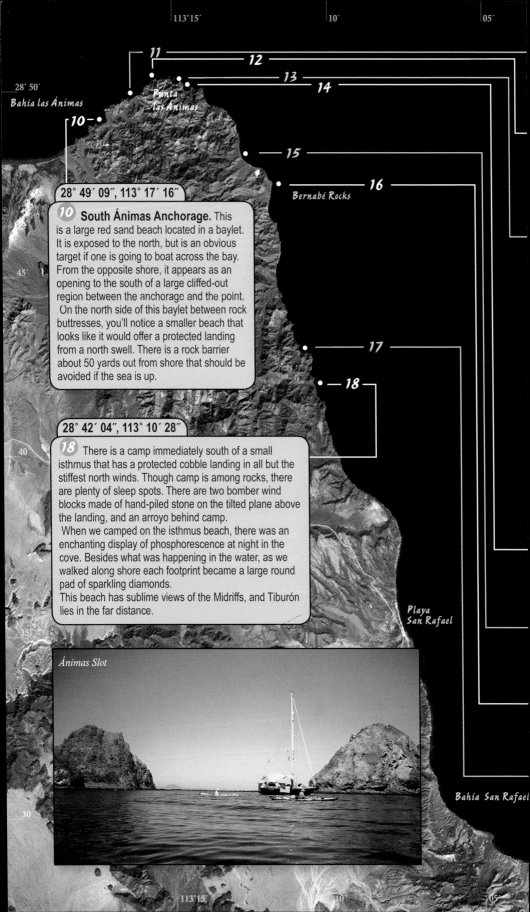

113°15′   10′   05′

28° 50′
Bahía las Ánimas

11
12
13
14

**Punta
las Ánimas**

10

15

16
Bernabé Rocks

28° 49′ 09″, 113° 17′ 16″

10 **South Ánimas Anchorage.** This
is a large red sand beach located in a baylet.
It is exposed to the north, but is an obvious
target if one is going to boat across the bay.
From the opposite shore, it appears as an
opening to the south of a large cliffed-out
region between the anchorage and the point.
On the north side of this baylet between rock
buttresses, you'll notice a smaller beach that
looks like it would offer a protected landing
from a north swell. There is a rock barrier
about 50 yards out from shore that should be
avoided if the sea is up.

17

18

28° 42′ 04″, 113° 10′ 28″

18 There is a camp immediately south of a small
isthmus that has a protected cobble landing in all but the
stiffest north winds. Though camp is among rocks, there
are plenty of sleep spots. There are two bomber wind
blocks made of hand-piled stone on the tilted plane above
the landing, and an arroyo behind camp.
When we camped on the isthmus beach, there was an
enchanting display of phosphorescence at night in the
cove. Besides what was happening in the water, as we
walked along shore each footprint became a large round
pad of sparkling diamonds.
This beach has sublime views of the Midriffs, and Tiburón
lies in the far distance.

**Playa
San Rafael**

Ánimas Slot

Bahía San Rafael

113°15′   10′   05′

28° 49′ 53″, 113° 16′ 15″

11 A good-sized but north-exposed beach.

28° 50′

28° 50′ 33″, 113° 15′ 06″

12 **Punta las Ánimas** can experience 4-5 knot currents and a tidal race. It should be approached with a watchful eye to the sea and wind conditions. The headland is comprised of beautiful jagged red cliffs interspersed with beaches. The backdrop is mountainous. Should the wind be up, it will make for adventuresome paddling getting around this long point. If you are boating wide because of surf, be wary of Bernabé Rocks down coast.

28° 50′ 17″, 113° 14′ 58″

13 **The Ánimas Slot** ✱✱✱ A perfect white sand beach protected from the worst of a north swell by an islet at its entrance. If you are coming into this sanctuary riding a strong norther, it is recommended you enter the harbor from the east side of the islet to avoid some submerged rocks. The background to the beach is comprised of dunes and red rock hills.
Well-protected camps after the Animas Slot are lacking until San Francisquito.

45′

Still heading south

40′

28° 50′ 04″, 113° 14′ 32″

14 **Puertecito de Enmedio.** A longish red sand beach somewhat protected in its upper corner. In the south corner, two large rocks out in the water guard the beach—these might offer a protected landing if you were talented enough to ride the swell in near them.

28° 48′ 21″, 113° 12′ 49″

15 Coming after a smaller but okay beach, this is a mile-long beach preceded by an arch at its northern end. It's a great camp if the east or north winds aren't up. If the north winds are up, you could make a tight landing just behind the arch on some steep cobble. By now the Midriff Islands are in view.

35′

28° 47′ 30″, 113° 11′ 45″

16 **Bernabé Rocks Point.** A cobble beach with some sand lies inside. Rocks a bit offshore of this point get dangerous with surf. Continuing on down bay, there are a few other exposed beaches and a couple sea caves.

28° 42′ 54″, 113° 10′ 54″

17 Heading towards a point of red rock, there is a gravel/cobble beach with a flat, sandy area for sleeping. There is a giant double arch on the north end of the beach. The landing is not north-protected.

30′

Punta Ballena

113°00′   55′   50′

19

28

San Rafael

20

Lower **Bahía San Rafael** has three nice beaches. I have only glassed them during the paddle across the bay, and they looked exposed. From Punta Ballena west into the bay, there is a very long beach. Not all of it would make for good camping, as there are sporadic sections of low bluff right behind shore. There is a large dry lagoon behind the center of this beach. Viewed from the middle of the bay, the distant Punta Ballena looks like a moray eel.

Bahía San Rafael

30

22

Punta Ballena

21-

23

2

28° 27′ 06″, 112° 53′ 00″

24 **Mujeres Cove, East Bight**. A good camp on a narrow beach, but the sleeping spots are not as nice as those in West Bight. The landing is also more exposed than West Bight's.

25

Francis

Sea cave shade break, Photo by: Dave Erskine

20

15

28° 36′ 20″, 113° 07′ 51″

19 Playa San Rafael. The top landing of Playa San Rafael. This is a good sand camp with some protection from swell. Farther down beach, nesting on a bluff next to some pretty dunes is the tiny community of San Rafael. A local told me there was water there, but I'm not sure if she meant at San Rafael or at the ranch where she lived, which was some five kilometers farther back. If you are desperate, I'm sure you could get some water.

28° 33′ 51″, 113° 07′ 02″

20 An east-northeast facing beach nestled between low cliffs of beige rock. Though the beach is not large, there is plenty of flat sleeping areas. The arroyo behind could be used too, but it is buggy. The land just behind San Rafael is low, but mountains make their way into the scenery behind the back of the bay.

28° 27′ 53″, 112° 56′ 10″

21 Big Beach. The water is shallow for a long ways out, so a north swell should come in as a graduated break. The area by some gray cliffs is rich in fossils, and there are more fossil beds inland.

28° 28′ 25″, 112° 54′ 08″

22 Punta Ballena. This is an exposed point with a possible tidal race extending off of it to the south. Usually tidal races are at their biggest when opposing wind and current collide. If the wind is not up, there can still be a race, but it won't be as large. On these windless days and if it is active, it is possible to boat inside the race hugging the shore.

28° 27′ 21″, 112° 53′ 15″

23 Mujeres Cove, West Bight ✳✳✳ This is a beautiful white sand beach in a small cove with a protected landing north of center. Cool looking granite formations on shore offer excellent snorkeling in the waters below them. There are views of the Midriff Islands all the way to the volcano on the south end of Tiburón from here. This cove is sometimes used as a fish camp and also as a yacht anchorage.

Mujeres Cove, West Bight

As you boat into the top bay of San Francisquito, there is a **light** and near it a very appealing, undeveloped white sand beach in the western corner of the bay.

Nestled some 2-3 hours by car via dirt road from either Highway 1 or L.A. Bay, **San Francisquito** is a picturesque outpost on the northern sea. It is not a town; there are no stores here, but there is *fresh water* available, a small cabana-style resort, some homes, and an airstrip. The water is trucked from a ranch inland. Sometimes there is a supply of bottled water.

San Francisquito is divided into two parts. The north part is Puerto San Francisquito in Ensenada las Palomas, a bay just west of Punta San Francisquito. This is a calm launch and land zone between two points that get tidal races. There are a few houses here and a major fish camp in season.

The southeastern half of San Francisquito is primarily the resort at Ensenada Blanca. It is on a long, heavenly beach with an airstrip behind it. Gringos who fly in for fishing are the most common visitors at the resort. Other than at the resort restaurant, you cannot purchase food in San Francisquito, so make sure you are stocked before you arrive.

San Francisquito is far from the highway; the roads into here are dirt and are all pretty bumpy and washboarded. From the north, the access is through L.A. Bay; this 85-mile long road is a notorious tire eater. The road from Highway 1 starting east of Guerrero Negro is direct but severely washboarded. A route up from Viscaino is the best and the shortest of all the approaches, if you are driving from the south.

28 °30′

Punta Ballena

Mujeres Coves

25

Punta San Francisquito

• — *26*

25

• ——— *27*

Ensenada Blanca

• ——— *28*

Hooked on sea kayaking

20′

San Francisquito

Puerto San Francisquito, Photo by: Doug Driskell

28° 25´ 33˝, 112° 51´ 49˝

25 **Puerto San Francisquito/Ensenada las Palomas.** This is a very functional beach in the back of a cove. It gets north winds but the waves are small. In fall, there is a large fish camp at its eastern end. The clamming in the cove is excellent.

Fresh water is available at the houses at the western end of the beach. Ask for Alberto's house. He is a helpful man who speaks English well; he knows the area intimately, and also does shuttles, either with panga or truck. His email is: betolucero2003@yahoo.com.mx. Should you be without a car, Alberto will drive his water truck down to the beach so you do not have to haul water. Camping on the beach is $5/person/night.

28° 26´ 33˝, 112° 50´ 42˝

26 **Punta San Francisquito**.
- Dave to fellow paddlers, "Watch out for whirlpools and big waves!"
- Fellow paddler, "Aye, and sea dragons and the end of the earth!"

A notoriously bad-ass point. It is beautifully rugged and gets some of the most dramatic waves of the sea. There can be a tidal race extending off the point and heading south. A very competent boater told me of his experience here: "I was glad I had confidence in my roll; it is equivalent to a Class IV river run." Local gringo fishermen half-jokingly call it "The White Wall of Death." They say that at times the waves are six feet, come in offset patterns, and are forceful enough to capsize a small motorboat. But it is not always desperate here. On one of our trips rounding the point, it was calm—we could have snorkeled. On another trip, the race was active but manageable. If you're dubious about peaked, wacky waves, it might be a good idea to talk to a local in Ensenada las Palomas about what they think the conditions are going to be like about the time you start for the point.

25´

28° 25´18˝, 112° 50´ 57˝

27 ✱✱✱ The beautiful **Ensenada Blanca.** This reading is for the protected northern corner of the beach. It is the only free camping available in the area. A fence up in the dunes marks the edge of private property to the south. It is a nice camp and close to good fishing.

28° 24´ 33˝, 112° 51´ 27˝

28 **San Francisquito Resort.** This is a tranquilo, slightly rundown establishment. A variety of small cabañas and a restaurant under a large palapa make up the complex. Camping with showers is available. In 2005, the price was $5/person/night. The restaurant likes advance notice if you are going to eat there. It is not cheap, but it's a fun experience. They have cold beer, and the food is good. They will cook your fish for you if you've been so lucky.

If you've got the time, this is a good place to chill. The shade under the palapa feels nice, and the cold beer running down the back of your throat as you gaze out on the sparkling sea is a welcome change from sitting in a kayak and grinding it out hour after hour.

South of the beach there is an area of rocks in the water just off the coast called "The Aquarium" that has great snorkeling.

Pelican patrol, Photo by: Lori Russell

The Unlikely Pelican

Sitting on a rock, a pelican is a most preposterous looking bird with a large, ungainly body on short, stumpy legs, and a long neck that supports his unnaturally long beak, from which hangs a most unlikely Santa's pouch. The beak and chin-pouch are so long and heavy that he must rest it flush against his neck so he appears to have no beak at all. But a pelican in flight is a thing of beauty. True masters of cruise control, they often don't actually fly but float just inches over the surface of the water, riding on the super dense layer of surface air which covers the earth. This "ground effect" method of flight uses a minimum of energy and allows the pelicans to float great distances without ever flapping their wings.

Pelicans cruise in large groups, flying in perfect formation, scoping the waters for schools of fish. Spotting some, a pelican will then fly up to 60 feet high, fold its wings and drop like a laser guided bomb, smashing the surface of the water and scooping up a mouthful of fish in its pouch. Their dive-bombing acrobatics are most impressive.

Pelican patrols can be seen in groups of five to a hundred as they migrate to the remote islands off the coast of Baja to breed and nest in the spring. Here they can rear their young in peace, free from the usual land predators, because pelicans put forward no protective behavior for their nest. They build simple mounds of sticks exposed on the ground, but within colonies sometimes numbering in the thousands, covering the slopes of the desert islands. They are very docile birds, and when threatened, they will fly off and abandon their young. So keep a good distance from their nest sites. It can be difficult in the spring to find an island campsite free of nesting pelicans.

The brown pelican seen in Baja and many sub-tropical waters was nearly extinct and listed as endangered in the 1970's. It was another victim of DDT, a chemical insecticide which found it's way into almost all food chains. The chemical made the eggshells of the pelicans and many other birds too thin and the eggs would crack before maturity. Today, as a protected bird, their populations are recovering.

– Lori Russell

A typical brown pelican family.

Camp on the backside of Isla San Lorenzo

```
SM |——————————|4.5——————————|9
NM |——————————|4.5|——————————|9
Km |——————————|4.5|——————————|9
```

The Midriff Islands are some of the least visited in the Sea of Cortez by kayakers because of the area's remoteness from an established town, the width of the crossing, and strong currents around the islas. But for some kayakers, the remoteness means fewer people. Though the islands are lacking in vegetation, the camping is good and the water offshore is often crystal-clear for snorkeling. However, because nearby currents dredge up cold water from the depths of the channels, swimming here is colder than any place else in the sea.

In spring the islands are major bird nesting areas. There are families of terns, boobies, gulls, oystercatchers, pelicans, and cormorants. This is good and bad for campers. Though charming and intriguing at times, the number of birds can also make camps less desirable because of noise, smell, or turf wars with the humans. There are less birds in the fall.

A healthy respect for the currents, which are accelerated by a funneling effect caused by the Midriff pinch, is necessary here; but the currents are manageable if coinciding atmospheric conditions are benign. Planning an appropriate launch time for any crossing is advised. A tide chart will assist in accounting for drift during a crossing, and unless you are very fast, at some point you will get drift. When the tide is coming in, the current in the channel runs to the north; when the tide is going out, the current runs to the south. Plan ahead for deflection away from your target, especially if you are launching during a new moon or full moon. An ill-timed launch that might have the current turn south on you a couple hours after a start from the south (San Francisquito, for instance) could result in a deflection into open sea. Along the island's shores, the current usually runs counter to the tide.

Crossing to the Midriffs may also involve breaking through a tidal race. Depending on where you launch from, a trip through a race might be unavoidable, if it means catching the right current in the channel. The races occur on the prominent points across from the Midriffs.

The Midriffs are permitted islands. The permit office in L.A. Bay and the parent office in Ensenada supplies them. Alberto in San Francisquito (see San Francisquito town page) also has permits. However, there is no permit enforcement on the Midriffs.

The area of San Francisquito is the best road-accessed launch point for a trip to the Midriff Islands.

la
e la
uarda

Isla Partida

Isla Rasa

Isla Salsipuedes

Isla las Ánimas

Isla San Lorenzo

Bahía
San Rafael

Punta
Ballena

29°00′

50′

28°40′

113°00′   112°50′

Isla las Ánimas is more or less a northern continuation of Isla San Lorenzo, as the space between them is only a couple hundred yards.

28° 41´ 51˝, 112° 55´ 49˝

1ᴀ A camp in a hook-shaped, very north-protected cove. The beach is gravel and is a sometimes-used fish camp. You'll find good hiking up the sparsely vegetated hills behind camp. Watch out for patches of Cholla cactus, however—this plant has ambush capability. I had the misfortune of getting a detachable segment stuck in my leg after I passed near a plant. Upon pulling it out, it stuck to my hand, and then upon flicking it away, it got embedded in my arm. I surrendered and cried for help. The currents on the outside of camp can be strong.

28° 42´ 19˝, 112° 55´ 58˝

2ᴀ A small beach at the very top of the island. It is sand and cobble and set back in a cove where it is protected from all weather but from due north, and then it probably sees a graduated break. There is great snorkeling nearby and direct views of Islas Salsipuedes, Rasa, and de la Guarda.

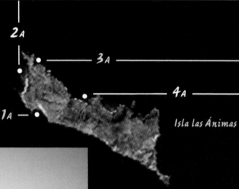

Isla las Ánimas

Paddling the Midriffs

28° 40´ 27˝, 112° 53´ 27˝

7sʟ ✻✻ This is a gravel spit offering some protection. It is the last good camp on the inside of San Lorenzo.

28° 39´ 47˝, 112° 52´ 38˝

6sʟ An unprotected but easily-landed gravel beach. On a glassy day, the Baja shore looks imminently close and reachable as if you could swim to it.

28° 39´ 11˝, 112° 52´ 03˝

5sʟ A small north-protected cove with a beach. It is a fish camp.

28° 38´ 27˝, 112° 50´ 53˝

4sʟ A north-protected camp just up from the prominent valley, but that doesn't get wind funneling over it. It is set against a wall of yellow and brown, with the sleeping spots scattered about. The beach is cobble and there is excellent snorkeling off it, as well as great views. Far to the south you'll see the volcanic cones of the Tres Virgenes, which look like islands in the sea.

28° 38´ 20˝, 112° 50´ 33˝

3sʟ The mouth of a valley that almost cuts the island in two. There can be much wind blowing out of it, so it is not a recommended camp. But it is a landmark and possibly a good hike.

28° 36´ 53˝, 112° 48´ 24˝

2sʟ A cobble beach with many scallop shells that have washed up from the ocean. There is sand camping in the back amidst a pretty cactus garden. Unfortunately, the gear carry is over large cobble.

Midriff Islands ~ Isla San Lorenzo, Isla las Ánimas

28° 42´ 27″, 112° 55´ 48″

3A A north-protected camp set between green cliffs. The beach is sand with some gravel, but it's a little trashy, as it is sometimes used as a fish camp. There is good hiking nearby.

28° 41´ 53″, 112° 54´ 58″

4A A gravel-bar beach with sleep spots in the valley behind. It is pretty with good views and some wave protection. There is a pelican rookery on the hill behind the beach in the spring, so don't expect privacy then.

The San Lorenzo/las Ánimas Channel. There is a surge through this channel when the tidal flow is strong. The surge creates long standing waves that you can sort of surf, but that dissipate not far from the channel. I have only been there during flood tide when the flow was from east to west. It is easy to get by the surge, but difficult to paddle against. At slack tide the channel is easily navigated.

28° 40´ 32″, 112° 52´ 42″

8SL ✸✸ A beautiful gravel beach surrounded by low-angle cliffs that are topped with a Cardón-studded hillside. Jagged rock arms extend out from each side of the beach forming a cove that settles some waves, though a strong north wind will send some onto the beach. There is great snorkeling nearby.

28° 39´ 35″, 112° 50´ 30″

— **9SL** —

9SL A fair-weather camp of great beauty set among cliffs and tumbling boulders. The beach is a mixture of dark sand and gravel.

40´

28° 36´ 56″, 112° 46´ 55″

10SL A fair-weather camp that wouldn't be safe in a big blow. It is low and backed by a towering cliff, leaving no retreat in contrary weather. There are two small tent sites among gravel and cobble.

3SL

28° 35´ 25″, 112° 45´ 14″

11SL A camp on the backside of a granite, cobble point on the southeast corner of the island. Wind can blow across the bar, but there is north-wave protection. High cliffs form the backdrop. There are great views of Islas San Esteban and Tiburón.

10SL

— **2SL** —

28° 35´ 12″, 112° 47´ 05″

1SL A potential landing site for a crossing originating in the San Francisquito area. Camp is in the back of a small bay near a patch of dunes that can be seen from a distance. It is well protected. The beach is a mixture of sharp granite gravel and some sand. The northern arm of the bay holds a small Cardón forest and a landlocked estuary.

11SL

— **1SL** — •

Isla San Lorenzo

35´

Isla San Lorenzo is a narrow, mountainous island with very steep relief on its southern end. This tapers to more relaxed hills in the north.

Isla Partida

—————————————— 1P ——————————————

Oyster Catcher hatching cycle

1R ——————————————

Isla Rasa

Adult Oyster C

The north inside corner of Salsipuedes is home to four camps. All of these camps are north-protected and all are a mix of gravel and cobble. Low features on land and small rock formations out in the water separate the camps. The area inland is comprised of pretty crags and low hills. Because they are so close together, only one camp is described.

28° 43′ 44″, 112° 57′ 34″

2s ✱✱✱ A small protected cove that could sleep a medium-sized group. From here there are great sunset views looking back to the Baja peninsula. The low hills behind camp afford a wonderful view of the islands to the north. There is splendid snorkeling and fishing right off the beach, but be cautious of the currents if you swim away from the protected zones near camp. Low tides can make big carries at this beach.

The outside of Isla Salsipuedes offers a few small but unprotected camps, one of which is quite pretty, and the north inlet camp which is the sister to camp #1. The inlet is long enough to moderate most north swells before they hit the beach.

Isla Salsipuedes

— 2s —•

Midriff Islands ~ Isla Salsipuedes, Isla Rasa, Isla Partida

28° 53′ 30″, 113° 02′ 20″

1p **Isla Partida** is made up of fractured columnar basalt and appears as two hills side by side when viewed from the north or south. There are cross currents north and south of the island. Camping is limited with one protected camp at this reading on the southeastern corner. The camp is a gravel bar; sleeping is on the edge of the desert behind the bar. There is a fish camp nearby. There is also an unprotected camp on the north shore of the island. On Partida, there is at least one good sea cave to explore, and for animal lovers, there is the fish-eating bat to check out.

28° 49′ 24″, 112° 58′ 46″

"It's alive." Fish-eating bat,
Photo by: Ann-Marie Hodge

1r **Isla Rasa.** You are normally not allowed to camp on Rasa, though sometimes it is possible with permission. It is a bird sanctuary overseen by biologists who live on the island part of the year. It was the first island in the sea to be protected by the Mexican government (1964) after a long fight initiated by American scientists and the Audubon Society. Before the government stepped in, people were harvesting the nesting birds' (Hermann's Gulls, Royal Terns, and Elegant Terns) eggs by the thousands annually and taking them to market. Rasa is the principal nesting area for these species of birds.

The topography of Rasa is low and barren, making the island hard to see from a distance. In the spring, it is wall-to-wall birds. It is difficult to walk, as there are so many birds and nests. A spectacle unfolds each nesting season as the terns and gulls fight each other for the limited terrain on the island. The gulls come first and lay their eggs, then the terns come and push back sections of the gulls by force of numbers, and then the gulls rebound by picking off tern eggs and re-occupying space on the perimeter of the tern zone. This goes on in cycles throughout the spring.

Isla Salsipuedes. Despite its name, which means, "Leave if you are able," this is a magical island. The name alludes to strong currents that can encircle the island and the problems they may cause; it was probably given when non-motorized sail-craft first visited the island. But for our trip in late springtime, we encountered no formidable troubles and had a wonderful time fishing, hiking, and bird watching. Though it is barren in appearance, there is an unexplainable, delightful feel to the place. The camps are deceptively beautiful.

Isla Salsipuedes

45′

28° 43′ 26″, 112° 57′ 05″

1s This very protected beach is located up a narrow inlet and is just opposite its twin inlet to the north. There is a camp behind and just a short walk over a sand bar of each inlet. The southern beach is a cobble fish camp and is not as nice as its northern sister camp.

The beach is a good starting point for a climb up the small cone nearby that is the defining vertical feature on the island. Up coast to the northwest a little bit is a nicer camp with more sand.

Las Tres Virgenes viewed from the west

Happy about a fine catch

San Francisquito

28 °25'

20'

Cabo
San Miquel

This rewarding run is most often done as
the second half of the L.A. Bay to Santa
Rosalia leg. However, the topography
changes quite a bit from the upper half
of the leg. The large bays of the upper
leg with long beaches inside and sharp
points outside with their tidal races soon
give way down here to a coast with fewer
sand beaches and fewer major points.
But there is one very significant headland
to navigate. It comes beneath some of
the grandest scenery anywhere in Baja:
Las Tres Virgenes (The Three Virgins),
a series of massive, dormant volcanoes.
These will grow to dominate the view as
you paddle closer to them. The headland,
Cabo Virgenes, is underneath the very
rugged but amazingly beautiful Cerro la
Reforma, and the paddle around it is
the crux and culmination of this leg.
It is an exposed and serious cape
should the weather be up, but it
is a mountain-gazer's delight
should the sea be calm.

10'

Punta
San Carlos

28 '00'

50'

Punta
Trinidad

40'

Cabo Virgenes

30'

Santa Rosalia

20'

Isla
San Marcos

10'

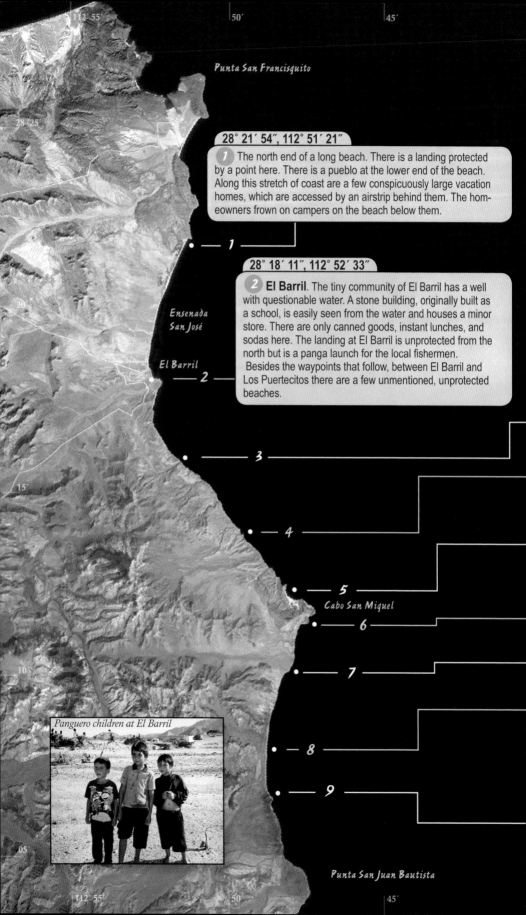

Punta San Francisquito

112° 55´ 50´ 45´

28° 25´

28° 21´ 54˝, 112° 51´ 21˝

1 The north end of a long beach. There is a landing protected by a point here. There is a pueblo at the lower end of the beach. Along this stretch of coast are a few conspicuously large vacation homes, which are accessed by an airstrip behind them. The homeowners frown on campers on the beach below them.

— 1

28° 18´ 11˝, 112° 52´ 33˝

2 **El Barril**. The tiny community of El Barril has a well with questionable water. A stone building, originally built as a school, is easily seen from the water and houses a minor store. There are only canned goods, instant lunches, and sodas here. The landing at El Barril is unprotected from the north but is a panga launch for the local fishermen.
  Besides the waypoints that follow, between El Barril and Los Puertecitos there are a few unmentioned, unprotected beaches.

20´

Ensenada San José

El Barril

— 2

15´

— 3

— 4

— 5

Cabo San Miquel

— 6

10´

— 7

Panguero children at El Barril

— 8

— 9

05´

Punta San Juan Bautista

112° 55´ 50´ 45´

28 °25′

20′

Mild day on the water, Photo by: Craig Miller

28° 15′ 52″, 112° 51′ 32″

3 There is a very pretty, narrow canyon behind this camp. A dry waterfall about a quarter of a mile up canyon requires some skill and good footwear to ascend. At times, the canyon is full of flowering Mimosas and Morning Glories. At night, the air blowing down the canyon and into camp is dressed with the scent of these flowers. A steep beach at the landing indicates a shore break.

28° 13′ 52″, 112° 49′ 33″

4 A small cove offering north and south wave protection. There is limited sleeping in the little arroyo here. Snorkeling is good around the low sandstone arms that form the cove. There is a sand/cobble/gravel landing.

15′

28° 12′ 13″, 112° 48′ 07″

5 **Los Puertecitos.** A large beach seen from El Barril. It is appealing in its duny/brushy setting. The landing is protected from most north sets by a rock point. If the sea were really up, camp would be back in either the arroyo or the desert.

28° 11′ 27″, 112° 47′ 17″

6 A protected beach around the backside of Cabo San Miquel with a less rocky landing than Los Puertecitos.

28° 10′ 05″, 112° 48′ 01″

7 A large arroyo that has a mildly protected landing.

10′

28° 08′ 00″, 112° 48′ 43″

8 A 2-mile long, east-facing beach.

The sand on this part of the coast begins to get darker about here. There are pretty cacti around, and rolling lowlands inland. Palo Blanco trees dot the hillsides. The large tidal fluctuations of up north begin to quiet down as you get away from the Midriff. The peaks of the massive Tres Virgenes are visible in the distance down coast.

28° 06′ 49″, 112° 48′ 40″

9 **Boca San Miquel.** The hiking track to the San Miquel mission is to the north of this reading in flatland scrub and is a little indistinct at first, but it soon develops into an easily followed road. This beach could be a camp, and gets some visitation from roving 4-wheelers and fishermen.

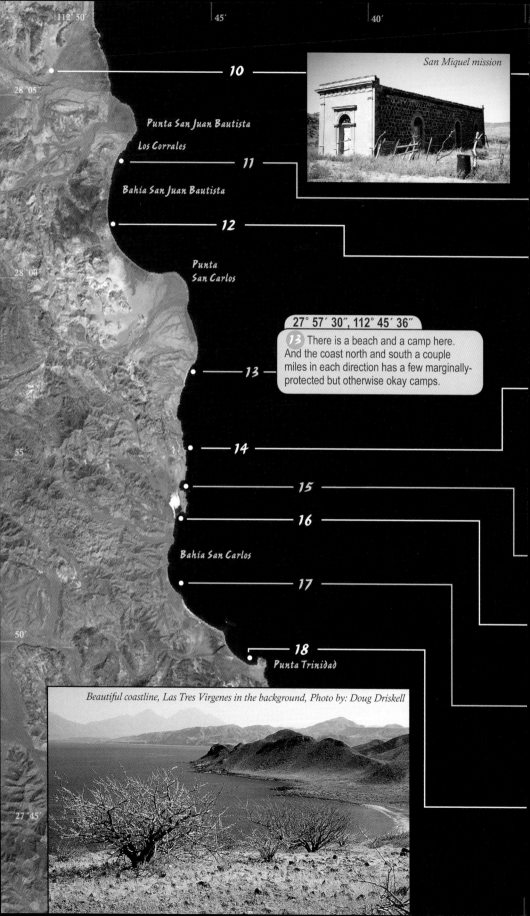

112° 50' 45' 40'

28° 05'

San Miguel mission

Punta San Juan Bautista

Los Corrales

11

Bahia San Juan Bautista

12

28° 00'

Punta
San Carlos

27° 57′ 30″, 112° 45′ 36″

13 There is a beach and a camp here.
And the coast north and south a couple
miles in each direction has a few marginally-
protected but otherwise okay camps.

13

55'

14

15

16

Bahia San Carlos

17

50'

18

Punta Trinidad

Beautiful coastline, Las Tres Virgenes in the background, Photo by: Doug Driskell

27° 45'

28° 05′ 41″, 112° 50′ 08″

10 **The mission of San Miquel.** The hike to the mission is enjoyable. Once there, you'll find stone walls and stone-lined irrigation canals, presumably built hundreds of years ago, that bisect the large plain around the mission. The mission itself is small and trashed on the inside but has some interesting architectural features.

28 "05´

28° 03′ 19″, 112° 47′ 57″

11 A scruffy little camp around the back of the low-lying Punta San Juan Bautista. It has a little north pro. A larger group can sleep on a big flat spot on the bluff behind the beach. There is a faint trail to this clearing. There are not many protected beaches in this area.

28° 01′ 29″, 112° 48′ 15″

12 A beach to the south of **Los Corrales,** which is a stone corral dating back to the mission days. This is a good camp but it's not north-protected. It is comprised of dark sand at the water's edge, gravel mixed with ground-up seashells in its mid-zone, and white sand higher up. Behind camp is a verdant field.

28 "00´

27° 55′ 18″, 112° 45′ 46″

14 ✱✱✱ A baylet with a nice beach that could hold a large group. It is north- and south-protected on all but big days by short arms of rock on either side. The north arm is an arch. Watch out for rocks in the bay when landing. This is a good camp for hiking as the terrain around it is moderately pitched and sparsely vegetated. Near camp are small hills of rich red rock and a valley of fluted, green sandstone formations.

55´

This part of the coast is a series of baylets with arms of rock extending from land to underwater. The shoreline is comprised of pretty sandstone bluffs with streaks of red rock mingled in.

27° 54′ 21″, 112° 45′ 48″

15 A south-protected trashy fish camp. There is a sea lion rock off the south arm of the bay.

27° 53′ 35″, 112° 45′ 52″

16 A north-protected, slightly trashy fish camp. The sleeping is on cobble unless one sleeps behind man-made wind blocks at the north end where there are some cleared sandy spots. This camp is mostly a long cobble bar that backs up to a large lagoon.

50´

27° 51′ 37″, 112° 45′ 53″

17 This big bay has a long beach, called **Playa la Palmita**, running from its center to its SE corner, where there is a small island, Islote el Racito. There is a shallow reef between el Racito and la Palmita that has a break over it in choppy conditions.

27° 49′ 24″, 112° 43′ 28″

18 **La Trinidad.** This is a fish camp protected from the south and the east. The beach is narrow; the best sleeping spots are in the dunes. It is an easy climb to the top of Punta Trinidad and the views are lovely. There is a north-protected beach on the backside of Punta Trinidad capable of holding a large group. To get to it, swing wide around the point, as rocks extend out in the water a ways.

27 "45´

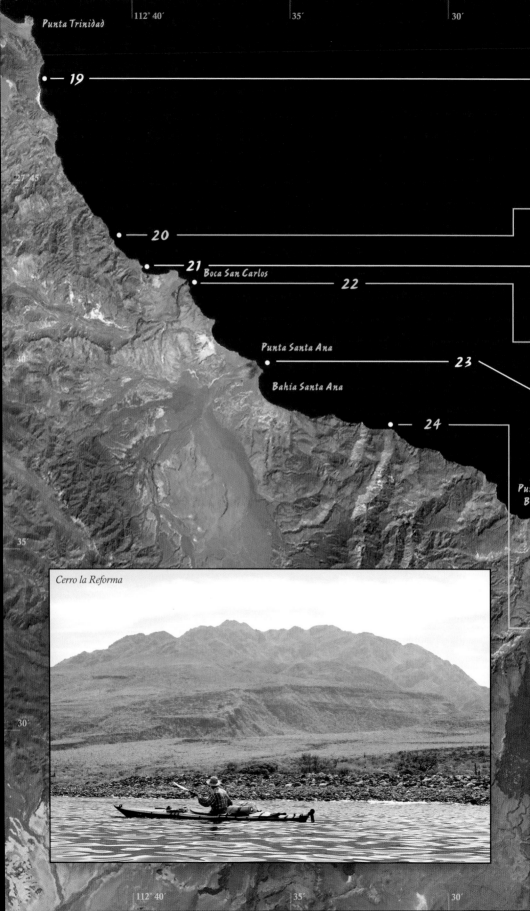

Punta Trinidad

112° 40′ 35′ 30′

27° 45′

• 19

• 20

• 21
Boca San Carlos

22

40′

Punta Santa Ana

• 23

Bahia Santa Ana

• 24

35′

Pu:
B

Cerro la Reforma

30′

112° 40′ 35′ 30′

SM
NM
Km

27° 47′ 58″, 112° 42′ 59″

19 **Ensenada Conchal.** The beginning of a long beach that will get some north pro from Punta Trinidad and from shoals and rocks that protrude just north of the beach. Swing wide to land. This beach is divided by a rock outcropping from another beach below it. This could offer some north pro, which is good because the lower beach is nicer than the upper one.

In general, this coast is marked by shallows and rocks out in the sea. Approach all landings head on and with caution. The beaches, particularly those of white sand, are loaded with stingrays, but make pretty camps and offer great views of the volcanoes to the south.

27°45′

27° 43′ 35″, 112° 40′ 44″

20 An exposed but very pretty gravel camp in a mountainous section of coast.

27° 42′ 43″, 112° 39′ 33″

21 A bay at the beginning of a lowland section of coast. There is a gravel beach deep enough in the bay to offer some protection from a north or south wind. I'm not sure of the sleeping zone, but it looked flat behind the gravel beach. This bay is before the low point seen from farther up north. The waters off the point, sometimes called Punta Baja, are shallow, so give the point a wide berth on a wavy day.

27° 42′ 22″, 112° 38′ 13″

22 **Boca San Carlos.** A narrow inlet that is guarded by shoals on both sides. Enter from dead center if you are going to make a landing. At low tide, entrance to the boca might be shut off by shallows. There is a fish camp in the boca with some shacks/houses. In the next bay there is a nice large, north-exposed beach.

40′

27° 40′ 05″, 112° 36′ 05″

23 **Punta Santa Ana.** The reading is from the backside of the point, which is low and is home to a distinctive patch of palms. The landing is gravel. The point lessens your exposure to surf. The lowness of the point would make it a windy camp on a bad day. It is scraggly here, though flat.

Bahía Santa Ana. A somewhat exposed beach in the back of the bay offers perhaps the last good camping before the stretch run around the craggy flank of Cerro la Reforma. There is a fish camp at the north end of the beach with car access. The sunsets from this part of the coast can be excellent with the towering volcanoes providing a grand backdrop.

After Bahía Santa Ana, there are twenty miles to the next north-protected landing. The paddle around the mountainous cape is magnificent. The background scenery borders on unbelievable as multicolored cliffs stagger upwards and steep canyons smite the hillsides. The shore is largely rugged. If the wind is not up, this stretch is a joy. If the wind is up, this is a long, unforgiving headland to paddle around.

35′

27° 38′ 16″, 112° 31′ 47″

24 **Punta Coyotitos.** A fair-weather camp with a landing on ankle-twisting rocks, but with sandy sleeping spots farther in.

Cerro la Reforma

Breakfast visitor, Photo by: Doug Driskell

30′

111

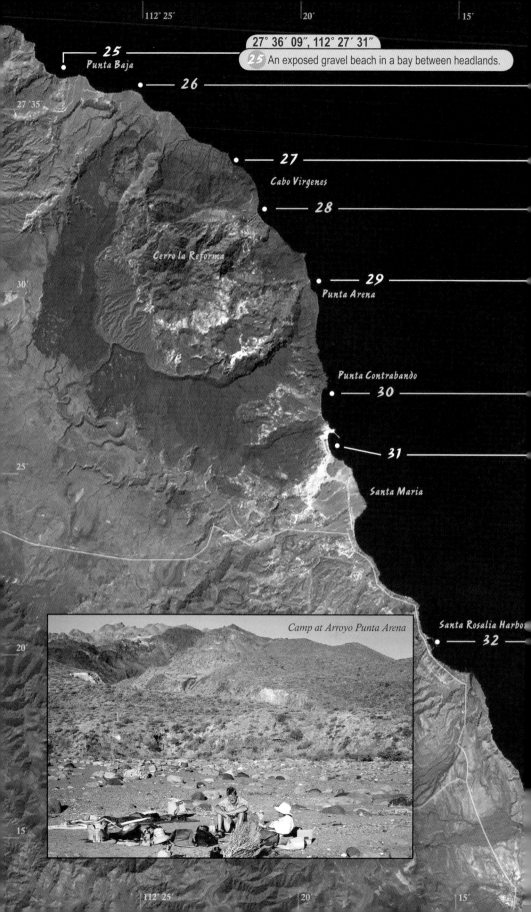

27° 36′ 09″, 112° 27′ 31″

25 An exposed gravel beach in a bay between headlands.

112° 25′

20′

15′

25
Punta Baja

26

27° 35′

27

Cabo Virgenes

28

30′

Cerro la Reforma

29
Punta Arena

Punta Contrabando
30

25′

31

Santa Maria

20′

Camp at Arroyo Punta Arena

Santa Rosalia Harbor
32

15′

112° 25′

20′

15′

27° 35' 27", 112° 25' 05"

26 After a south-protected beach, you'll encounter this low, gravel landing. There is a fish camp here. A giant arroyo is directly behind.

27 '35'

27° 33' 28", 112° 22' 04"

27 **Cabo Virgenes.** A **light** is nestled in a little bay that is exposed but quite pretty. A steep beach is surrounded by beautiful geology—including a cliff striped in yellow, red, and black. This could be a hard-luck camp on gravel. The landing is on rock and the carry up would not be easy.

27° 32' 16", 112° 21' 19"

28 A fish camp guarded by shoals offering some wave protection. The camp zone is rock and gravel.

27° 30' 15", 112° 19' 41"

29 **Arroyo Punta Arena.** A northeast exposed camp with a gravel landing. There are good sleep-spots of hard, dark sand behind the beach. If conditions are favorable, this is a very good camp and one of the last for enjoying the volcano. Behind camp, there is a beautiful hike up a large canyon with red and yellow walls. South of Punta Arena is an exposed, steep, long black sand beach fronted by gravel.

30'

27° 27' 18", 112° 19' 18"

30 The second beach in from the point. The first beach is a fish camp. Both beaches are north-protected. A large rock in the water marks the second beach, which is gravel and wedged between cliffs. This pretty little camp could hold more people than you would think. Two other beaches, each progressively bigger but also progressively less protected, follow as you go further into the bay.

27° 25' 30", 112° 19' 00"

31 **Mine.** This is a large gypsum mine and sees a fair amount of activity. Hundreds of acres in back of the coast have been stripped for the mineral. Large tanker ships dock up to the pier, which is well lit at night.

25'

The little community of **Santa Maria** following the mine is the last place to land before Santa Rosalia. I have heard of one kayak group storing a car here while they did their trip.
North of Santa Rosalia, currents and waves of a minor tidal race pick up. From up high, the race looks like a river. A paddler that hugs the shore here can be on flatwater, while just 100 yards out another paddler can be in choppy whitewater.

27° 20' 23", 112° 15' 56"

32 **Santa Rosalia Harbor.** The harbor is the best place to land in Santa Rosalia. Entrance to the stone-enclosed harbor is from the south. Land on the yacht docks where space is available. This is a secure place to leave your boats while you go into town, and the yachties here are friendly. It is also possible for a small group to sleep on the docks for a minimal fee. Work out the details at the harbor house just up from the gated dock. Beer in the fridge is available to all at $1 apiece or stock the fridge with your own. I advise you to have one immediately. You'll find a clean bathroom with a cold shower in the harbor house, too. The proprietor is Ricardo; he is a helpful man and also offers affordable car storage at his place down coast in San Bruno.
You are in **Baja Sur** now, set your watches forward.

20'

Punta Concepción

15'

Close Encounters of the Giant Kind

 A few hundred yards offshore in the glistening morning calm, immense domes of the great finback whales broke the surface and spouted for air. We watched intently from our beach camp through binoculars and decided this could be a rare opportunity for some closer observation. We canned our plans to pack camp and make miles and hopped in our empty kayaks with just a powerbar (Darn! Forgot the camera!) and paddled to where they had been. But it was a half hour before we saw another rise, this time just a hundred yards away and then he sunk back into the deep. Slowly and quietly, we paddled in the whales' direction, readying ourselves for a closer view, but nothing could prepare me for the overwhelming jolt of adrenaline felt as this giant freight train surfaced just twenty feet from my little boat with a great "spoosh" as he spouted for air. His huge length arched through the water and then the waves collapsed in around him as he dove. Any closer and surely my kayak would have been sucked into his vortex.

 The feeling is stunning, marvelous and frightening at the same time. Surely we are witnessing one of the great natural wonders of the world. The finback is cousin to the largest animal on earth, the blue whale, and one of the largest ever to have lived, larger than most dinosaurs.

 We continued paddling for a couple of hours in large circles, scaring ourselves with several more close encounters, watching them swim under our boats, and sometimes in front of us, heading right at us and diving at the last instant. I got the distinct feeling they were checking us out too. Finally, they cruised away, faster than we could paddle, looking for the next great clouds of krill they feed on.

Whale Biology

 There is perhaps no better place to go whale watching than in Baja, as the number of tour outfitters will testify. There are more species of whales seen in the Sea of Cortez and along the Pacific Coast than any other single place in the world. The warm waters of the sea and the lagoons off the Pacific produce thick harvests of plankton, krill, and various minnows, which are dependable food source for the whales.

 There are two types of whales, both found in Baja: the toothed whales which include the sperm whale, killer whale, and dolphin; and baleen whales which include the blue, the grey, the fin, and the humpback whale. Baleen refers to a keratinous membrane, which forms hundreds of filtering plates on the roof of the whale's mouth, instead of teeth. These plates filter small organisms from mouthfuls of water, while the toothed whales hunt larger fish, birds, and sea mammals in their teeth.

Finback whale, Photo by: Mike Acebo

Whale Biology (Continued)

Most people understand that whales are mammals and like humans, they give birth to live babies—unlike birds or fish, which lay eggs. They care for their young by nursing them with milk. And even though they spend their lives in water, they must breathe air from above the water, unlike fish that filter air molecules directly from the water.

Many baleen whale species come to Baja in the fall to breed, calve and feed in the food-rich waters, although there are numerous individuals that remain as year-round residents. In the spring, grey whales form strong family groups and begin the 4000-mile migration to the Arctic to feed on the rich plankton blooms there in summer. Some species reverse the seasons, migrating to the Antarctic summer in November.

The blue whale is the largest animal on earth, growing up to a hundred feet and weighing 180 tons—that's over 350,000 pounds. The grey, fin and humpback whales are a bit smaller. As baleen filter feeders, they must consume 8000 lbs. of krill a day. And in Baja immature schools of fish, shrimp and squid swim in clouds so dense, they turn the water black for hundreds of yards. The baleen whales scoop up thousands of gallons of water in a mouthful and filter out the krill. A young nursing calf must consume a hundred gallons of milk a day suckling its mother, in between surfacing for air, and grows 8 lbs. per hour.

Until 1868, whales were not in great danger from whalers because they could outrun most ships, swimming at 30 miles per hour. But the development of the steamship and then the exploding harpoon changed all that. By the 1900's, floating whale factories were slaughtering up to 30,000 blue whales alone in one season. By the 1930's, the large baleen whales became so scarce that whalers shifted their focus to other species. Once numbering in the hundreds of thousands, it is estimated that as few as 10,000 blue whales survive today. The International Whaling Commission has tried to enforce a whaling ban, but population recovery is slow and poaching by some countries continues.

– Lori Russell

Santa Rosalia is a colorful place with frontier, sea-town architecture and a local, as opposed to tourist, flavor. In its former life it was a company town for a large copper mine owned by a French firm. The homes built by that firm have a somewhat uniform look but modern dwellers have given them a colorful paint job. Though the French owned the mine, copper buyers came from all over the world, especially Germany and England. Large ships from around the globe used to tie up to the pier to pick up copper or drop off coal. While they did so, officers and company officials would gather on the outskirts of town in elegant homes to socialize and visit with company administrators that lived in Santa Rosalia. You

'Up' Street (Calle Obregón)

can visit some of these homes (most of which are in bad shape these days), as well as the old company office (now a museum) and the stately French Hotel, if you walk up the hill to the north of the downtown area. The French Hotel is open for business and is a great place for breakfast or to just chill out on the airy veranda and gaze at the bay. The hotel does not serve dinner.

Back downtown, there is a church that is made of steel which was prefabricated in France. Alexandre Eiffel (of Eiffel Tower fame) created this church. Other parts of town bear the mark of the copper days in the form of decaying processing plants and loading docks. You can see these structures on the drive into town from the north. Some are being remodeled into new retail businesses.

The core district of Santa Rosalia is designed primarily around two streets that run the course of the town's narrow valley. Calle Obregón and Calle Constitución are known to gringo locals as the "Up Street" and the "Down Street", because they are "one way only" streets; you can only go up one and down the other. If you are in a car, you constantly get stuck in the traffic patterns these streets produce—if you miss the store you're aiming for, it's often not easy to get back to it; it's simpler to park and walk if you're anywhere close to where you want to be.

To get your shopping done in Santa Rosalia, you have to surf several small stores that are scattered around the central district. There is an internet café downtown. There is

Santa Rosalia from the south

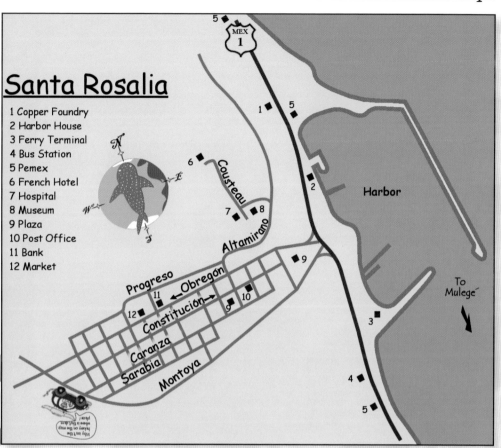

Santa Rosalia

1 Copper Foundry
2 Harbor House
3 Ferry Terminal
4 Bus Station
5 Pemex
6 French Hotel
7 Hospital
8 Museum
9 Plaza
10 Post Office
11 Bank
12 Market

one hardware store where you can purchase white gas (gasolina blanca); it is located on the 'Up' Street and only sells Coleman gas by the gallon. Buy it if you need it because there is possibly no other place close by to purchase it. Santa Rosalia is also home to a great smoothie shop, a bakery, and a couple of good restaurants. Recommended is the restaurant El Muelle, towards the bottom of the 'Down' Street, and Terco's one block west of the plaza on the 'Up' Street.

The coast south of Santa Rosalia is craggy and exposed. Along it, the Hotel El Morro looks like as good a place to stay as any if you want a modern motel on the water, or at least overlooking the water. A few kilometers farther south of Santa Rosalia you'll come upon a campground on a tidal inlet called Las Palmas. Camping and car storage here are possible but pricey. The rock bar guarding the estero to Las Palmas is unprotected from surf and its rocks are exposed except at high tide.

Ricardo, the proprietor of the harbor in town, offers car storage at his house in San Bruno, which is 14 miles south of Santa Rosalia. The price is very reasonable, and you can hitch, take the bus, or get a ride with Ricardo when he gets off work. Besides the usual modes of transportation—kayak, car, or bus—you can also get to Santa Rosalia by ferry from Guaymas on the Mexican mainland.

San Marcos village church

SM
NM
Km

Isla San Marcos is a somewhat-ignored kayaking destination for Baja, and that's a pity because it is worthy. Most boaters drive by it while on Highway 1 on their way to some greater destination or they boat past it on their north to south coastal adventure, not having the energy or the time for a San Marcos detour. Maybe the site of the large gypsum mine and the small community nestled at its base on the southwest shore deter some. However, San Marcos is a surprisingly good little trip. In particular, the north end and the outside coast of the island have great camps and fascinating geology including large sea caves. The yellowtail fishing can be sweet, and the mine area is an interesting visit if you look at it in the right light.

North coast of Isla San Marcos

20′

15′

Isla San Marcos

San Lucas

San Bruno

Isla San Rafael

10′

Punta Chivato

27° 09′ 42″, 112° 09′ 30″

SB **San Bruno.** This is a small and friendly village south of Santa Rosalia and makes the best launch point for a trip to Isla San Marcos if you are driving. There is no restaurant in town, though you can get beer and some minor foodstuffs at one of a few tiny tiendas scattered about. If you drive into town, follow the path of least resistance to the small panga harbor. There are a couple of places to stash a car near here. There is a beer store next to the harbor, whose owner (Jorge) will look after a car; and at the end of the road, behind a fence and north of the harbor is a home on a lot with palm trees where you might store a car. I have heard of one group also being allowed to camp there for a modest fee. One can launch from the tiny harbor or the panga beach just south of the harbor.

Note: There are a number of car-camp spots south of town, some with access to the water. The area is a bit of a featureless plain with a maze of dirt roads over it. It is not recommended to leave a car here.

05′

112°10   05′   112°00′

27° 14′ 54″, 112° 06′ 08″

4 A very cool paddle-through sea cave at low tide. There is a camp just north of this cave. A bit farther up coast is another massive paddle-through sea cave, really an arch. Behind it is a gravel beach. It could be a camp for a small group, but is limited on views because it is almost entirely encircled by rock. Unfortunately, the beach is trashy sometimes due to its popularity as a local motorboat-accessed lunch spot.

There is a **light** on a small island off the tip of **Punta Bufechero**. The fishing here can be exemplary.

Boating around **Punta Piedra Blanca** you enter into the wonderful north coast region of San Marcos. It is very pretty with richly colored red and brown rock, backed by sparsely vegetated hills that are easily hiked. There are the typical rugged north shore headlands here, but there are an atypical number of good camping spots for a north end.

Punta Bufechero **5**

4

Punta Islote

27° 14′ 14″, 112° 06′ 30″

3 A **light** on a rock islet. There are a couple of small islands near here that front nice fishing terrain.

3

Punta Piedra Blanca

27° 14′ 06″, 112° 06′ 07″

2 A very small cobble-camp in a cute cove protected from north swells. There is a well-used fish camp just north of here. There are small caves and arches in this area, and the snorkeling is good.

2

27° 13′ 22″, 112° 05′ 31″

1 A good camp far enough north of the mine to put it out of the picture, though the end of the mine's pier is visible. This camp is in a small arroyo visible from the main shore. Look approximately a half-mile south of a white splotch in the cliffs. The landing is cobble mixed with stone and is protected from north swells and north wind.

There are plenty of sleep spots on the gravel floor of the narrow arroyo. False figs and pipe organ cactus grow in the arroyo forming a pretty background. Nearby, the middle part of this inside coast has sections of very red cliffs.

1

Punta Coloradito

10

Punta Blanca

Isla San Rafael

North shore sea cave

27° 11′ 14″, 112° 04′ 46″

10 **The mine/town**. There are rumors the mine may close soon, but until it does, and probably even after it does, this is a very industrial place. It is also a village, replete with houses, a church, a medical clinic, and a store. The people here are friendly and they don't mind you being around. A walk around here is a different kind of day hike. Landing is at a protected beach on the south side of the large tanker dock. There is a lot of hustle and bustle going on at the mine, as the operation is constant. Trucks move back and forth while large earthmovers work the pit behind town and pile gypsum near the dock. On a windy day, town is a swirl of white dust.

Isla San Marcos

27° 15′ 29″, 112° 05′ 11″

5 ✳✳✳ Just southeast of Punta Bufechero is a north-protected beach that looks like an excellent camp. In this corner of the island are three other possible and worthy camps.

27° 14′ 58″, 112° 04′ 38″

6 A dark sand beach nestled among orange rock with a landing protected from north swells. Before the next reading are some minor camps offering varying degrees of landing protection and one large beach facing north/northeast.

27° 14′ 12″, 112° 03′ 55″

7 **Starfish Bay** ✳✳✳ An awesome beach, somewhat divided in two by a minor ridge. This beach is big and beautiful and has a craggy backdrop of red and brown hills. There is some Cardón in the valley behind as well. Jagged rock prominences on either side of the beach protect it from the majority of north or south wave activity.

27°15′

Down coast and around **Punta Gorda, Bahía el Burro** unfolds. Surprisingly, there is no good camping in this bay. The bay is divided into two beaches. The northern one has a protected landing but is all large rocks with no flat spots to set up camp. The southern beach might be a camp, but it gets some north swell and has a rocky landing.

Punta Gorda

Bahía el Burro

Punta Cinco de Mayo

27° 11′ 46″, 112° 03′ 01″

8 A north-protected, small beach of white sand mixed with rocks. The sleep spots are on the bench above the beach. A short bluff provides some wind protection for cooking, but the sleeping area would probably get breezy. This is an occasional fish camp, and many ray jaws and large crab shells litter the area.

27° 10′ 47″, 112° 04′ 18″

9 **Puerto Viejo.** This is a completely north-protected bay. High walls rim it with a couple of steep arroyo breaks in between. This reading is at a good-sized beach with a large palapa on it. You'll find more privacy east of the palapa. There is road access to the mine village.

Punta Chivato can be seen down channel, in the middle of which is Isla San Rafael also called Isla Lobos. I presume there is a sea lion colony there. A paddle to the islet would make a good day trip if you wish to extend your San Marcos visit.

There are a couple of landing spots above **Punta Blanca**. One in particular is a low gravel bar with a palapa on it. The landing is good but the beach is not wind-protected. To the north of this landing is another possible small camp with north protection at an abandoned house.

10′

ta
ra

North shore sunset

Sssthings that Sting

Spiders

Of all the nasty "S's" of Baja, spiders are the least worrisome. They have an undeserved notoriety probably because of their grotesque appearance with multiple eyes, legs and hairy faces. But also because of a gross exaggeration of their toxicity. The most notable poisonous spider, the Brown Recluse, is found more to the north. The Baja Recluse is not venomous. Neither is the Tarantula. But he is large and scary looking, and he will bite, leaving an itchy bump, like most spiders. The most interesting thing about spiders is the way each species traps it's prey, often in a web. They will then inject it with venom, which will digest the prey before sucking up the juices.

Scorpions

Scorpions are another potentially serious camp visitor. Usually their sting will only cause a minor irritation, with swelling and discomfort. But in some rare cases, depending on individual susceptibility, people have died from severe allergic reactions by respiratory failure, most often in the very young and old. Consult your doctor on your personal allergies.

Scorpions are one of the oldest critters on earth, with fossils over 400 million years old. It is thought they may have been one of the first animals to crawl out of the sea. They are in the class of Arachnids, related to spiders. Species have adapted to all climates, from hot desert to high mountains and tropical forests. Shaped like miniature lobsters (but no relation), they can effectively grasp their prey in their front claws while they deliver a fatal sting by swinging their tails over their heads. Species range in size from one inch to four inches and they prefer to dine on insects, other scorpions, and sometimes small rodents.

Even though they are not often seen, the best protection is knowing their behavior. They prefer to live in rocky or bushy areas where they hide in the day, rather than on beaches. You might find one under the rock you pick up to make a fire ring. They only come out at night to hunt, so be sure to wear shoes when making night calls. In the morning, always shake out shoes and blankets, and look under tents and anything they might be able to crawl under. Never leave open gear bags on the ground at night. If you should find one under your tent, it will scurry quickly for the nearest cover. So just stand out of its way.

Snakes

Rattlesnakes can be very dangerous and potentially fatal, so they are worth mentioning here. But in fact, they are rarely seen and more people die each year from bee stings.

There are about 30 species of rattlers, including the Baja Rattler (Crotalus enyo), with a wide variety of sizes and colors, but most are identified by their wide, triangular heads and the rattlers on their tails. The distinctive buzzing noise of the rattle will usually warn you from a safe distance. But young rattlesnakes have no developed rattles, and have just as much venom as adults so they can be more dangerous. Rattlesnakes have coloring that amounts to a blotchy camouflage when viewed indirectly, so they are hard to see; pay extra attention when hiking in rocky or grassy places. Be especially wary at night when they are out and about, like their prey, which are mice and lizards. Like most desert animals, they hide in shady cover during the hot day.

A rattlesnake bite is rarely fatal, but always painful and always potentially serious. They can inject either hemotoxins or neurotoxins that can destroy blood tissues or nerve tissues, causing paralysis or damaged limbs. Immature rattlers leave venom (a "wet" bite) more often than adults, as the adults tend not to use their venom when defending themselves, but save it instead for prey. The best rescue in the event of a wet bite is to evacuate to a medical facility as soon as possible. This is tough to do in the more remote areas of Baja. Use of a radio or flagging down a boat or panga would be advised in this case.

Stingrays

On some of the sandier, silty-bottomed beaches and harbors of Baja, you will see small stingrays, about four to six inches long. They like to lie flat on the bottom sands, camouflaging themselves from predators. But beware and be savvy—learn the "Baja Shuffle." This is where you enter the water shuffling your feet along the bottom, penguin-style, to scare away anything that lies hidden there, like stingrays. Because, small as they are, they pack a mean sting. Should you step on one, at first it will just feel like a hefty bee sting. But within minutes, the poison will creep up your leg and suddenly you will feel a burning like someone is cutting off your leg with a dull, rusty knife. The pain can be so intense, it will bring water to your eyes, and your only thought is 'get me to the hospital.' Not an easy option at most remote beaches in Baja. But have courage; the poison is not life-threatening or long term. In about one to two hours, the poison will dissipate and the pain will be gone entirely. You'll feel like swimming again if you haven't passed out in the meantime. Otherwise, a few aspirin and soaking the wound in warm water may ease the discomfort a bit.

– Lori Russell

Canyon wall north of Santa Rosalia, Photo by: Doug Driskell

nta Rosalia

SM
NM
Km

27°20′

This is a short leg and somewhat
developed. There are a few small
communities dotting the coastline, the most
prominent being Punta Chivato; wilderness
beaches are hard to find unless you go
via Isla San Marcos. Highway 1
parallels a portion of the leg, but
views up coast to the dramatic
peaks of the Volcáns las Tres
Virgenes make up for a lot. It
is a pleasant leg despite the
nearness of civilization.

15′

Isla San Marcos

10′

San Bruno

Punta Chivato

05′

27°00′

26°55′

Mulegé

112°15′   10′   05′   112°00′   111°55′

125

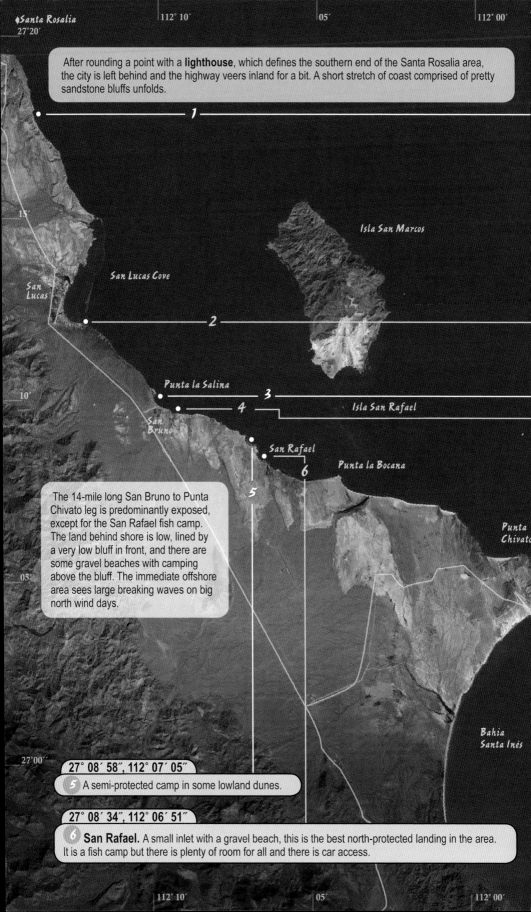

After rounding a point with a **lighthouse**, which defines the southern end of the Santa Rosalia area, the city is left behind and the highway veers inland for a bit. A short stretch of coast comprised of pretty sandstone bluffs unfolds.

1

15′

Isla San Marcos

San Lucas Cove

San
Lucas

2

10′

Punta la Salina

3

4

Isla San Rafael

San
Bruno

San Rafael

6

Punta la Bocana

5

The 14-mile long San Bruno to Punta Chivato leg is predominantly exposed, except for the San Rafael fish camp. The land behind shore is low, lined by a very low bluff in front, and there are some gravel beaches with camping above the bluff. The immediate offshore area sees large breaking waves on big north wind days.

*Punta
Chivato*

05′

*Bahia
Santa Inés*

27°00′

27° 08′ 58″, 112° 07′ 05″

5 A semi-protected camp in some lowland dunes.

27° 08′ 34″, 112° 06′ 51″

6 **San Rafael.** A small inlet with a gravel beach, this is the best north-protected landing in the area. It is a fish camp but there is plenty of room for all and there is car access.

27° 18′ 00″, 112° 13′ 54″

1 This would be an interesting camp in fair weather for a small group of open-minded boaters. It is in the middle of the bluffs and quite pretty, but the sleeping is on sandstone shelves, so it is not for the Ritz Carlton crowd. There is a protected landing on cobble.

San Lucas Cove. The outer arm of San Lucas Cove is a low rock bar with one tiny hill on its north corner. The exposed bar makes for poor camping.

Inside the cove, there is a military base, a trailer park/campground, and a panga launch/beach at the north of the cove. All campers in the cove will have no problem waking up early, as a very loud, corny-sounding reveille is played from the military base's loudspeakers before dawn.

15'

27° 12′ 06″, 112° 12′ 14″

2 A cleared boat landing in an otherwise rocky shore leading to an opening under a set of palms. There is some protection from north swell. There are two old concrete holding tanks here, and it sees occasional car traffic. If nobody is hanging out here already, the clearing makes a pleasant enough camp considering the lack of options around, and offers a beautiful view of the volcanoes up north.

27° 10′ 11″, 112° 10′ 00″

3 **La Salina.** A small **light** and a panga launch on the inside of a jetty. There are a few private property signs nearby, so I'm not sure if camping is allowed, but the area is wave-protected and has a beach with enough places to sleep. It can see heavy panguero use, however.

10'

27° 09′ 42″, 112° 09′ 30″

4 **San Bruno.** San Bruno is a small, peaceful town with fresh water but limited food or other supplies. The harbor is tiny with a panga beach just south of it. The panga beach is good for landing but not camping, and sees some surf on windy days. San Bruno is discussed more in the Isla San Marcos chapter, as it is the probable launch point for a trip out to that island.

San Bruno panga launch

05'

27°00''

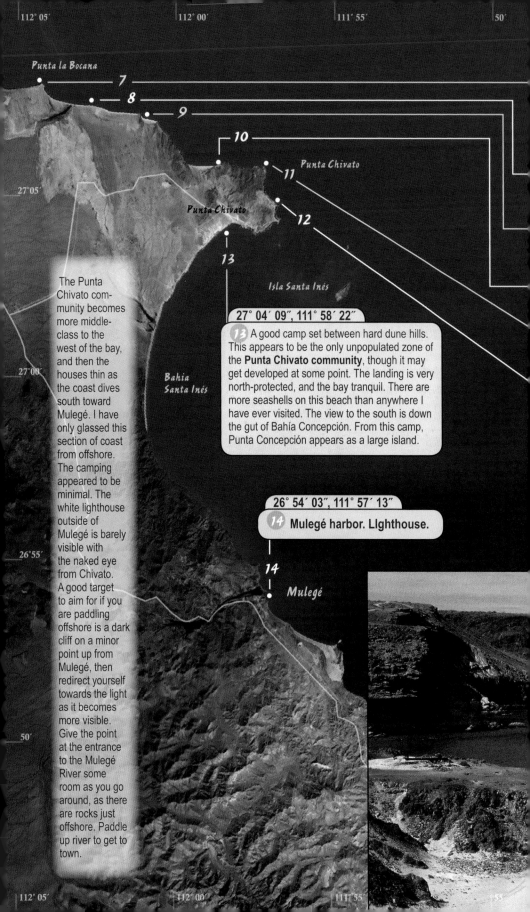

Punta la Bocana

7

8

9

10

Punta Chivato

11

Punta Chivato

12

27° 05′

13

Isla Santa Inés

The Punta
Chivato com-
munity becomes
more middle-
class to the
west of the bay,
and then the
houses thin as
the coast dives
south toward
Mulegé. I have
only glassed this
section of coast
from offshore.
The camping
appeared to be
minimal. The
white lighthouse
outside of
Mulegé is barely
visible with
the naked eye
from Chivato.
A good target
to aim for if you
are paddling
offshore is a dark
cliff on a minor
point up from
Mulegé, then
redirect yourself
towards the light
as it becomes
more visible.
Give the point
at the entrance
to the Mulegé
River some
room as you go
around, as there
are rocks just
offshore. Paddle
up river to get to
town.

27° 00′

Bahia
Santa Inés

27° 04′ 09″, 111° 58′ 22″

13 A good camp set between hard dune hills.
This appears to be the only unpopulated zone of
the **Punta Chivato community**, though it may
get developed at some point. The landing is very
north-protected, and the bay tranquil. There are
more seashells on this beach than anywhere I
have ever visited. The view to the south is down
the gut of Bahía Concepción. From this camp,
Punta Concepción appears as a large island.

26° 54′ 03″, 111° 57′ 13″

14 **Mulegé harbor. LIghthouse.**

26° 55′

14

Mulegé

50′

27° 08´ 00˝, 112° 04´ 17˝

7 **Punta la Bocana.** A scruffy lowland point. There is supposed to be an estuary, Boca de Magda-lena, just south of the point according to some maps and the satellite image; but if there is one, it is hard to spot from the water. The entrance might be blocked by a land bridge.

27° 07´ 24˝, 112° 02´ 38˝

8 An exposed but beautiful, long beach. The landing is over low blocks of sandstone, which are soft-ened on top by algae growth. This would not be a good landing if there were any waves, but if it's calm, this beach makes a great camp. From here, the sunset views of the volcanoes up north are special.

27° 07´ 08˝, 112° 00´ 59˝

9 A charming white sand beach around a small point. There is a residence here above the area of most protection.

27° 05´ 41˝, 111° 58´ 30˝

10 **Ensenada Muerta.** An attractive bay with a beach at the back of it.

27° 05´ 44˝, 111° 57´ 13˝

11 **Punta Chivato. Lighthouse.** This is the first of a series of headlands that make up the point. The geology is beautiful red and orange rock. The snorkeling opportunities look promising, though Chivato is rumored to be somewhat of a shark hangout. In 2004, local fishermen mistakenly caught an 18-foot great white in their nets. A second great white was caught off the point later that fall.

27° 04´ 48˝, 111° 56´ 56˝

12 ✹✹ A gorgeous orange and black rock point with nice beaches. The beach to the north of this reading has better sleep spots, but this one has a more protected landing. This point is easily accessed from the community right around the corner, so it may not be as private as it looks.

Around the point, you will enter north-protected waters, but shore is largely developed. Upscale homes sit above a thin beach. There is one pay campground towards the east end of the settlement. A handsome hotel in from the point has a great patio with sublime sunset views; the drinks are not totally pricey, though the atmosphere is chic and the clientele primarily European. There is a small store behind the hotel.

Punta Chivato south beach, Photo by: Doug Driskell

Mulegé

Mulegé is one of the "big four" sea kayaking towns of Baja, the others being Bahía de los Ángeles, Loreto, and La Paz. But it is not a big town, just an important town. It sits at the top of Bahía Concepción, which is a great training ground for kayakers; and is the start for one of the major sea kayaking legs along the peninsula, "Mulegé to Loreto."

Mulegé is about as cute as a town gets in Baja, with small, tight streets running amongst older buildings. It is sandwiched in a narrow valley busy with palm trees and bougainvilleas, and there is a spring fed river lying in it. Most amenities are available in town, but it is not overflowing with shopping. And that is a good thing—the stores are small and the mail doesn't always go out on time. Some non-boating draws to Mulegé are a mission built in 1766 and ancient cave paintings in the not-to-far-away interior.

In September 2006, Mulegé was the scene of a devastating flood. When the remnants of Hurricane Juan parked themselves over the mountains surrounding town, twenty inches of water rained down in one day. Mudslides cascaded into the swollen river, sending torrents of silt and debris downstream into houses, restaurants, and campgrounds. Town is recovering slowly, and parts of the river corridor will be a long time rebuilding and rebudding before things return to normal.

The restaurant in Mulegé I find myself returning to time and again is Las Casitas. It is located east of the plaza on Calle Madero. It has a garden terrace with water features and parrots, and they serve killer Margaritas. A restaurant I have yet to check out but hear good things about is Los Equipales on Calle Moctezuma. The taco stand of choice is Donie's Tacos just inside the entrance to town where a tasty and inexpensive meal can be had; you can't miss it if they are grilling their meats in the smoker outside on the sidewalk.

Downtown Mulegé is not located directly on the sea; it sits inland more than a mile, though there is access to the sea either with a short drive or by boating down river. If you are using Mulegé as a staging ground for a "Mulegé to Loreto" leg, it is best to camp near town. Though there are some picturesque camps on Bahía Concepción south of town, they are probably best left for travelers driving farther south or wanting to kayak Bahía Concepción. Listed here are three places off the highway south of town that are good to start a trip from, or to stay at if you are passing through town.

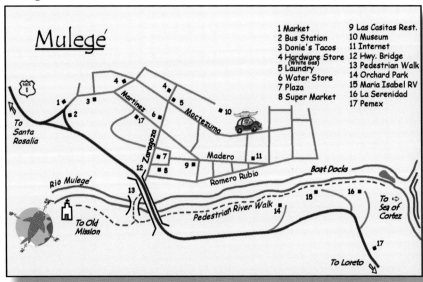

Orchard RV Park

Mulegé Plaza, Photo by: Lissoni Associati

26° 53′ 42″, 111° 58′ 30″

14ᵗʰ Orchard RV Park. Orchard has long been a favorite for kayakers launching from Mulegé. It is clean, has beautiful trees, good showers, is on the river, and is a just a pleasant walk into town via the river path. Sad to say, however, that Orchard's days as a camp are numbered, due to its being subdivided and developed into small home sites. It might only be around as a camp for a couple more years. Orchard management says they will continue to allow car storage for the public however, even after build-out of the houses. In 2005 it was $3.00/day to leave a car there.
 A few words about the river: don't swim in it because of questionable water quality, and if the tide is coming in, paddling to the mouth is an uphill battle. This can hinder a trip planning to cross the top of the bay to Punta Concepción. Also, if it seems a little windy up river near town, it can be really windy out on the sea.

26° 53′ 54″, 111° 57′ 53″

15ᵗʰ Villa Maria Isabelle RV Park. Good, friendly, clean, and convenient. There is access to a river ramp. The walk to town is longer than Orchard's. If you were set on not driving, it might be easier to boat into town, but leaving boats unattended in town could be sketchy.

26° 53′ 56″, 111° 57′ 34″

16ᵗʰ La Serenidad. La Serenidad is on the river and is a good place to camp, launch, or leave a car. It is a bit of a hike to town without a car, however. There is a restaurant and a pool here, as well as a hotel. There is a traditional Saturday night pig roast, and a big Halloween party every year. The proprietors are Don Johnson and his daughter, Diana.

"Bahía Concepción

The 25-mile long Bahía Concepción is a good sheltered paddling environment for the beginner to intermediate sea kayaker. More adventurous paddlers might find it a bit tame and too built up. A large portion of the west shore is developed, though the east shore is not (for now) and provides a getaway feeling. Because it is almost encircled by land, the sea conditions in Bahía Concepción are milder than those found on the outside of the bay. Large breaking surf seldom happens, though a windy day can still test a paddler. Also, the waters of the bay are more turgid and occluded than the outside sea— visibility for snorkeling is reduced more often than not. On a personal note, I have less success fishing here than in the clearer waters outside.

Upper Bahía Concepción from Isla Coyote, Photo by: Doug Driskell

Though developed, the western shore of the bay is pretty. Never far away, the highway twists up and down and in and out of hill-lined coves dotted with houses and campgrounds. Some of the coves are home to small hotels or restaurants. Although there may be bottled water at or near some camps, do not count on it; bring enough drinking water for however long you plan to be away from town. From January through March there is an influx of RV and car-campers at these beaches.

There are five or six islands within the upper portion of the bay, all of which are easily paddled to from the western shore. Unfortunately there are only a few camps possible on them.

Mulegé   Punta Concepción

Bahía Concepción

Rio Mulegé

111° 55′

1

2

Isla el Gallo

Punta Hornitos

26° 51′ 35″, 111° 54′ 45″

3 This is a cobble beach set between small hills south of Punta Gallo. There are deposits of clam and conch shells here. It is road accessible and might have car-campers at certain times of the year. There is a boat landing cleared from tide-zone rocks. It is semi-protected from north waves by Punta Gallo.

3

Bahía Concepción

26°50′

Punta San Pedro

Sea of tranquility

Punta Arena

4

5

26° 43′ 15″, 111° 54′ 34″

9 **Playa Coyote/ Coyote Bay.** A picturesque but mostly private community, often seen with yachts moored in front of it. Pay camping is toward the south near palapas and at a more isolated beach at the bottom of the bay. The main beach is north-protected. There is often some jake-brake noise from trucks gearing down hill behind the bay. There is a hot springs near camp.

45′

Punta Piedrita

Isla Ramón

Isla Pitahaya

6

Isla la Liebre

Isla la Cueva

7

8

Isla Coyote

Bahía Coyote

10

9

Isla Blanca

Punta Santa Barbara

111°55′

26° 53´ 34″, 111° 57´ 03″

1 The north end of a large, brown sand beach; possibly the best free camping close to Mulegé. It is not right on the road but car-accessible and slightly trashy. Though it faces north, the landing is partially protected by a small jut of land off the beach's north end. Were one to have boated down coast and chosen this camp over the RV parks in Mulegé because it is free, it is a bit far from town for convenient shopping. A paddle up the river from here to town or a hitchhike in are possible, though leaving any gear unattended might be risky.

26° 52´ 36″, 111° 55´ 08″

2 The southern half of the beach described above, but away from the trashy zone of the northern end. It is exposed to north waves, but one could paddle behind the **light** off the point to calmer water and a beach just south of the point, though that is not as attractive a beach.

South of the previous reading, up until Punta Arena, the coast is generally rocky and there are scattered pockets of private property. I've missed boating this section, but from satellite images, it looks like there could be a couple of camping opportunities along the way.

26°50´

26° 46´ 47″, 111° 52´ 08″

4 North of this reading, on a low point, there is cabaña camping at $6.00/night; nearby is a small restaurant. This area can see quite a bit of wind scraping across it.
The settlement of **Punta Arena,** adjacent to this reading, has a nice protected beach, but does not want campers. Their entrance sign reads, "*Solo los Permanentes.*"

26° 45´ 47″, 111° 53´ 08″

5 **Playa Santispac.** A very protected beach in a picturesque cove. It is a bit busy here and not far from the road—quieter camping can be had up the cove arm to the east. On the outside of this arm is a beach that is owned by the Santispac people and probably has less road noise than the cove beach.

26° 44´ 50″, 111° 53´ 24″

6 **Isla la Liebre.** A tiny, low, dirty camp that is north-protected. Of more interest is a beach across from this island that is white sand and removed from the highway a kilometer or so.

26° 44´ 33″, 111° 54´ 04″

7 **Playa los Cocos.** A nice enough white sand beach that has a few palapas on it but no facilities other than latrines. It is a pay beach. A negative to this area is a mangrove swamp nearby that collects standing water and breeds fleas.

26° 43´ 53″, 111° 54´ 32″

8 **Playa el Burro.** A pay beach lined with casitas. There is a rural-quality restaurant here. Ice and cold beer are for sale at the tiny tienda across the street. The office is by the Mexican flag at the back south end of the beach.

45

26° 43´ 22″, 111° 53´ 11″

10 **Isla Coyote ✳✳✳** Grotesquely sculpted lava rock and a steep hillside ringed with a garden of desert plants form the backdrop to a beautiful cove and a small strip of white sand beach. This is the nicest camp in Bahía Concepción and would be five-star if it wasn't open to the north. An oddity to this otherwise pristine camp is that it is also a pet cemetery. Behind the beach are graves and monuments placed by wandering gringo sailors who have lost that special animal.

The Santa Barbara stretch of coast is behind the rocky headlands south of Coyote Bay and is the only lengthy, undeveloped section of coastline of the northern half of Concepción's western shore.

Bahía Coyote — 11 —

Punta Amolares

— 12 —

Punta Santa Barbara

• — 13 —

Bahía Concepción

26°40′

— 14 —

Rio Mulegé Great White Heron

— 15 —

Isla el Requesón

—17— 16 —

Playa Armenta
— 18 —

26° 38′ 06″, 111° 49′ 30″

17 **Playa la Perla** ✶✶✶ A white sand beach in a small cove off the highway. There are palapas, a couple of trees, and a pretty cactus garden between camp and the highway. La Perla is kept very clean and is *muy tranquilo.*

35′

26° 37′ 30″, 111° 48′ 34″

18 **Playa Armenta.** This is another small, nice campground with a white sand beach. There are three palapas in the primary zone and an additional, hike-to palapa on a small point.

Below Playa Armenta the coast loses its beaches. There is a lesser camp halfway towards the end of the bay, north of the giant seashell sculpture that is a landmark alongside the highway, and then a lowland forms the bottom of the bay. This southern shore is rocky—kayak camping is possible, but not attractive. I have heard of a fresh water source at km 87 of the highway near a pull-off and under a tree, but I was not able to find it when I investigated.

26° 42´ 13˝, 111° 53´ 04˝

11 **Playa Santa Barbara, north beach**. This beach has pretty views of the islands out in the bay but has minimal camping. Sleeping would probably be among the scrub vegetation behind the thin beach. The beach is low here and might receive some of the sea if the weather is horrible. There is an abandoned white house behind camp.

26° 41´ 57˝, 111° 52´ 52˝

12 **Playa Santa Barbara, south beach** ✱✱✱ A beautiful beach with a riot of palms in its center. It gets some waves on a windy day but they are small. A large group could camp here.

26° 41´ 51˝, 111° 52´ 09˝

13 A pretty gravel/shell beach with a feel of wilderness due to Highway 1 taking a dip inland away from camp. Unfortunately it is north-exposed. The beach is good only for a small group.

26° 39´ 37˝, 111° 50´ 58˝

14 This is a beach I haven't landed on but it looked okay from the water. There is what looks like a small abandoned house nearby.

26° 38´ 37˝, 111° 50´ 43˝

15 **Playa Buenaventura.** There are two private beaches, a restaurant, and a small hotel in this cove. You'll notice some houses behind the beaches. The hotel is cute and clean. There are casitas perched on stilts near the restaurant that are available for rent at a modest price. Inquire at the restaurant for pricing details.

26° 38´ 18˝, 111° 49´ 54˝

16 **Playa Requesón** ✱✱✱ A beautiful white sand spit that juts out into the bay. The top of the spit is a small island that forms coves north and south of the beach. It is a car-accessible camp with palapas; someone will come by in the evening to collect the small camping fee.

There is a mountain south of Requesón with a twisting lava rock formation on its face that was trimmed with white paint by an ambitious solo artist some years ago. I'm not in favor of decorating the wilderness, but this looks quite cool from a certain perspective.

Flame mountain south of Playa Requesón

Bahía Concepción

The **east shore** of Bahía Concepción is mostly a low, Cardón-filled plain rising to meet rugged mountains on the interior. These mountains offer nice viewing and some hiking opportunities for the Concepción adventurer. The dirt roads that snake along the lower coast and then into the mountains are popular with the Mulegé ATV crowd.

26° 51´ 45˝, 111° 50´ 44˝

19 **Bahía Santo Domingo** ✲✲✲ This is a narrow but pretty white sand beach that can be distinguished with the naked eye from the west Concepción coast. The bay is protected from north swell. There is a large, colorful fish camp up coast inside of Punta Hornitos, but it is separated from this camp by a low bluff. There is a chance for a fabulous sunset view from here, as well as from other camps down coast.

East shore of Bahía Concepción

26° 46´ 46˝, 111° 49´ 16˝

21 A point with a baylet under it. A rusted car bumper embedded in the ground marks a protected but somewhat low camp. Views of the rugged mountains inland are very pretty, and there is a trail behind camp leading up into them.

26° 46´ 25˝, 111° 49´ 06˝

22 A high-ground camp among small trees. Large square rocks form a semi-permanent fire ring and seats. An old refrigerator on shore indicates a possible fish camp.

26° 42´ 55˝, 111° 48´ 41˝

23 The bay south of **Punta Amolares**. There is a good camp here, sometimes used by kayak outfitters from across the bay.

The next four miles of coast are very low with no camps. North of the next reading is the El Salto ranch, a landmark of sorts, with a dirt track and a fence leading down to the water.

26° 40´ 34˝, 111° 45´ 53˝

24 Here there is a camp inside and north of **Punta Cardóncito**. It is a southwest-facing beach of shell fragments and piles of small scallop shells. There are good flat sleeping spots. There is a dirt road directly behind camp that parallels the lower half of this coast. The mountain behind camp is a dark peak with a vertical intrusion of white rock. South of this reading the coast is bland and the mountains on the interior are smaller than those to the north, so camping is less desirable.

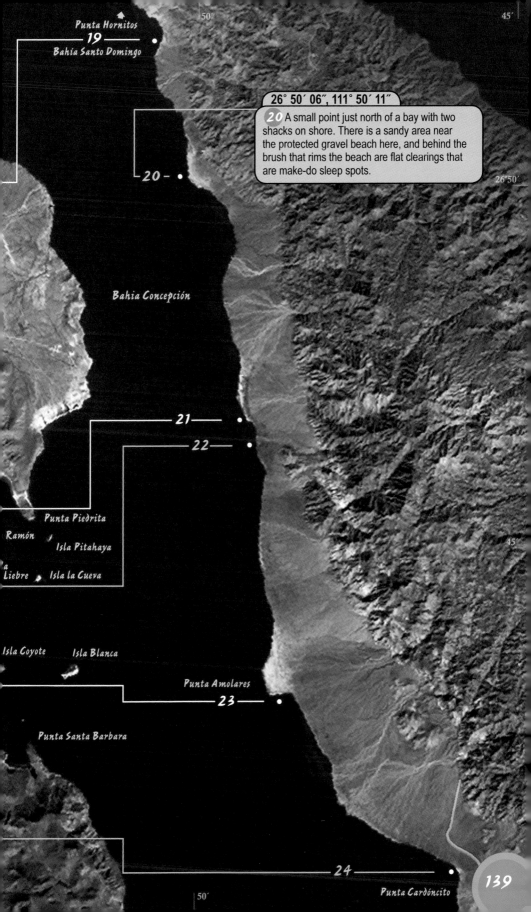

Punta Hornitos
—— 19 ——
Bahía Santo Domingo

26° 50′ 06″, 111° 50′ 11″
20 A small point just north of a bay with two shacks on shore. There is a sandy area near the protected gravel beach here, and behind the brush that rims the beach are flat clearings that are make-do sleep spots.

— 20 —

Bahía Concepción

— 21 —
— 22 —

Punta Piedrita
Ramón Isla Pitahaya
ᵃ
Liebre Isla la Cueva

Isla Coyote Isla Blanca

Punta Amolares
— 23 —

Punta Santa Barbara

— 24 —
Punta Cardóncito

50′   45′
26°50

45′

50′

Sunrise outside of Mulegé, Photo by: Doug Driskell

Mulegé

Punta Concepción

Punta Gallo

Punta Hornitos

26°50'

Punta Santa Teresa

40'

Bahía Concepción

Bahía San Nicolás

Punta el Pulpito

30'

This is a great kayak leg. At this time, the outside of the Concepción peninsula is still relatively undeveloped. For now, the coast is composed of unpopulated sections interspersed with a few small communities. It is semi-wilderness, abundant with white sand beaches, and dotted by mountains on the interior.

This is the southern Sea of Cortez, and conditions are more user-friendly than up north. Temperatures are warmer, tidal fluctuation at most is 2' to 4', currents are moderate, and the waves somewhat smaller than in the northern sea. But it still gets big enough down here when the weather goes sour. It's not Easy Street if a blow comes in, just easier, perhaps. There are still significant points to negotiate. A noticeable feature of the southern sea, however, is the lack of noteworthy tidal races, making the navigation of these points somewhat of a less risky proposition than up north.

The beginning of a "Mulegé to Loreto" trip is probably the hardest day of the trip, as most groups will try to cross Bahía Concepción to Punta Hornitos or beyond. It is eight miles from Mulegé to Hornitos, with the crossing coming in the second half, and it is hard to get an early start on day one of any trip—the boats are confusing to pack, a last minute shopping event might need to occur, or the tide might be against you in the Rio Mulegé, the common launch area. The beaches around Punta Gallo on the main peninsula offer a bailout point should things not get off to a timely start from town.

The crossing accomplished, the next decision is whether to hang out at a good camp on the inside of the Concepción peninsula or to go for it, clear Punta Concepción, and make Caleta los Pilares on the far shore in the same day as the crossing. Though possible, camping is marginal between the two points. If you have begun your day from Mulegé, there is a chance people are tired, if the wind is up from the north, you might want to play it conservatively and call it an early day and camp on the inside.

San Juanico

20'

10'

Isla Coronados

Loreto

26°00'

111° 50'   40'   30'   20'

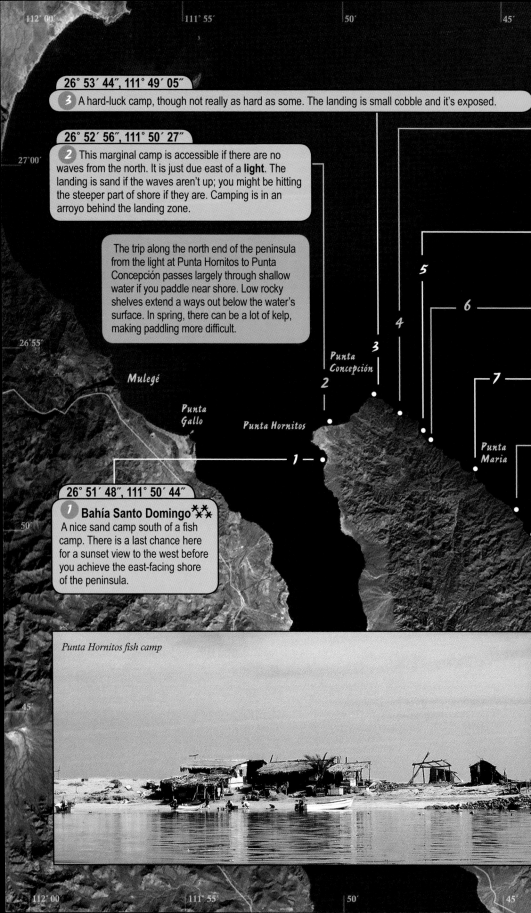

26° 53′ 44″, 111° 49′ 05″

3 A hard-luck camp, though not really as hard as some. The landing is small cobble and it's exposed.

26° 52′ 56″, 111° 50′ 27″

2 This marginal camp is accessible if there are no waves from the north. It is just due east of a **light**. The landing is sand if the waves aren't up; you might be hitting the steeper part of shore if they are. Camping is in an arroyo behind the landing zone.

The trip along the north end of the peninsula from the light at Punta Hornitos to Punta Concepción passes largely through shallow water if you paddle near shore. Low rocky shelves extend a ways out below the water's surface. In spring, there can be a lot of kelp, making paddling more difficult.

Mulegé

Punta Gallo

Punta Hornitos

Punta Concepción

Punta Maria

26° 51′ 48″, 111° 50′ 44″

1 Bahía Santo Domingo✳✳
A nice sand camp south of a fish camp. There is a last chance here for a sunset view to the west before you achieve the east-facing shore of the peninsula.

Punta Hornitos fish camp

26° 52′ 29″, 111° 47′ 28″

6 A long gravel beach partitioned by small gravel hills into three camp-worthy alcoves. There is good snorkeling here. There is a section of coast with shallow sea caves between this reading and the next.

26° 51′ 42″, 111° 45′ 58″

7 **Punta María** has exposed cobble camps on either side. South of the point you'll find geology of small red-brown hills pockmarked by cave-like indentations, a trait that repeats itself often in southern Baja.

26° 50′ 37″, 111° 44′ 48″

8 **Las Palmas.** A small arroyo with palm trees at the shore. It is not a camp, but there is fresh water seeping down the shore wall that is hard to gather but very tasty. I used a dive fin held into the rock to divert a trickle away from it. To get water in any sizable quantity would take some time.

26° 49′ 54″, 111° 44′ 12″

9 A cobble camp, probably not good on a wavy day, as the sleeping zone is not very high above the water. However, this is a nice part of the coast. There is a fish camp just around the southern corner of this camp.

The section of coast to Punta Santa Rosa has a number of cobble camping opportunities, some better than others and all a bit exposed to northern weather. Towards the point the landings get ugly as the cobble turns soccer ball-sized and is unstable at water level.

Punta Santa Teresa

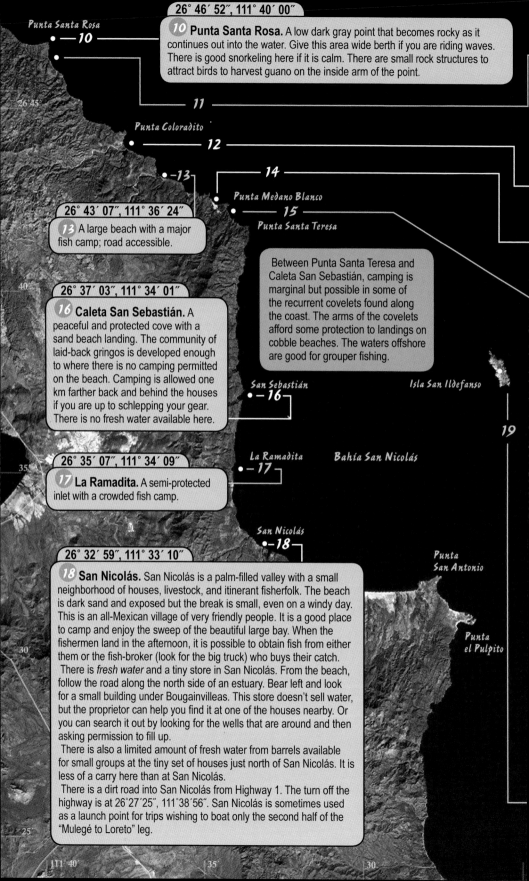

26° 46′ 52″, 111° 40′ 00″

10 **Punta Santa Rosa.** A low dark gray point that becomes rocky as it continues out into the water. Give this area wide berth if you are riding waves. There is good snorkeling here if it is calm. There are small rock structures to attract birds to harvest guano on the inside arm of the point.

Punta Santa Rosa
• —*10* ——

26° 45′

11 ——

Punta Coloradito
• —— *12*

• —*13*

14 ——

26° 43′ 07″, 111° 36′ 24″

13 A large beach with a major fish camp; road accessible.

Punta Medano Blanco
• —— *15*
Punta Santa Teresa

Between Punta Santa Teresa and Caleta San Sebastián, camping is marginal but possible in some of the recurrent covelets found along the coast. The arms of the covelets afford some protection to landings on cobble beaches. The waters offshore are good for grouper fishing.

40′

26° 37′ 03″, 111° 34′ 01″

16 **Caleta San Sebastián.** A peaceful and protected cove with a sand beach landing. The community of laid-back gringos is developed enough to where there is no camping permitted on the beach. Camping is allowed one km farther back and behind the houses if you are up to schlepping your gear. There is no fresh water available here.

San Sebastián
• —*16*

Isla San Ildefanso

19

26° 35′ 07″, 111° 34′ 09″

17 **La Ramadita.** A semi-protected inlet with a crowded fish camp.

35′

La Ramadita
• —*17*

Bahía San Nicolás

San Nicolás
• —*18*

26° 32′ 59″, 111° 33′ 10″

18 **San Nicolás.** San Nicolás is a palm-filled valley with a small neighborhood of houses, livestock, and itinerant fisherfolk. The beach is dark sand and exposed but the break is small, even on a windy day. This is an all-Mexican village of very friendly people. It is a good place to camp and enjoy the sweep of the beautiful large bay. When the fishermen land in the afternoon, it is possible to obtain fish from either them or the fish-broker (look for the big truck) who buys their catch.
  There is *fresh water* and a tiny store in San Nicolás. From the beach, follow the road along the north side of an estuary. Bear left and look for a small building under Bougainvilleas. This store doesn't sell water, but the proprietor can help you find it at one of the houses nearby. Or you can search it out by looking for the wells that are around and then asking permission to fill up.
  There is also a limited amount of fresh water from barrels available for small groups at the tiny set of houses just north of San Nicolás. It is less of a carry here than at San Nicolás.
  There is a dirt road into San Nicolás from Highway 1. The turn off the highway is at 26°27′25″, 111°38′56″. San Nicolás is sometimes used as a launch point for trips wishing to boat only the second half of the "Mulegé to Loreto" leg.

Punta
San Antonio

Punta
el Pulpito

30′

25′

111° 40′   35′   30′

SM
NM
Km

26° 45'

26° 46′ 19″, 111° 39′ 58″

11 ✱✱ A nice, semi-protected camp on gravel. It could hold a large group. This section of coast is full of ospreys.

Between the camps on Punta Santa Rosa and Punta Coloradito, there are three fair-weather camps: one is at the mouth of an arroyo, one is partially protected between a brown cliff and a pink cliff, and one is a large cobble beach. The shoreline has many rocky alcoves that provide nice snorkeling opportunities.

26° 44′ 03″, 111° 37′ 38″

12 A sandy beach just south of Punta Coloradito. It is more protected than others in the area.

26° 42′ 27″, 111° 34′ 50″

14 **Medano Blanco** ✱✱✱ An ultra-beautiful wilderness beach. It is exposed to the north, but the break is moderate—if you are going to crash and have a yard sale, you couldn't ask for a prettier place. The top of the beach has some protection, but watch out for rocks in the bay above and below the anvil-shaped entrance rock. The north landing is on cobble with sand and has an arroyo behind it for sleeping. There is very pleasant hiking on a trail along the **lighthouse** point south of the beach.

40'

26° 42′ 19″, 111° 34′ 23″

15 A protected camp just around the corner from Medano Blanco. It is cobble, but there are enough cleared spaces for a medium–sized group to sleep on. There is pretty slickrock at water level.

Medano Blanco

35'

30'

26° 37′ 52″, 111° 25′ 43″

19 **Isla San Ildefanso** is a rocky but picturesque islet with caves and bird colonies; however, there are no camp spots. There is good fishing for large cabrilla off the island at about 100-feet deep.

On a section of coast dubbed El Carricito, there is an exposed, duny, pleasant looking camp two miles past San Nicolás. Just down from that there is a long, low beach ending a half-mile before Punta San Antonio.

San Nicolás

Bahía San Nicolás

El Carricito

Punta San Antonio

26° 32′ 17″, 111° 27′ 46″

20 **Punta San Antonio.**

—21—

Punta el Pulpito

—22—

—23—

—24—

26° 22′ 54″, 111° 25′ 44″

26 Caleta Almeja ✗✗✗ A beautiful cove with cliffs on the west arm, a white sand beach in the back, and low crags descending to boulders and tall grass on the east. There is morning shade under the eastern cliffs. The surf-break in the cove is gradual and landing in weather should be okay. This is a picture perfect spot, and big enough for the largest of groups.

—25—

—26—

Punta San Basilio

27 *Ensenada San Juanico*

Punta Mercenarios

26° 22′ 09″, 111° 25′ 49″

27 ✗✗✗ Ensenada San Juanico, called **Ensenada San Basilio** on some maps, is one of the highlights of the entire coast. It is beautiful and magnificent in its natural state, though it is slightly developed and at times busy with sailboats and car campers. But even if the primary beaches at the back of the bay are full (winter), there are large outlying beaches on the bay's southern arm that see little traffic.

Boating into the bay, two rock formations immediately catch your eye. In the center/back of the bay is a small island of enchanting-looking rock towers. To the north is a graceful sloping arm of sandstone coming down from a hill into the water. Above it a few houses are perched, and though I hate shoreline development, I would love to own one of them. When you are deep into the back of the bay and then turn around and look out to sea, you look past the rock tower island to the jagged pinnacles of Punta Mercenarios off the southern arm. It is quite a view.

The camping configuration of the bay is: Two beaches in back, separated by a small hill. These are road accessible. Along the bay's southern arm are three more beaches. The western one has a small structure on it and is possibly lived on. The two outermost beaches are away from the action (yachts, Zodiacs, and car campers). They could see wave activity during a north blow, but are beautiful and have gradual breaks.

✦✦ The bay between the low Punta San Antonio and the high Punta el Pulpito holds three or four nice sand beaches. They have varying degrees of exposure; none with complete protection. There is a reef in the bay that can help break up surf before it hits shore. If you wish to land in weather, stand off until you have defined the reef and your route around it. These beaches have access to a trail up Punta el Pulpito. Overall, this area is a very special place; you are "out there," and it is beautiful.

26° 31´ 03″, 111° 26´ 28″

21 Punta el Pulpito. A "point of points." There are a few tougher places to navigate in the Sea of Cortez, but this is pretty stout. Pulpito's headland is dark and dramatic. Approach this area with caution in stormy seas. On one occasion paddling by Pulpito, I had surf from the east and a fish on my line; things got complicated as we floated towards the rocks but worked out when the fish broke away just before I had to grab my paddle and back off from the point. A strong north blow would be worse, I'm sure.
Almost hidden below the bastion of rock are two arches, one large and buried in an alcove, one smaller and just around the backside. After passing the second arch, there is a small beach that makes a nice landing for a hike up the point. It would be a great camp if it weren't narrow and backed by a cliff.

30´

Punta el Pulpito

25´

26° 30´ 23″, 111° 27´ 24″

22 A canyon camp down from Pulpito. Though the camp is approaching the marginal category, it is very north-protected and has a five-star cave for napping in the shade. Camp has sandy spots among cobble with room for up to four tents max. The landing at high tide is smooth but it's rocky at low tide. Just up from here you'll find a smaller camp with a clearing amongst cobble that could hold two tents. The cactus inland of both camps is bountiful and grabby and makes a hike to Pulpito a real chore even though the distance isn't great.

20´

26° 28´ 39″, 111° 27´ 47″

23 Saquicismunde. A protected but permanent fish camp with two beaches, the bigger of the two coming just south of this reading. Camping possibilities are limited here, and are probably best left for a hard-luck situation. A third beach a little farther down and uninhabited might be camp worthy.

26° 27´ 35″, 111° 28´ 16″

24 Las Tinajas. A canyon hike that narrows into a box, looks like it's going to end, but keeps going. There is a trickle of fresh water coming down a wall farther back.

15´

26° 23´ 45″, 111° 27´ 07″

25 Boca San Juanico. A large fish camp; road accessible.

111° 30′ **25′** **20′**

26° 20′ 47″, 111° 24′ 49″

28 The outermost beach in San Juanico. It is comprised of fine white sand. There is a reef in front of it that might cut down surf on a weather day. Approach camp from the west if there is north swell. There are two other camps west of this camp, one near a big arroyo and the other near a small arroyo. The beach in front of the big arroyo has a lagoon behind it, which might mean it's buggy.

28

Punta San Basilio

Ensenada San Juanico

29

Punta Mercenarios

There are beautiful multi-colored cliffs along the shoreline south of Mercenarios. Landing opportunities until Punta Mangle are limited to a couple of emergency-only alcoves.

26° 20′

Cerro Mercenarios

Punta Mangle
30

15′

31

Punta San Bruno
32

10′

33

Cacti basking in the sun

Punta Bajo

Isla

05′

Loreto
34

111° 30′ **25′** **20′**

SM
NM
Km.

10′
05′
111° 00′

26° 20′ 56″, 111° 24′ 12″

29 Punta Mercenarios.
This beautiful point can be negotiated inside or outside of the pinnacle formations. If you're coming up shore from inside the bay and there is swell from the north, the reef mentioned in the previous reading must also be dealt with, in which case the point might best be taken wide.

Punta Mercenarios

26° 16′ 42″, 111° 23′ 26″

30 The bay inside Punta Mangle is protected and has beaches but there is development here. A small hotel/big house sits on a cliff above one beach, and a small house sits near the other.

26°15′

26° 13′ 54″, 111° 23′ 11″

31 ✱✱ This is a big white sand beach situated in front of several dunes and set between low cliffs. It is easily seen from Punta Mangle. It does catch north swell, though the landing is not difficult in moderate seas.

26° 12′ 56″, 111° 22′ 39″

32 Boca San Bruno. Easily identified by a few palm trees. There is a fish camp on the north end of the beach though there is enough room to camp on the other end of the beach. There is a little more swell down here. A bar off the north end of the beach breaks surf on windy days. There is a lagoon behind the beach. It is rumored San Bruno will be the next big Loreto area development.

The coast south of San Bruno is ultra scenic but short on camping spots. Boating is along a rugged coast under mountains. Rock formations nestled in steep valleys halfway up the mountains are towers of dark, pockmarked stone. The visuals of these are fantastic when backlit by an afternoon sun. The beaches are best suited for a lunch stop only. Most of the landings are on steep cobble. A fellow guide has identified one small arroyo as a camp and good hike at approximately: 26°07′44″, 111°21′12″.

10′

26° 06′ 02″, 111° 19′ 26″

33 Punta Bajo. Up coast from Punta Bajo you'll find an exposed cobble beach with a sandy arroyo behind that makes a possible camp. On the point itself sits an abandoned, domed stone building and a **light**. It is possible to land on a cobble beach just on the north of the building. There could be camping here if so desired, but it would be up on dirt and semi-trashy. A road that leads to Loreto runs through here, so expect some local traffic.

Coming into Loreto, there are a few camp spots at either deserted private property or on small pull-offs from the coast dirt road. The coast is low at this point and there are multiple landing opportunities. The water is shallow for a long ways out and is popular with free divers looking for Chocolates, a delicious brown-colored, medium-sized clam. Surf is minimal due to the sweep of the land and protection from Isla Coronados.

05′

26° 00′ 54″, 111° 20′ 15″

34 Loreto Harbor.

Isla Carmen

149

10′
05′
111° 00′

View from the hammock

Sea Lions

  If you see a cluster of dark, dorsal-type fins sticking out of the water, it's not a shark convention. It's probably a raft of floating, snoozing sea lions, hanging their fins in the air. The difference between sea lions and seals is that sea lions have ears and walk on their fins. Sea lions are very social and enjoy swimming, hunting and lounging around together, even sleeping on top of each other. They are very playful and will even come out to meet and swim with kayakers.

  Clumsy and awkward on land, they are elegant and powerful in the water and are efficient hunters. So efficient that often they wait until you have snagged a fish, then come in and grab the helpless prey before you have had a chance to land it.

  You can enjoy snorkeling with sea lions, but keep a safe distance. The youngsters are curious and want to play with humans, but the large males are territorial and the mothers are very protective of their young. Sea lions mate in May and June and then give birth one year later. So this early summer period is when they are the most aggressive, especially the large males, who can grow up to 800 pounds. The males gather a harem of 10 to 20 females and guard them with loud howling. You will see their colonies on many beaches in Baja, with the males bellowing back and forth at each other all night long. You don't want to camp near a sea lion colony if you want to sleep.

– Lori Russell

Photo by: Lori Russell

Lying on a plain under the towering Sierra la Giganta, **Loreto** is an important location in Baja sea kayaking—it is in the center of the two most popular coastal runs, "Mulegé to Loreto" and "Loreto to La Paz," and also sits alongside a fantastic archipelago of islands that make up the body of the Loreto National Marine Park. Town is quaint, friendly, and easy to get around. It is accommodates visitors well with a variety of hotels, restaurants, outfitters, and a dive/fishing shop. Shuttles by car or bus are easy to do out of Loreto. There is also an airport with flights to other Mexican cities and to Southern California.

Loreto's history dates back to the 1600's when it was a Jesuit mission settlement. The mission is still present downtown. Later it became the first capitol of Baja. Its modern heyday was in the 1970's as a sport-fishing town, but billfish in the sea became scarce and some hotels in the core district lost business and now sit abandoned. For the time being, Loreto is relatively laid-back and is a good place for sea rats to chill. But the future appears to be different—developers are re-igniting business in Loreto and a couple of big projects outside of town are planned, including a massive "sustainable" home/golf course/village complex south of the airport that is presently under construction. When built out, it will undoubtedly change Loreto forever. How anybody can have the gall to call golf courses in the desert sustainable I will never know.

As far as restaurants go, there are a bunch: Café Olé has long been the favorite for breakfast, McLulu's Tacos is a fun experience (the proprietress has tremendous personality), another taco restaurant just east of there is a good place to eat budget food, and Lindo's on Av. Hidalgo across from McLulu's is good for any meal and docs a great Sunday brunch.

The mission tower above downtown Loreto, Photo by: Lori Russell

Landing/Launching at Loreto:

There is a hotel/house district along the beach north of the center of town. The Hotel La Pinta, a good but pricey place to stay, is one of the last buildings on the beach before the malecón (Ave. Lopez Mateos), which is the seaside road and walkway. Though La Pinta has plenty of parking, they do not allow car storage.

Just north of La Pinta you'll come upon an alley where you can get a car to the beach. A marsh behind the beach here precludes building so there is some privacy. It is possible to car camp here, but leaving gear unattended without a car to lock it in is not recommended. The yellow building to the north is a smaller hotel that looks nice and is cheaper than La Pinta. Some public shade palapas between La Pinta and the malecón provide a possible loading/unloading zone.

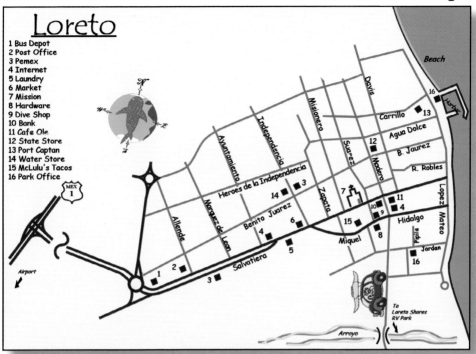

Loreto

1 Bus Depot
2 Post Office
3 Pemex
4 Internet
5 Laundry
6 Market
7 Mission
8 Hardware
9 Dive Shop
10 Bank
11 Cafe Ole
12 State Store
13 Port Captan
14 Water Store
15 McLulu's Tacos
16 Park Office

A little farther south is Loreto harbor (26° 00' 53", 111° 20' 20"). One of the Marine Park offices is located at the harbor, though it is often closed. There is also an office here where you can obtain a fishing license. The harbor is small, active, and primarily for pangas and other motorcraft. Loading or unloading sea kayaks here is not recommended. However, there is a tiny beach immediately south of the harbor that is very protected and can be used as a landing zone, though access to this beach is over rocks which line the malecón. Across the malecón from this spit of a beach is a reasonably priced hotel, the San Francisquito.

Inland from the harbor area a few blocks on Ave. Rosenda Robles is the cheapest place to stay downtown, the El Morro RV Park. It is one of the best places for coast running kayakers on a budget to hang, though doing so involves ferrying gear a few blocks. Adjacent to the core district of town, El Morro is a small courtyard of a place that has showers, a little camping area, and a few motel rooms. El Morro offers car storage.

South of the harbor, the shore is rocky for a ways until the malecón ends. Below the malecón there is a great looking hotel that I have not stayed at, the Oasis. It is a little cheaper than La Pinta, has a nice looking restaurant, and has shaded hammocks strung in front of the rooms.

Loreto Shores RV Park (25° 59' 54", 111° 20' 15") is a good landing/launch point for the camp-minded crowd. At the southern edge of town, it is just inland of a palm-dotted beach and behind and between two townhome complexes. Camping is on a grassy area at the back of the park, which is often full of RV campers during the second half of winter. The showers are excellent, the water is potable, and there is an enclosed public kitchen. Long-term car storage is available only in the shoulder seasons.

Note: Many trips putting-in for the "Loreto to La Paz" run or an "Isla Carmen" trip do not launch from Loreto, but launch farther down coast in the Puerto Escondido area. This is because the coast for 15 kilometers south of Loreto is either bland or a resort and the crossing to Carmen from Loreto is long. Near Escondido the crossing is shorter and there is car storage and a boat ramp. For more on the Puerto Escondido area, see page 179.

The waters around Loreto and the beaches of its nearby islands, from Isla Coronados to Isla Catalina, are part of the Loreto Bay National Marine Park. The Park was established by the federal government in 1996 to help preserve the area biosphere. A big push was made to get commercial fishing trawlers out of the area; it was successful for a while (to some danger of the unarmed enforcers), but, as far as I can tell from personal observation, the directive isn't always obeyed. I also question how there can be significant development allowed around the shores of a marine park when there is a symbiotic relationship between the land and the water. Adding thousands of fish-hungry human beings, hundreds of motorized watercraft, and tons of condos to a coast where shorebirds used to live is counterproductive to a healthy marine life.

Isla Catalina valley with Cardón, Giant Barrel, and Cholla cacti.

SM
NM
Km

But the fact there is a Park is a commendable step. The beaches on the islands have been cleaned up for the most part, and rules are in place to keep them nice. Some of the Park regulations are: no campfires (stoves only), human waste disposed of in a porta-potty (which seems optional depending on the size of the group and whether it is commercially guided), and camping in designated sites only. (There is a map of Park campsites following this introduction.) Most of this chapter's descriptions of campsites within the Park have the official campsite numbers included with them. There are also descriptions of places that are not official camps—this is to provide options for lunch spots, forced landings due to weather, and other exigent circumstances. Occasionally, Marine Park camp names are not always the names other maps or even longtime locals give certain places.

You can obtain a permit at the Park's main office south of the corner of Pipila and Fernando Jordan in Loreto or sometimes at their secondary office at the harbor, though this office is often closed. In 2007, camping costs were $2.00 U.S./person/night. You will be asked to go to the bank to pay and get a receipt to bring back to the Park office, so make sure you time your permit run during local banking hours. You'll receive a bracelet to wear that indicates you're permitted to stay in the Park.

On a trip in 2002, I was asked to list an itinerary with campsite for each day of a ten-day trip. I did, but deviated from the itinerary somewhat during the actual trip. In 2005, Park personnel only asked for a length of stay in the Park, not an itinerary, but this was for a shoulder season trip, when things were less busy. On the "Formato de Registro," accompanying this blurb, there is a place to list an itinerary. After completing business with the Park officials, groups with a commercial guide are then asked to go to the Port Captain. I have heard that he will try to charge you something extra on top of the Park fee so avoid going to the Port Captain unless it is necessary.

Park camping permits and regulations are enforced loosely at times and heavily at other times. I have had a Park panga pull directly in front of the beach I was camped on and not ask for anything, but on the other hand, I've also heard of groups camped in the Park being shaken down quite aggressively and asked to show their permits.

Isla Coronados

Loreto

Isla Carmen

Puerto
Escondido

Isla Danzante

Isla Monserrat

Isla Catalina

Agua Verde

10′

26°00′

25°50′

40′

30′

111° 20′   10′   111° 00′   110° 50′

155

Parque Nacional Bahía de Loreto
Blvd. Adolfo López Mateos Esq. Atanasio Carrillo
Col. centro, Loreto Baja California Sur. México. C.P.23880
Tel/Fax 01 613 13 5-04-77 y 13-5-14-29
Correo electrónico:
loreto@conanp.gob.mx

FORMATO DE REGISTRO PARA TURISTAS
(PARTICULARES)

Fecha (date):	¿Equipo personal? (personal equipment)?:	Equipo rentado (leased equipment): (company):	
/ /			

Lugar(es) a visitar (place(s) to visit):

	Day/month site	Day/month site	Day/month site	**Periodo de estancia** (Visit period):
1 (/)	4 (/)	7 (/)		
2 (/)	5 (/)	8 (/)		
3 (/)	6 (/)	9 (/)		

Actividades a realizar (Planned activities):

Responsable del grupo (head of the group):	**Firma** (signature):	
Dirección (address):	**Teléfono** (phone number):	**Correo-e** (e-mail):

No.	NOMBRE (name)	EDAD (age)	PROCEDENCIA (origin)
1			
2			
3			
4			
5			
6			
7			
8			
9			
10			
11			
12			
13			
14			
15			
16			
17			
18			
19			
20			
21			
22			
23			
24			
25			

Folios boletos verificados:	Folios boletos vendidos:
al	al

COMISIÓN NACIONAL DE
ÁREAS NATURALES
PROTEGIDAS

PARQUE
NACIONAL

BAHIA DE
LORETO

COMISION NACIONAL DE
AREAS NATURALES
PROTEGIDAS

SITIOS DE CAMPAMENTO TURISTICO

ZONA COSTERA

CT- 01 PARSIDE
CT- 02 BEATRIZ
CT- 03 SANTO DOMINGO
CT- 04 EL NIDO
CT- 05 LOS NIDOS
CT- 06 LA PALMITA
CT- 07 SANTA ROSA N
CT- 08 SANTA ROSA
CT- 09 EL VERDE
CT- 10 COLORADITO
CT- 11 SAN LINO
CT- 12 SAN LINITO
CT- 13 MEDANO BLANCO
CT- 14 TERESA
CT- 15 SAN SEBASTIAN
CT- 16 SAN NICOLAS
CT- 17 JACOBO
CT- 18 SAN ANTONIO
CT- 19 PULPITO
CT- 20 FLASH FLOOD
CT- 21 SAQUISISMUDE
CT- 22 LAS TINAJAS
CT- 23 SAN JUANICO
CT- 24 PUERTO ALMEJAS
CT- 25 SAN BASILIO
CT- 26 EL MANGLE
CT- 27 SAN BRUNO
CT- 28 PLAYA EL TIBURON
CT- 29 LORETO
CT- 30 LA SALINITA
CT- 31 NOTRI
CT- 31 CHUENQUE (JUNCALITO)
CT- 34 PUNTA COYOTE
CT- 34 PUERTO ESCONDIDO
CT- 35 EL QUEMADO

Continua...ZONA COSTERA

CT- 36 TRIPUI
CT- 37 TECOMAJA
CT- 38 LIGUI
CT- 39 EL ESTUCHE (E. BLANCA)
CT- 40 PUERTOCITOS
CT- 41 ENSENADA EL ESTUCHE N
CT- 42 ENSENADA EL ESTUCHE
CT- 43 EL AGUJILLO N
CT- 44 EL TRIUNFO N
CT- 45 EL TRIUNFO
CT- 46 EL TRIUNFO S
CT- 47 EL COYOTITO
CT- 48 LA DIGUNTITA
CT- 49 PLAYA LA BALLENA
CT- 50 EL MALECON
CT- 51 EL CARRIZALITO VENTANA
CT- 52 EL CARRIZALITO PALMAS
CT- 53 EL CARRIZALITO S
CT- 53 AGUA CALIENTE
CT- 54 SAN COSME
CT- 55 SAN COSME E
CT- 56 PLAYA SAN FERNANDO
CT- 57 ESTERO SAN COSME
CT- 58 AGUA VERDE N
CT- 59 AGUA VERDE CENTRO
CT- 60 AGUA VERDE S

I. CORONADO

CD- 01 BARRA ARENOSA S
CD- 02 EXTREMO BARRA ARENOSA
CD- 03 EXTREMO BARRA ARENOSA N
CD- 04 NORTE DE BAHÍA HONDA
CD- 05 ENSENADA BLANCA
CD- 06 ENSENADA BLANCA N
CD- 07 LOS METATES

I. DANZANTE

DZ- 01 CALETA DEL AMOR
DZ- 02 PUNTA ELEONORA N
DZ- 03 PUNTA ELEONORA N
DZ- 04 NORTE DE BAHÍA HONDA
DZ- 05 BAJA HONDA N
DZ- 06 BAHÍA HONDA
DZ- 07 LAS CUEVAS
DZ- 08 EL ARROYO
DZ- 09 PUNTA ARENA
DZ- 10 PUNTA ARENA N
DZ- 11 LOS HONGOS
DZ- 12 LOS HONGOS II
DZ- 13 PLAYA LAS GRAVAS
DZ- 14 EL MANGLE
DZ- 15 LUNA DE MIEL

I. CARMEN

CN- 01 LOS CIRIOS
CN- 02 PIEDRA HUNDIDA
CN- 03 EL ARCO
CN- 04 LAS CASITAS
CN- 05 LAS CASITAS S
CN- 06 (SIN NOMBRE)
CN- 07 (SIN NOMBRE)
CN- 08 EL CANTIL N
CN- 09 EL CANTIL S
CN- 10 LOS COLORINES
CN- 11 LAS CORONAS
CN- 12 LOS TRIANGULOS
CN- 13 LOS TRIANGULOS O
CN- 14 PLATA SALINAS
CN- 15 PLAYAS SALINAS O
CN- 16 LOS PAREDONES
CN- 17 AGUA CHICA
CN- 18 GAVILANES
CN- 19 NORTE DE ARROYO BLANCO
CN- 20 ARROYO BLANCO
CN- 21 PUNTA COLORADA N
CN- 22 PUNTA COLORADA
CN- 22 SAN FRANCISCO
CN- 23 LAS COLORADAS
CN- 24 PUNTA BAJA N
CN- 25 PUNTA BAJA
CN- 26 PUNTA BAJA O
CN- 27 PUNTA BAJA NO
CN- 28 PUNTA ARENA
CN- 29 EL FARO
CN- 30 PLAYA GARAYZAR
CN- 31 BAHÍA MARQUER S
CN- 32 BAHIA MARQUER
CN- 33 LOS CARDONES
CN- 34 BAHÍA BALANDRA
CN- 35 PLAYA LA CHOYA
CN- 36 BAHÍA OTO
CN- 37 LA PALMA
CN- 38 EL REFUGIO

I. MONTSERRAT

MS- 01 PLAYA SAN LAZARO
MS- 02 PLAYA LA HERRADURA
MS- 03 PLAYA LAS GRAVAS
MS- 04 PLAYA ANTARES
MS- 05 LOS QUESILLOS
MS- 06 PLAYA SUR
MS- 07 LOS MURILLOS
MS- 08 ENSENADA BAJA
MS- 09 ENSENADA BAJA N
MS- 10 PLAYA NOROESTE
MS- 11 PLAYA PAULINA
MS- 12 PLAYA DAVIS

I. CORONADOS

I. CARMEN

I. MONTSERRAT

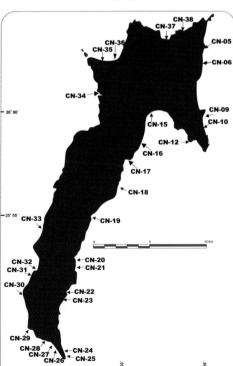

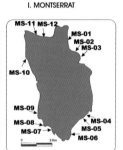

I. DANZANTE

I. CATALANA

Ensenada Blanca

26° 07′ 06″, 111° 17′ 14″

3 Los Metates, CD-07. A small beach inside the northern arm of the bay. There is a tin shack indicating the sometimes-possibility of a fish camp. It is very protected from north swells.

26° 06′ 42″, 111° 16′ 46″

2 Playa de Coronados, CD-05 ✱✱

This is the primary beach on the island, and it is beautiful! In a serene, small bay (Ensenada Blanca), this very protected beach faces west. There are views of the Sierra la Giganta to the southwest and a handsome mountain up the main coast to the north. On the beach are three palapas. One has a table in it and a barbecue pit built into the rocks behind it. There is a composting toilet here as well. The beach is white sand and there are an abundance of clams out in the shallow bay. The only drawbacks to this idyllic place: it gets day use from pangas carrying tourists, and yachts sometimes anchor in front of the beach. After experiencing one motor yacht in the cove leave its generator running all night so that its occupants could be air conditioned, I demoted this beach from five to four stars.

The cone of the old volcano is behind the beach. A trail goes up the first rib of the mountain to the east of camp. There are a few other camp possibilities in this bay, though none are as nice as this.

Ensenada Blanca beach

26° 06′ 16″, 111° 18′ 16″

1 Isla la Chollita. La Chollita is a tiny, low island with a **light** on it. The islet is largely composed of lava rock. There is a cleared landing in the south cove creating a good lunch spot.

Marine Park Islands ~ Isla Coronados

Isla Coronados is one of the better short kayak trips in the Sea of Cortez. This beautiful volcanic island is a minimal distance from a primary launch town, Loreto, but far enough away that the presence of town is not strongly felt when you are on the island. Coronados has limited but very nice camping, and its beaches front great geology. The island has a 500' high volcano that sits in a back corner and makes a wonderful day hike. The perimeter of the island can be circumnavigated by kayak in a day, during which the scenery changes from low beaches on the southwest corner to large rock formations on the steep northern end. On calm days, you can park on the rocks on the outside of the island and go snorkeling in canyons off the edge of the island. Sunsets from the white sand beaches look out across the looming mountains behind Loreto, and are sometimes breathtaking.

Punta Bajo is a good launch for a trip to Coronados if you are just out from Loreto for a few days and don't want to do the upwind paddle from town. Another good, intermediate-length trip would be San Juanico (page 146)-Coronados-Loreto. It's 35 miles if you circumnavigate the island and has a lot of good scenery in its short distance. Hire a taxi with a roof rack to get you out from town if you don't have transportation or a guide service.

26° 08′ 06″, 111° 16′ 42″

4 A big, freestanding rock—seen from miles away if you came down the main peninsula. It is the first of a few prominent geologic formations on the north end. This is the surf-exposed part of the island, but it is lovely paddling here on a mild day. Be aware of some conflicting currents creating strange wave patterns. If you are not a strong swimmer, you might not want to venture too far from shore or your boat.

10'

4

Isla Coronados

Around the northeast corner of the island is a sea lion rookery. Continuing down the eastern shore of the island, the dramatic north end formations recede into lower angle slopes coming off the volcano. There are no camps in this zone, though there are some landing possibilities on rocky beaches.

3 —
Ensenada Blanca
2 —

1 — *7 —*
ta o
Barra Arenosa
6

— 5 —

26° 06′ 19″, 111° 15′ 46″

5 Lighthouse.

26° 05′ 57″, 111° 17′ 50″

6 **Extremo Barra Arenosa, CD-02.** The outside of the southwest tip of Coronados, This is a small beach with a fish camp and a Park sign informing visitors of the rules.

05'

26° 06′ 06″, 111° 17′ 42″

7 **Bahía Honda, CD-04.** This is the inside of the southwestern tip. There is a long white sand beach here, but it is very narrow. There are a couple of tent sites above the beach among some small dunes. Just west of this reading is another camp on a tree-dotted beach in a covelet.

26° 05′

Isla Carmen is a top target destination for sea kayakers in Baja; it is the main feature within the Loreto Marine Park. Because of its proximity to Loreto, its mid-large size and manageable crossing, Carmen yearns to be explored. And it is explored—a lot. I'm not sure of the actual number of kayakers that visit each year, but I have looked through the Marine Park's reservation book and there are many names penciled in for the winter high season. Numerous commercial groups boat Carmen, and often the better inside beaches are reserved in advance. But Carmen has many beaches, and it is still only lightly kayaked in the spring and fall shoulder seasons.

Some of Carmen's features include: a town (or the remnants of one), plus mountains, flats, and a fresh water source, making it different from many of the islands in the sea. There are some lovely beaches, one with a giant sand dune, and there is also a large sea cave to play in. The island's interior is being used to reintroduce Desert Bighorn Sheep to the Baja environment; though I have also heard it said that the reason for the implanting of the Bighorns is to turn Carmen into a private hunting ground.

Isla Carmen is privately owned, at least in part by the salt company that built the small town on its east side and mined the flats there. The mining operation is defunct now. Visitors are asked to stay on the beaches and not venture into the interior of Carmen. Should you wish permission to explore the interior of the island, contact: Enrique Grajeda Cazarez at igrajedac@vitro.com.

Isla Carmen's long north end is a unique feature compared to most Sea of Cortez islands. This north coast is comprised of three distinct points: Puntas Cholla, Tintorera, and Lobos. These points and the distance between them create a potential navigation hazard if the weather comes from the north. But this is not the wilderness of say, Isla de la Guarda; smallcraft traffic on the north end of Carmen is frequent, and there are semi-permanent fish camps at each corner of the north coast, so help is not far away.

Carmen is most easily approached from the Puerto Escondido area south of Loreto. From Escondido (page 179), where it is possible to leave a car and where there is a protected launch, Carmen is five miles out, with Isla Danzante offering a midway stopping point. The southern tip of Carmen has a number of camps, making it a desirable day-one target.

The shallow Carmen channel gets active in a wind. Should the waves in the channel build, they sometimes become awkward and seem to come at your boat from different directions simultaneously—a phenomenon sometimes known in this book as "wacky waves." Traditional navigation calls this a "confused sea."

26° 00′

25° 55′

50′

Loreto

Puerto Esc

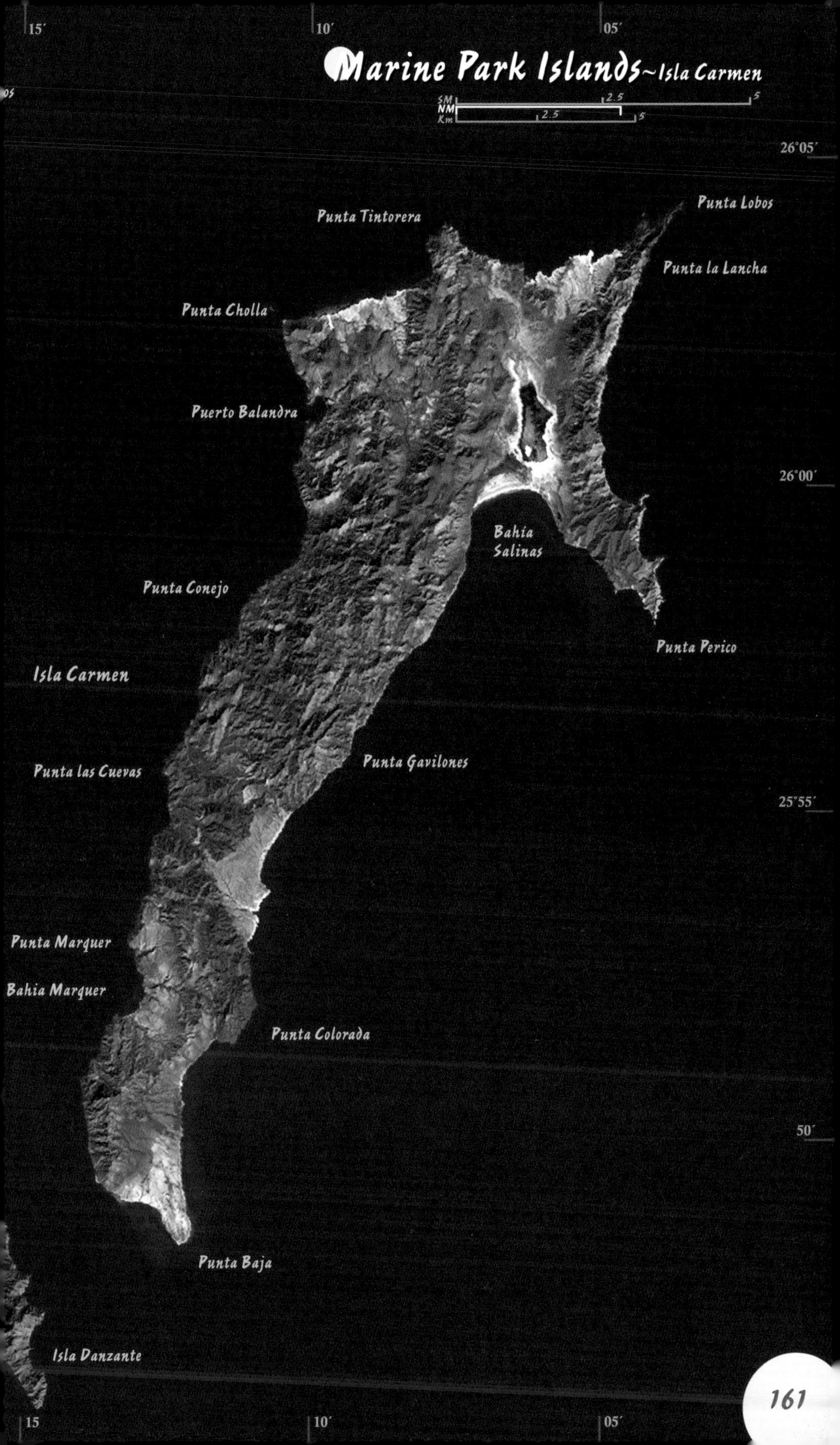

SM
NM
Km

2.5

2.5

2.5

5

5

15′   10′   05′   26°05′

Punta Lobos

Punta Tintorera

Punta la Lancha

Punta Cholla

Puerto Balandra

26°00′

Bahia
Salinas

Punta Conejo

Punta Perico

Isla Carmen

Punta las Cuevas

Punta Gavilones

25°55′

Punta Marquer

Bahia Marquer

Punta Colorada

50′

Punta Baja

Isla Danzante

15   10′   05′

Sunset over the Sierra la G...

25° 56' 10", 111° 12' 17"

6 An approximate reading of a gravel beach facing northwest. It is located in a bay with a valley behind it.

25° 52' 04", 111° 13' 07"

5 Bahía Marquer, CN-31 and CN-32. The primary camp here is a large gravel beach in the back southern corner of the bay. This NW-facing beach aspect repeats itself in the other bays in the mid-section of this inside coast, and it leaves them all somewhat prone to northerlies. Another gravel beach a half-mile up from this offers more protection from north waves.
 Intermittent smaller bays, backed by rising planes dotted with Cardón, appear after Bahía Marquer as you head north.

25° 49' 46", 111° 13' 50"

4 Gorilla Head. This unofficial name came from the hill behind camp, which with its rich brown color and corrugated ridgelets above small caves resembles the furrowed brow of our jungle brethren. This topography is encountered often on Carmen. The camp is protected from northeast winds. The landing is gravel/rock, but there is a smooth (though small) area in which to camp.

25° 49' 20", 111° 13' 39"

25°50'

3 El Faro, CN-29. Lighthouse. (Most maps call this Punta Arena, though the Park map lists CN-28 as that point.) This is a nice sand and gravel beach with some interesting-looking balanced rocks scattered around. Shelves in the cliff behind the beach make a good kitchen area. There is late sun in the morning and a cave for shade in the afternoon. The sunset views of Sierra la Giganta can be spectacular. At night, you can faintly hear truck traffic down Highway 1 through the mountains.

Isla

111° 20'

Puerto Escondido

8 – •

Isla Carmen

26° 00′ 25″, 111° 10′ 17″

8 A fish camp in an inlet behind and to the north of a red knob of rock.

Bahía Salinas

7 — •

25° 59′ 00″, 111° 10′ 29″

7 A 2-mile wide bay. There are two camps in the lower inside corner of the bay, separated by a horn of rock. The landing is gravel/sand and is okay for glass boats. A line of rocks protruding in front of camp (but easily avoided) quiets north waves just before the landing. There is good fishing off these rocks if there is no surf. The eastern camp has an elevated sand area good for the kitchen at the mouth of an arroyo, and good hiking opportunities exist behind camp.

Punta Conejo

6 – •

Punta Gavilones

Punta las Cuevas

25°55′

Bahía Marquer

5 – •

Punta Colorada

25° 49′ 03″, 111° 12′ 59″

2 **Punta Baja Norte, CN-27.** This low part of the island is hard to decipher from a distance. As you get closer, you'll see a number of beaches. CN-27 is somewhat long and narrow; it doesn't offer much protection from a high sea. A better sleeping area is an eight-foot climb up a bank behind the beach where you'll find some flats. In the spring, the beaches on this part of the island get inundated with washed-up algae, which smells quite bad. You can somewhat avoid the smell by camping on the flats. There is a pretty peak to the north of camp.

50′

–•

25° 48′ 34″, 111° 12′ 31″ ~ Approx.

1 **CN-26.** A nice, white sand cove on the southwest end of Carmen up coast from Punta Baja.

3 – •

Arena

2 – •

1

163

Punta Baja   10′

111° 15'

SM
NM
Km 1.5

26°10'

El Refugio

There is another possible camp one mile east of Playa la Cholla, it is **Bahía Oto, CN-36.** After this, there are no landings until east of Punta Tintorera. which is a long, rocky headland that should be given wide berth on surf days.

26° 03´ 34˝, 111° 07´ 18˝

12 This interesting camp is guarded by two horns of rock. With surf, a landing is possible but challenging. The surf lies down as you near the beach, but it's a thread-the-needle approach with a cobble landing so it might not be a good glass boat beach. There is plenty of sleep space and a nice twisting arroyo behind camp. Your tents will feel the wind, but the same is true for all beaches of this aspect.

26° 02´ 35˝, 111° 09´ 45˝

11 **Playa la Cholla, CN-35** ✗✗ This is a big white sand beach that can conceivably hold multiple groups. The landing is open to the north. On a surf day, land with caution to avoid rounded rocks that partially line the beach. The break is gradual for the most part, but some smaller waves hit shore. Behind this fine beach is a long sandy arroyo with dunes on each side. There is a smaller beach to the east separated from Playa la Cholla by a low hill and a short cliff at sea level. At low tide you can walk the sand strip between the beaches. The hills behind the beaches are devoid of significant cactus growth and are easily hiked.

05'

26° 02´ 40˝, 111° 10´ 42˝

10 **Isla Cholla. Light.** This small rock island off the northwest tip of Carmen offers a safe landing on its southwest corner. There is no camping here, as the area is an oft-used fish camp. The climb up the light yields fantastic views, and also provides a view of the surf and landing zones for the northwest beaches of Carmen. The north end of Isla Cholla is a major bird chill zone.

Carmen north end. This is a 7½ -mile stretch that involves rounding three points. There are sanctuaries on wind days, yet the ruggedness of both the mid-point and the final point warrants a heads-up attitude and an eye to the weather.

26° 01´ 12˝, 111° 09´ 45˝

9 **Puerto Balandra, CN-34.** This is a significant harbor that opens up after a bottleneck entrance. Yachts and even small cruise ships commonly visit. It is exposed only to the west. There are four or five possible camps, though the Marine Park has it listed as only having one. As you enter the harbor, you'll see two small beaches on the south arm. The long main beach is located in the back of the inlet. It is a slightly trashy beach, but you can at least cool off under some trees that are located near a SEMARNAT sign. A smaller and cleaner beach to the south and a fish camp to the north flank this beach. The large flat arroyo behind the main beach has a well-worn trail leading into it, but there is a NO TRESPASSING sign there as well. It looks like a worthy valley to explore, and I think the eco-cruise folks get to take a hike up this trail. In this arroyo the Cholla cacti yield edible fruit. When cutting them open, handle the small globules only with gloves, as miniscule, almost invisible quills coat the outside of the fruit.

26°00'

111° 15'

26° 03′ 06″, 111° 06′ 13″

13 **La Palma, CN-37.** The beach here is very rocky. Landing is possible only in a small, man-made alcove in the SE corner—only this spot is surf-protected. Camp is located near the remnants of an old village where the foundations of buildings still sit. The area is a little trashy and not very nice, but there are level spots for tents. There is a NO TRESPASSING sign nearby, but the best camp spot and one that could hold a large group is just behind this sign.

The ravens at this camp are smart and aggressive. Leave no food items or containers out if you decide to wander off. And hide your water; the determined birds recognize water jugs and will attempt to peck through them to get a drink. A dirt road descends into camp from the low hills to the south and is traveled by vehicles occasionally. The road goes over a low pass, through the town dump, and into the salt pond village at Bahía Salinas.

26° 03′ 19″, 111° 05′ 07″

14 **El Refugio, CN-38** ✶✶✶ This is one of the more ideal camps on Carmen. The beach is made of white sand and sits to the back of a narrow inlet; walls of sheer rock stand on either side. The cove resembles a small fjord. Camp could accommodate the largest of groups, and the beach is semi-protected from northerly waves by a slight twist in the cove. If it is windy, waves flop against the inlet's cliffs and then refract back in a haphazard fashion, creating a wacky ride until the landing, which sees some surf but has a calm eastern corner. There is a 100-foot high sand dune behind the camping area. The large dune provides a very fun short hike, or just a thing of beauty to behold from the cocktail area.

26°10′

26° 04′ 06″, 111° 04′ 15″

15 An islet/large rock just off the coast west of Punta Lobos. This unique landmark takes you by surprise at first. Unfortunately, it is a major fish camp otherwise it would make a great kayak camp. A large cave on the southeast corner of the islet houses a rotating crew of pescaderos, some lounging, others out fishing. The inside passage beneath the islet offers a respite from any wind that might kick up.

05′

Isla Carmen

Punta Tintorera

12

13   14

15   *Punta Lobos*

16

11

lla

9

Balandra

26° 04′ 23″, 111° 03′ 33″

16 **Punta Lobos. Light.** There are gravel beaches in a small bay just before the point that could be used as camps, but you are exposed to the fish camp to the east and also any north winds. This rocky point can get active and tricky on a north wind day. It is an uphill paddle to the sharp point, and you have to fight to stay away from shore. There is a wind shadow behind Punta Lobos, but it is small. The next seven miles of coast to the south, though having some campsites, are largely a series of dramatic headlands.

26°00′

Bahía Salinas

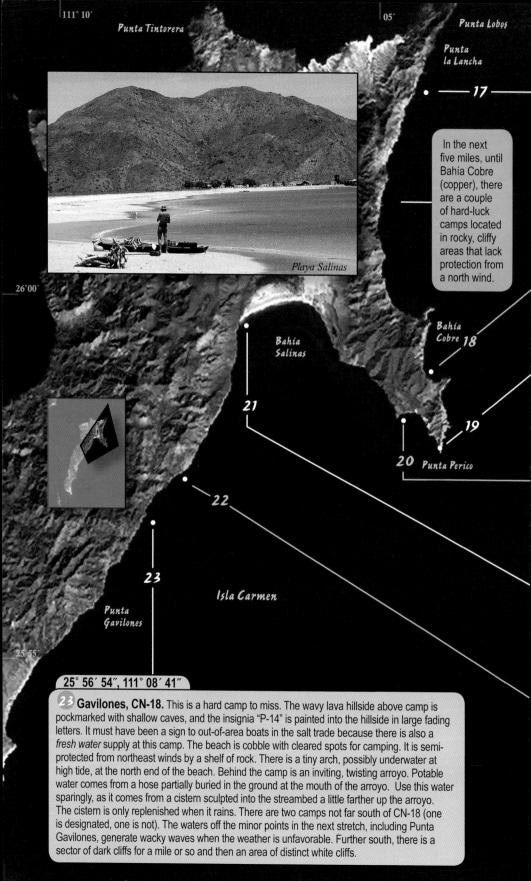

111° 10′

Punta Tintorera

05′

Punta Lobos

Punta
la Lancha

— 17 —

In the next
five miles, until
Bahía Cobre
(copper), there
are a couple
of hard-luck
camps located
in rocky, cliffy
areas that lack
protection from
a north wind.

Playa Salinas

26°00′

Bahía
Salinas

Bahía
Cobre 18

21

19

20 *Punta Perico*

22

23

Isla Carmen

*Punta
Gavilones*

25°55′

25° 56′ 54″, 111° 08′ 41″

23 Gavilones, CN-18. This is a hard camp to miss. The wavy lava hillside above camp is pockmarked with shallow caves, and the insignia "P-14" is painted into the hillside in large fading letters. It must have been a sign to out-of-area boats in the salt trade because there is also a *fresh water* supply at this camp. The beach is cobble with cleared spots for camping. It is semi-protected from northeast winds by a shelf of rock. There is a tiny arch, possibly underwater at high tide, at the north end of the beach. Behind the camp is an inviting, twisting arroyo. Potable water comes from a hose partially buried in the ground at the mouth of the arroyo. Use this water sparingly, as it comes from a cistern sculpted into the streambed a little farther up the arroyo. The cistern is only replenished when it rains. There are two camps not far south of CN-18 (one is designated, one is not). The waters off the minor points in the next stretch, including Punta Gavilones, generate wacky waves when the weather is unfavorable. Further south, there is a sector of dark cliffs for a mile or so and then an area of distinct white cliffs.

SM
NM
Km   1.5   3

26° 02′ 49″, 111° 04′ 28″

17 Las Casitas S, CN-05. South of Punta la Lancha, which is a big green promontory, is a series of campsites. The first and most protected, tucked in behind the promontory, is a fish camp. South of that, across a small bay, is a large cobble beach suitable for a big group. (But it is less wave-protected than the fish camp and also in view of it.) Just south of this, around a small corner, you'll notice a sizable black rock in the water and across from it a smaller, more private beach that has less of an uphill carry than its larger sister beach to the north. The sunset views of distant Isla Catalina and the multi-hued hills of la Lancha are sublime.

25° 58′ 54″, 111° 04′ 11″

18 Los Colorines, CN-10. Though exposed to the north, there is a good camp in this southwest corner of the bay above Punta Perico. It is a sometimes-used fish camp. The beach is yellow sand, and it leads up to ochre-colored cliffs that stretch to the north.

25° 57′ 56″, 111° 04′ 04″

19 Punta Perico. I do not know what the paddle around Perico is like on a big wind day, but I have boated it in a mid-strength blow, and it wasn't too difficult. Perico has a large red rock and a lesser one just south of that sitting close off shore. Depending on the wind and tide, you can squeeze between the rocks or take them wide and long. When you round the point, you are protected from north winds; however, if you chose to paddle up Bahía Salinas, you will encounter the winds again if they are blowing due to low land north of the bay.

26°00′

25° 58′ 24″, 111° 04′ 37″

20 Los Triangulos, CN-12 ✴✴✴ A small bay inside of Perico protected from north winds. This cove often sees yachts at anchor. The beach is gravel, but three or four spots have been cleared down to sand for tents. There is good snorkeling at a reef off the west arm of the bay.

Carmen northeast coast

Attractive, horizontally striped cliffs color the coast northwest of Perico. On the way up Bahía Salinas, there is a picturesque old red- and white-striped concrete lighthouse. There is some hard-luck camping north of the **light.**

25° 59′ 44″, 111° 07′ 04″

21 Playas Salinas, CN-15 ✴✴✴ This is a huge, arching white sand beach. The aquamarine water of the north-protected bay quietly laps against the shore. Camp is on the western end of the beach, away from a small village. At the village, a long pier juts out into the water, and the wreck of an old cargo ship lies in the bay. A few houses and a small church comprise the settlement, with two residences permanently occupied. There is a small marine biology station here. This village was once the producer of large quantities of salt, coming from the evaporative pond inland.

25°55′

25° 57′ 30″, 111° 08′ 12″

22 Agua Chica, CN-17. There is a *fresh water* well here, but you'll have to pass a NO TRESPASSING sign to get to it. Sometimes this sign is fallen over and lying face down in the sand. As you boat along the coast, this camp appears at a break in some cliffs. The beach is cobble/rock with an arroyo behind it. There is one palm tree here. The small beach is a mixture of protruding orange and green basement rock and gravel. Sticking out into the bay are a few old rusted supports that used to carry a pipe out into the water. The course of the ghost pipeline runs up into the arroyo and to a low concrete well. The well is large and not too deep, but you need your own bucket and rope to fetch the water. The sides of the well are precipitous and the timbers nearby rotten, so watch your footing. The water is potable, but should be purified before drinking.

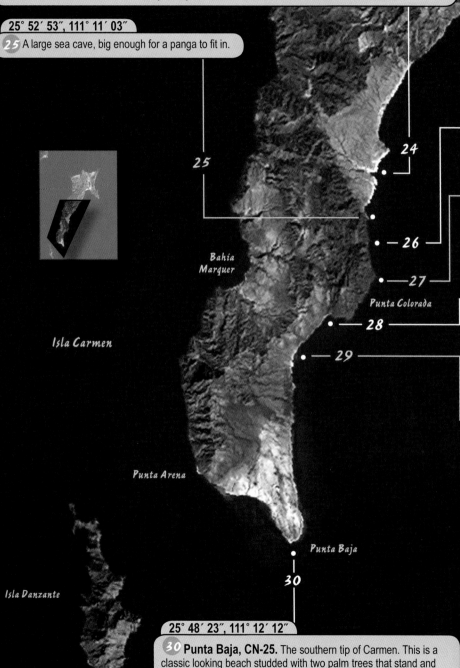

25° 53′ 29″, 111° 11′ 00″

24 **Arroyo Blanco, CN-20** ✖✖✖ This is a perfect cove, set in a limestone arroyo facing east-southeast. The beach is cobble and sand. It is only 30 yards across, but there is plenty of sleeping space. Short, pleasant hikes are possible on the limestone shelves surrounding the cove. The water in the cove is clear and calm; the bottom is mostly sandy but has a few rocks that attract fish.

25° 52′ 53″, 111° 11′ 03″

25 A large sea cave, big enough for a panga to fit in.

25°55′

Pu
Ga

25

Bahia
Marquer

Isla Carmen

24

26

27

Punta Colorada

28

29

50′

Punta Arena

Punta Baja

30

Isla Danzante

25° 48′ 23″, 111° 12′ 12″

30 **Punta Baja, CN-25.** The southern tip of Carmen. This is a classic looking beach studded with two palm trees that stand and sway side by side. The beach is so low it looks like an atoll when viewed from the water. It offers views of both the sunrise and sunset; however, it also gets wind from multiple directions and there is no sanctuary. The place looks idyllic, but only camp here on a calm day.

Marine Park Islands~Carmen

SM
NM
Km

25°55′

View of Carmen from above Ligui

25° 52′ 30″, 111° 11′ 01″

26 CN-20 or 21. A maroon-colored cobble camp with sand spots. It has a great shade cave with accompanying arch. Tall Cardóns grace the backdrop.

25° 52′ 01″, 111° 10′ 53″

27 Punta Colorada. This is a formation of dark maroon cliffs 75 feet high stretching for a mile north and then a little ways south of the point. There is a giant shelf of rock extending underwater from the cliff 200 feet or so before abruptly falling off into deep water.

25° 51′ 31″, 111° 11′ 38″

28 San Francisco, CN-22. This protected beach is all gravel and cobble, but in spaces the small rocks have been cleared to accommodate sleepers, cooks, and eaters. Some of the spaces have developed into alcoves, almost rooms, as the rocks get piled up in small walls a little sturdier and higher each year. There are Palo Verde and Ironwood trees near the campsite and a very cool looking hill looming in the background. In this camp, we encountered large lizards and a big orange snake slithered between us during morning coffee. CN-22 is actually the second camp in from the point. The first camp is similar to it, but there are no cleared rooms.

25° 50′ 56″, 111° 12′ 11″

29 Las Coloradas, CN-23. A white sand beach mixed with cobble. The backside is slightly duny. A nice looking gorilla hill sits behind the small dunes.

50′

The bottom of the island gets progressively flatter. From places, including a possible small arroyo camp north of Punta Baja, there are views over to the Sierra la Giganta and the peaks of Isla Danzante.

Fat camper

Isla Danzante (Spanish for "dancer") is a dramatic small island lying between the southern tip of Isla Carmen and the peninsular coast south of Loreto. For an island of its size and steepness, it has a plethora of camps and packs a lot of great scenery into a small place. Danzante is an easy one- or two-day visit, and is a good intermediate stop for a trip to or from Carmen if you are launching from the Puerto Escondido area.

25° 48′ 45″, 111° 15′ 36″

1   **Light nearby.** The northwest corner of Danzante. This point is a little more than half way to Carmen from Escondido. It is not a camp but it is a good rest spot. There is a low saddle where you can park and walk over to the east side of the isle to check on the conditions in the channel between Carmen and Danzante. **DZ-01, Caleta del Amor**, is east of this reading. It is a north-facing beach in an impressive setting.

25° 48′ 36″, 111° 15′ 35″

13   **Honeymoon Cove, DZ-15**. A small beautiful camp in an inlet protected by the north arm of Honeymoon Cove. A red rock stands behind the off-white sand beach. There are small pockets of roped-off vegetation here. The Honeymoon Cove area is a much-protected harbor popular with the yacht crowd. There is another beach in the vicinity, but it is designated "No Camping." The area is also home to an oyster farm, marked off by a line of orange floats. Don't dive here or you might have some angry fishermen to deal with, and they'll only warn you once.

25° 47′ 43″, 111° 15′ 32″

12   **DZ-12.** The southern cove in the large bay on the northwest side of the island. Sailors call it Pyramid Cove. It is home to an attractive west-facing beach good for a smaller-sized group. Another camp of gray sand is found to the north. It is probably **DZ-13, Las Gravas.**

25° 47′ 35″, 111° 15′ 29″

11   **DZ-11.** A very charming, small cove with two gorilla head hills above it. The area around here is known as Los Hongos (The Mushrooms).

Isla Danzante

Honeymoon Cove   *Punta Eleonora*

Bahia Honda

25° 46′ 41″, 111° 15′ 24″

10   **Punta Arena, DZ-09.** A sandy point that can hold a large group, though the wind might blow across it on a bad day. There is a mushroom-shaped rock on the south end and signs posted with information about the care and use of the island.

Waiting for crumbs

25° 46′ 17″, 111° 15′ 01″

9   **DZ-08.** Set in a turquoise bay, this is a sandy beach big enough for a mid-sized group.

Ligui

Ensen... Blanca

25° 46′ 02″, 111° 14′ 52″

8   **Las Cuevas, DZ-07.** A small but pretty beach tucked under brown hills pockmarked with shallow caves. It offers sunset views of the Sierra la Giganta.

25° 50′

Marine Park Islands ~ Isla Danzante

Isla Carmen

25° 47′ 57″, 111° 14′ 59″

2 **DZ-02.** There is only one official camp here, though there are a few landings. The beaches are gravel. There is an arm of land leaving shore with an interesting rock formation at its point.

25° 47′ 36″, 111° 14′ 59″

3 **DZ-03.** A small protected cove with a cobble beach set among splendid maroon rock. There is afternoon shade here.

25° 46′ 49″, 111° 14′ 50″

4 **Norte de Bahía Honda, DZ-04** ✗✗ This beach is in a small bay surrounded by fantastic rock formations, which for whatever reason conjure up images of Druids for me. A giant arch at water's edge adds to the dramatic scenery.

25°50′

Danzante on a north wind day, seen from Playa Ligui

25° 46′ 41″, 111° 14′ 52″

5 **DZ-05.** The beach just south of the arch. It is sand/gravel mix with a shade cave at its north end. It is large enough for a medium-sized group.

25°45′

25° 46′ 30″, 111° 14′ 47″

6 **DZ-06** ✗✗ The southern-most camp in Bahía Honda. Good for large groups. Giant rock blobs that look like immense sand castle drip-formations and short spires dot and flank the beach. With steep hillsides in the background, the overall effect is very engaging.

25° 45′ 54″, 111° 14′ 39″

7 **Light.** The southern point of Isla Danzante. A significant reef with a wave break protrudes from the end of the island.

Isla Monserrat. This is a smallish island of low relief with good to excellent camping. Hiking up high is possible without too much difficultly in a few places. At shoreline, the waters around the island are startlingly clear when snorkeling. Monserrat is said to be bountiful in scorpions, but I encountered none on my visit. On my one trip to Monserrat, I spent time on the west and north coasts before taking a window of opportunity and paddling to Isla Catalina. I had planned to come back to Monserrat and explore its southern end after circumnavigating Catalina, but a stay on Catalina extended by a windstorm and then a northerly breeze on my return paddle constrained me to divert to Agua Verde. Monserrat is on the verge of being "out there," and has no short access point from which to launch. The closest points across from it are wilderness camps that are 9+ miles away. A possible launch area is Ligui, where it is not too hard to find someone to look after a car. Other car access launch points might be Puerto Escondido or Agua Verde, though the road into Agua Verde is fairly rugged.

25°45′

25° 42′ 27″, 111° 03′ 10″

② MS-11, MS-12 ✳✳✳ The north bay on Monserrat has two wonderful beaches. In the middle is an arroyo leading to a canyon of golden-colored rock. The western beach, MS-11 or **Playa Paulina**, is a large dark sand beach suitable for big groups. A rock arm on its west rim protects it from westerlies. Should there be northerlies, both these beaches will get surf, but the break is graduated on account of a shallow approach. Playa Paulina has more camp areas in a high sea than its eastern sister, Playa Davis. MS-12, **Playa Davis**, is white sand with a low orange sandstone rock in the middle. The views from here are great, and changing light from long sunsets behind the Sierra la Giganta adds to their magnificence.

25° 41′ 42″, 111° 03′ 27″

① MS-10 vicinity. These are a series of beaches on the western coast. They are of a variety of aspects and size, one being mostly sand, but none with significant protection. Rocks at low tide are a problem in the area. Vertical sandstone fins welded together dot the landscape, and overall the coast is rather pretty without being overly dramatic, however there are great views of the mountains across the channel.

Landed at Playa Davis

SM
NM
Km   1.51   3

Isla Monserrat viewed from the west

25°45′

25° 42′ 13″, 111° 01′ 56″

3 MS-1, Playa San Lazaro ✷✷
A bay with a beach that gets protection
from north swells by a short jetty of
rock. The beach is composed of
brown sand and lightly spaced cobble,
and there is a view from the beach to
Isla Catalina to the east.
   You'll find another good beach in a
larger bay to the south of MS-1, but
there is possible exposure to the
north here. It is probably **MS-2, Playa
la Herradura.** There are a couple of
lesser beaches on either side of it.
South of la Herradura the coast
becomes cliffed-out for a while.

Isla Monserrat

Ensenada Baja

40′

25° 38′ 59″, 111° 01′ 46″

4 Monserrat southern end. (These notes are from a glassing of the south end taken from atop
the light on Marcial Rock off Punta Marcial.) There are some nice looking beaches on either side of the
light on the south end of Monserrat. These would be Park beaches **MS-4 to MS-9.** East of the light, there
is a large beach of white sand, which appears to be a major camp. There are possibilities of a few lesser
camps up the coast from there. The camps west of the light seem smaller, but there is probably still a
significant beach there somewhere. Above this the coast is a long, low white cliff.

173

25°45′

Isla Catalina is one of the remotest islands in the Sea of Cortez. Its northern end is 15 miles from Isla Monserrat and 29 miles from Ligui, and its southern end is 18 miles from Agua Verde. Unlike many of the other islands, Isla Catalina has never been attached to either the mainland or the peninsula, so life on Catalina has taken on some unique features—one of which is that it is home to the rattleless rattlesnake. Catalina is a beautiful island and worthy of the trip for the adventurous paddler. Pay heed to the crossing, as there is the possibility of large seas in the channel between Monserrat and Catalina, particularly in the fall and winter. Northerlies are common at that time of year, and there is also the possibility of a westerly, which could hurt your return trip. Catalina's wide distance from anywhere exposes the paddler. Have ample water in the event of a forced layover.

25° 40′ 02″, 110° 47′ 57″

1 This reading is from a beach north of a prominent prow of dark rock that is visible a long ways off to the west; it's a good landmark to focus on if you're crossing from Monserrat. Currents get conflicted off this headland and a strong northerly compounds this problem, so approach with caution or divert south in times of weather.

This is a good camp, and careful landings can be achieved with north or south swell, as it is inset in a small cove. There are actually two beaches here—the northern one is the more worthy of the two. The landing is rocky but manageable and has a short carry onto coarse sand. The vegetation around camp is accented by tremendous Barrel Cacti dotting the steep hillsides. They are visually spectacular. There is Cardón in the arroyo floor, as well as an edible Cholla.

South bay arch

40

25° 38′ 50″, 110° 48′ 12″

8 (Between here and waypoint #7 are two possible camps I haven't been able to check out.) This is a beach south of the rock prow mentioned above. The landing is a bit gnarly at low tide and the cobble of the beach is a pain but the site is nice and has enough sleep spots for a mid-sized group.

25° 36′ 29″, 110° 47′ 12″

7 ✴✴✴ A small cove protected from north and south winds with a gravel beach and a sand interior. Buttresses of beige and orange rock guard the rims of the cove. There is a small arch in the north buttress. The twisting arroyo behind the beach has a kitchen spot that is protected from a westerly. There are enough sleep spots in the arroyo for a large group.

25° 36′ 00″, 110° 46′ 35″

6 ✴✴✴ This bay has multiple camping opportunities. There are sea caves on its eastern side and a giant arch towards the west corner. With complete protection from north swells and a dreamy view of Isla Santa Cruz to the south, it adds up to one of the more pleasant bays in the sea.

You'll find a four-star camp with a lot of character in the east arm of this bay. It doesn't look like much from the water, just a small cobble beach set in cliffs, but the cobble gives way to a bedrock kitchen area with a sandy sleeping spot alongside it. There is a steep, tiered canyon behind it. The first two easy-to-climb tiers each have room for one tent.

Up bay and east of the arch is the big camp for the area. The best part about it is the direct view of the arch. The kitchen zone is sand mixed with rock. More sleep spots exist farther up the arroyo. The landing is cobble and for whatever reason is a magnet for dead fish. There are fleas here too. It's not a bad camp, but I wouldn't take it unless I was forced to by the size of my group.

Just west of the arch is a cobble camp. It's more than passable for a small group, but it is impossible to escape the cobble. (Cobble camp joke: "Hey, there's a rock under my mattress!") This is a very protected cove and has walking access to the arch at low tide. The arch is a fun playground and has a righteous cliff-diving spot at its end. There is a fish camp on a beach just west of this cove.

Marine Park Islands ~Isla Catalina

SM
NM
Km _____ 1.5 | 3 | 3

25° 42′ 51″, 110° 46′ 29″

(2) My paddle around the north of the island was on a breezy and wavy day, but I felt I had to make a move after being pinned down at the previous camp for two extra days by wicked north wind. The northwest coast was rugged and steep; I would have loved to fish it on a calm day. I did pass a couple of possible landings in bays up the inside top corner, though I declined the opportunity to land due to my slow progress against the waves. I don't remember the top of the island well because things were a bit hectic during my paddle around, but I do remember the northeast corner and the rocks leading out from it. Boat it quite wide if there is a wind. The surf gets large and controlling here. I thought I was smart about rounding corners in a blow, but I almost bought the farm here after starting my turn a bit too soon and then having a powerful set of three rogue waves come in behind me.

My voyage down the outside coast was a surf and not entirely fun because I had sun in my eyes and felt small and vulnerable that far out. This was accented by the recurring thought that I had no real idea of where I was heading, not knowing anything about the island except for having scanned it on a large scale topo. I stayed out from the coast until reaching the next camp whereupon I boated around a line of surf off its eastern point and then made a good landing on the south side in oblique waves.

Isla Catalina

25° 41′ 19″, 110° 45′ 53″

(3) A large plain on the upper east coast. It juts out into the water in a low triangle from the flank of the mountainous interior. Though some protection from waves is possible here, it's hard to get out of the wind when making camp. The beach is serious cobble, but the interior is sand and small brush offering a little more wind protection the farther back you go. There is plenty of roaming area on the plain for a stroll.

South of waypoint #2 the coast is mostly rugged. Steep mountains fall abruptly to the sea. There are two lesser points to negotiate before the end of the island. After the first point, you'll encounter two nice looking beaches that I didn't land on due to wind and time considerations; however, the surf looked manageable and there are sand landings.

25° 36′ 03″, 110° 45′ 24″

(4) First refuge around the southeast point. A marginal camp of sloping cobble in a protected cove. There is a spire in the middle of the small beach.

25° 35′ 45″, 110° 45′ 33″

(5) The **light** at the southern end of the island.

Punta Sur

175

So that the Isla San José grouping of islands can be included near where they lie relevant to the rest of the coast, the "Loreto to La Paz" leg has been broken up into two chapters: "Loreto to San Evaristo" and "San Evaristo to La Paz." San Evaristo was chosen as the break point in the leg because it is the largest village encountered on the leg; it is the northern terminus of the coast road from La Paz; and it is the most common launch point for an Isla San José trip.

Dawn start from Ligui

Loreto

Isla Carmen

SM		14.5		29
NM			14.5	29
Km		14.5		29

25°50′

Puerto
Escondido

Isla Danzante

Isla Monserrat

40′

Isla Catalina

30′

Agua Verde

Punta Marcial

20′

Loreto to San Evaristo

Though it appears a number of beaches around Loreto and some north of La Paz are losing their solitude and accessibility to development, "Loreto to La Paz" is still one of the major Baja sea kayaking trips. It is among the top four in popularity, the others being "Isla Espíritu Santo," "Isla Carmen," and "Mulegé to Loreto." "Loreto to La Paz" is long (140 miles), but convenient because of an easy Highway 1 shuttle. The leg has gorgeous mountain scenery along a beautiful coastline. There are stops at villages along the way. Agua Verde, Timbabichi, Los Dolores, Los Burros, and San Evaristo all have fresh water, and some lesser ranches along the coast also have well water.

Conditions on the sea vary from place to place during the leg. There are 2- to 4-foot tides south of Loreto. The waves at the start can be some of the largest of the trip, as north winds funnel down the Loreto-Isla Carmen channel and cause the sea to bounce up off its shallow bottom. The points to navigate around are generally of moderate difficulty; Punta Marcial south of Agua Verde is the primary exception to this, and is nasty with weather.

It's a good idea to get an early start from Loreto, as the camping for the first 14+ miles is slim. The shoreline south of town is primarily a non-descript, brushy, cobble coast interspersed with development, though the views of the Sierra la Giganta to the west are some of the most memorable in Baja. Many trips will choose to launch from the Puerto Escondido area south of Loreto as a way to skip the first developed miles.

Isla Santa Cruz

10′

25°00′

Isla San José

24°50′

San Evaristo

40′

30′

Isla Espíritu Santo

20′

La Paz

10′

177

111°20′   10′   111°00′   110°50′   40′   30′   20′

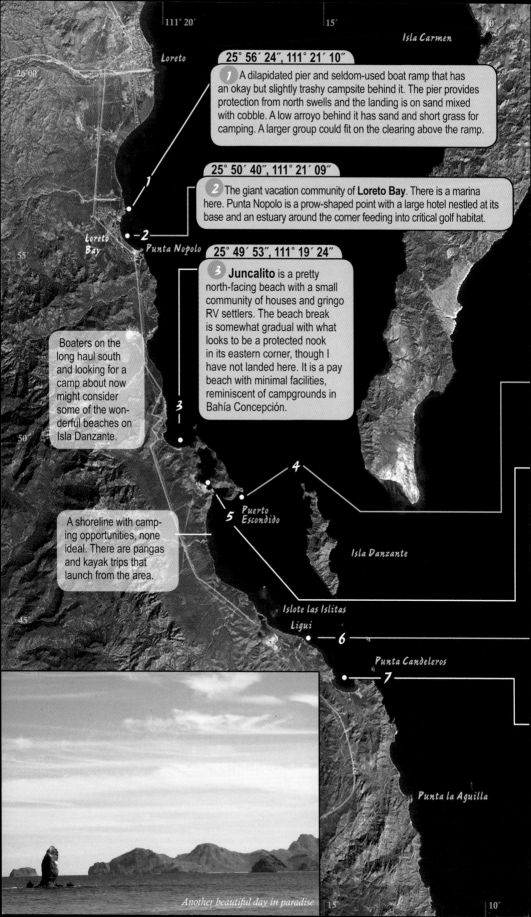

111° 20´   15´   10´

Isla Carmen

Loreto

26°00

55

Loreto Bay

Punta Nopolo

50

45

25° 56´ 24″, 111° 21´ 10″

1 A dilapidated pier and seldom-used boat ramp that has an okay but slightly trashy campsite behind it. The pier provides protection from north swells and the landing is on sand mixed with cobble. A low arroyo behind it has sand and short grass for camping. A larger group could fit on the clearing above the ramp.

25° 50´ 40″, 111° 21´ 09″

2 The giant vacation community of **Loreto Bay**. There is a marina here. Punta Nopolo is a prow-shaped point with a large hotel nestled at its base and an estuary around the corner feeding into critical golf habitat.

25° 49´ 53″, 111° 19´ 24″

3 **Juncalito** is a pretty north-facing beach with a small community of houses and gringo RV settlers. The beach break is somewhat gradual with what looks to be a protected nook in its eastern corner, though I have not landed here. It is a pay beach with minimal facilities, reminiscent of campgrounds in Bahía Concepción.

Boaters on the long haul south and looking for a camp about now might consider some of the wonderful beaches on Isla Danzante.

A shoreline with camping opportunities, none ideal. There are pangas and kayak trips that launch from the area.

4

5   Puerto Escondido

Isla Danzante

Islote las Islitas

Ligui

6

Punta Candeleros

7

Punta la Aguilla

Another beautiful day in paradise

15´   10´

South of Candelero Chico

55′

25° 48′ 41″, 111° 17′ 40″

4 Punta Coyote. A small but north-protected beach with a great view. It might be better suited as a lunch stop. The **light** and entrance to Puerto Escondido are just around the corner. Another good lunch spot is on the small Islote las Islitas to the south.

50′

25° 48′ 45″, 111° 18′ 30″

5 Puerto Escondido. Entered from the south, this natural harbor, fortified by concrete walls, was historically a major launch spot for trips heading south or out to Islas Danzante and Carmen. In 2006, new owners of the port took over and are turning it into a major marina. The prices to launch have skyrocketed up to $35 U.S./kayak. There is secured parking, but the fee for that is probably steep, too. There is significant public outcry about the high-end privatization of the harbor and it's boat ramp—perhaps this will lead to some compromise on pricing in the future. There is *fresh water* available here, also for a fee.
A better launch option is now to use the **Tripui Hotel and RV Park** facilities just west of Escondido on the access road. They are landlocked but do shuttles to a beach less than 2 miles away and have car storage, as well as camping with showers.

25° 44′ 31″, 111° 15′ 34″

45′

6 Ligui. This community of good people is difficult to see from the water, as the village is closer to the highway. The beach is gravel and not protected from surf, though it is not a shore break. The best camp spots are clearings in the small trees behind the beach. However, these are usually taken by "never say winter" gringos in RV's and campers. They are nice folk, however, and I'm sure you could fit in.

25° 43′ 13″, 111° 14′ 10″

7 Ensenada Blanca/Candelero Ensenada. A significant bay with an arcing white sand beach. The break on the main beach is graduated. There is a protected landing and panga launch in the upper west corner, though a developer has recently shut off road access to this end of the beach. There are buildings in the center of the shoreline that house a kayak outfitter, but soon much of the beach will be claimed by the developer and a new hotel will be erected.

Isla Monserrat

40′

Leaving Ensenada Blanca you are getting away from populated shores for a while. The scenery from here to San Evaristo is mountainous and very striking. Abrupt towers of rock hovering over white sand beaches punctuate the views between large bays. Fresh water is available at reasonable intervals.

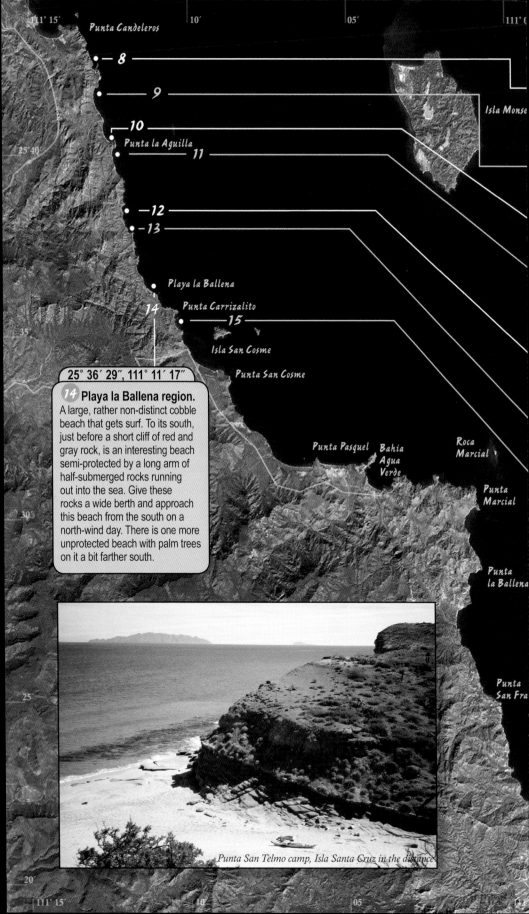

Punta Candeleros

8

9

10

Punta la Aguilla

11

12

13

Isla Monse

25' 40'

Playa la Ballena

Punta Carrizalito

14   15

Isla San Cosme

Punta San Cosme

35'

25° 36´ 29˝, 111° 11´ 17˝

14 Playa la Ballena region.
A large, rather non-distinct cobble
beach that gets surf. To its south,
just before a short cliff of red and
gray rock, is an interesting beach
semi-protected by a long arm of
half-submerged rocks running
out into the sea. Give these
rocks a wide berth and approach
this beach from the south on a
north-wind day. There is one more
unprotected beach with palm trees
on it a bit farther south.

Punta Pasquel   Bahía
                 Agua
                 Verde

Roca
Marcial

Punta
Marcial

30'

Punta
la Ballena

25'

Punta
San Fra

Punta San Telmo camp, Isla Santa Cruz in the distance

20'

SM
NM
Km

25° 42′ 22″, 111° 12′ 52″

8 **Candelero Chico** ✲✲✲ A cove nestled under steep walls. It faces north, but waves diminish during the ride in. The eastern arm of this baylet is actually an island at high tide. Camp here is a mixture of gravel and sand, and it can hold a large group.

25° 41′ 50″, 111° 12′ 53″

Isla Catalina   25°40′

9 An alternative camp to Candelero Chico for a small group. It gets no seas on a day with a northerly. There is a pleasant view of Isla Monserrat and an awesome down-coast vista, as well as a shade tree.

From here to Agua Verde, the coast gently undulates in a mixture of minor points and bays. Give the points good berth on wavy days. Some campsites in the bays are not listed, as they are not protected.

25° 40′ 21″, 111° 12′ 28″

10 A lovely south- but not north-protected camp that doesn't get morning sun until late. The beach is coarse dark red sand. Punta la Aguilla, just around the corner, has excellent snorkeling.

25° 40′ 08″, 111° 12′ 23″

35′

11 **Playa Triunfo** ✲✲✲ A beach popular with commercial groups. Prevalent donkey poop cost this camp a fifth star. The best camping is on the north end where a tall red-rock wall provides wind protection. Out in the sea is the landmark Roca Blanca, which is not white rock but often stained white by guano until a hurricane cleans it off. Chocolate-drop fantasy rock formations shape the magnificent scenery down coast.

25° 38′ 34″, 111° 12′ 03″

12 A little rescue beach around a point. A good place to lunch or relax if you have had seas from the north and need a break. South of here is a bay with a fenced palapa up on a hill. There are a few camping areas nearby, though none with great protection.

25° 37′ 55″, 111° 11′ 47″

30′

13 An interesting point of gray and red rock. There are two beaches; one is a cute cove with a fish camp on the north side, and the other is a gravel beach around the corner.

25° 35′ 28″, 111° 10′ 23″

15 South of **Punta Carrizalito** there is a small bay with a tiny island set back into it. The island is so close to shore that it is almost indistinguishable if you are out on the water. Between the island and shore there is a shoal that appears at low tide; the shoal is home to a hot spring. There is a narrow beach to land on behind the island, but it is probably too narrow to camp on. There are a few possible camps near the hot spring, none ideal, though the scenery is very pretty here with Isla San Cosme in the foreground and Catalina and Monserrat in the distance.

25′

Grouper caught with a handline, Roca Vela in the background

110° 55′   50′   45′

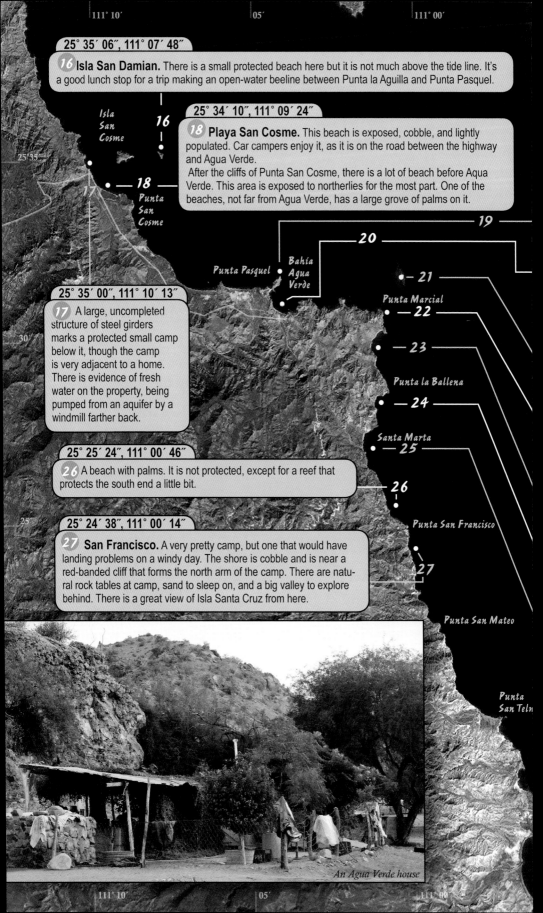

25° 35′ 06″, 111° 07′ 48″

16 **Isla San Damian.** There is a small protected beach here but it is not much above the tide line. It's a good lunch stop for a trip making an open-water beeline between Punta la Aguilla and Punta Pasquel.

Isla San Cosme   **16**

25′35′

25° 34′ 10″, 111° 09′ 24″

18 **Playa San Cosme.** This beach is exposed, cobble, and lightly populated. Car campers enjoy it, as it is on the road between the highway and Agua Verde.
After the cliffs of Punta San Cosme, there is a lot of beach before Aqua Verde. This area is exposed to northerlies for the most part. One of the beaches, not far from Agua Verde, has a large grove of palms on it.

18
Punta San Cosme

19

20

Punta Pasquel   *Bahía Agua Verde*

21

25° 35′ 00″, 111° 10′ 13″

17 A large, uncompleted structure of steel girders marks a protected small camp below it, though the camp is very adjacent to a home. There is evidence of fresh water on the property, being pumped from an aquifer by a windmill farther back.

Punta Marcial
22

30′

23

Punta la Ballena

24

25° 25′ 24″, 111° 00′ 46″

26 A beach with palms. It is not protected, except for a reef that protects the south end a little bit.

Santa Marta
25

25′

26

25° 24′ 38″, 111° 00′ 14″

27 **San Francisco.** A very pretty camp, but one that would have landing problems on a windy day. The shore is cobble and is near a red-banded cliff that forms the north arm of the camp. There are natural rock tables at camp, sand to sleep on, and a big valley to explore behind. There is a great view of Isla Santa Cruz from here.

Punta San Francisco

27

Punta San Mateo

Punta San Telm

An Agua Verde house

SM
NM
Km

Isla Catalina

25° 31′ 52″, 111° 04′ 07″

19 **Punta Pasquel** marks the turn into Agua Verde. There is an exposed camp of nice sand on the northwest face. You can hike across this beach to another beach on the inside of the bay. From that beach there is a trail/road into Agua Verde.
As you approach the point you gain sight of Roca Vela, the beautiful sentinel of rock that stands at the mouth of Bahía Agua Verde.

25° 30′ 54″, 111° 04′ 08″

20 **Agua Verde** is a funky, peaceful fishing community. The harbor offers some protection from north seas but the landing in front of the village does get waves. There is more protection and privacy the closer you are to the north arm of the bay where there is a separate, protected beach that has a palapa and a house on it. This is also a panga launch, and yachts moor just offshore. The back of the bay is divided into two beaches by a ridge/islet formation. There is the village beach to the north of the ridge and an undeveloped beach to the south. The "privacy" beach to the south of the islet is sand with small shade trees behind it. On a big water day a lot of this beach might be underwater.
Town is a loose hodgepodge of basic residences built among palm trees and rock outcroppings. Some structures are integrated into the rock ridges that intersect town. There is *fresh water* from an artesian well about 200 yards up from the south end of the village beach. There is also a very small store in the back northwest corner of the village. It is up against a hill about three houses to the west of a tidy white church. The store is sometimes mistaken for a residence (which it also is) so you have to look closely if you want to find it. The people of Agua Verde are friendly; it is a great place to hang.
One mile east of Bahía Agua Verde is an exposed sand beach that would be a nice fair-weather camp. Another exposed but lovely beach farther along toward Punta Marcial has palms on it.

25° 31′ 47″, 111° 00′ 20″

21 **Marcial Rock.** There is a **light** here, as well as a sea lion colony.

25° 30′ 56″, 111° 00′ 57″

22 **Punta Marcial** is the crux navigational hazard of a "Loreto to La Paz" run. Besides the lofty point extending dramatically out into the sea, there is a significant reef in the waters south of it. The point generates confused waves on mild wind days. It can be hazardous with a strong north wind. On a big day, you need to boat either very high and wide or tight and low to avoid the reef break. If you were in Agua Verde preparing to head south, and looked out at Roca Vela and saw waves slapping against its side and rising up its face, you might want to lay up a day.

25° 29′ 55″, 111° 01′ 22″

23 Around the south side of Marcial are three protected coves. The third and least protected is the best for camping. It is a gravel beach with sleep spots in the arroyo behind.

25° 28′ 32″, 111° 01′ 11″

24 **Inside Punta Ballena** ✳✳✳A beautiful and very protected beach with a wide, sandy area. A palapa from a part-time fish camp sits in the back. A sea cave is on the inside of the point, and a multi-colored banded cliff forms the outside arm of camp. This beach is popular with commercial outfitters.

Isla Santa Cruz

25° 27′ 08″, 111° 01′ 36″

25 **Santa Marta.** A mild surf landing onto a big east-facing beach where colored hills form the backdrop. There is less surf towards the north end of the beach. There is a ranch with brackish water at the south end. Its owner requests that campers use a portable toilet system and build no fires on the beach.

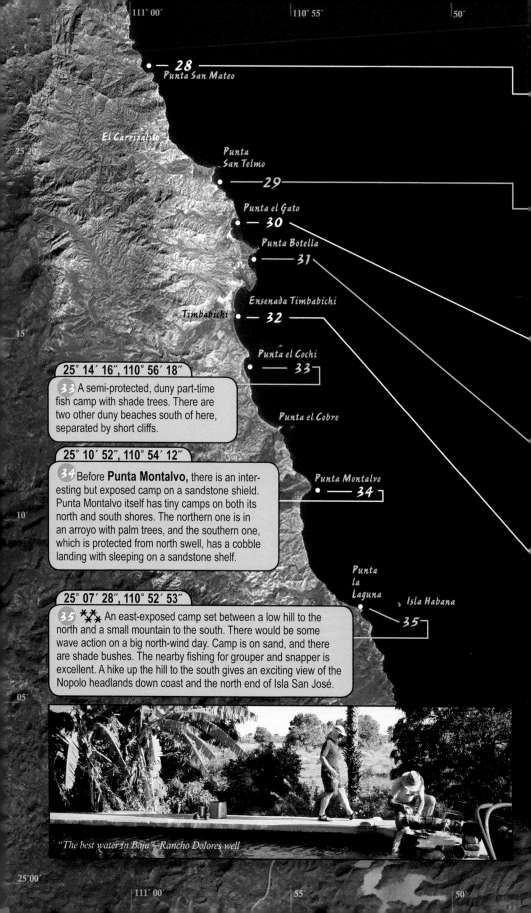

28
Punta San Mateo

El Carrizalito

25° 20′

Punta
San Telmo

29

Punta el Gato
30

Punta Botella
31

Ensenada Timbabichi

Timbabichi
32

15′

Punta el Cochi
33

25° 14′ 16″, 110° 56′ 18″

33 A semi-protected, duny part-time
fish camp with shade trees. There are
two other duny beaches south of here,
separated by short cliffs.

Punta el Cobre

25° 10′ 52″, 110° 54′ 12″

34 Before **Punta Montalvo,** there is an interesting but exposed camp on a sandstone shield.
Punta Montalvo itself has tiny camps on both its
north and south shores. The northern one is in
an arroyo with palm trees, and the southern one,
which is protected from north swell, has a cobble
landing with sleeping on a sandstone shelf.

Punta Montalvo
34

10′

Punta
la
Laguna   , Isla Habana

25° 07′ 28″, 110° 52′ 53″

35 ✸✸ An east-exposed camp set between a low hill to the
✸✸
north and a small mountain to the south. There would be some
wave action on a big north-wind day. Camp is on sand, and there
are shade bushes. The nearby fishing for grouper and snapper is
excellent. A hike up the hill to the south gives an exciting view of the
Nopolo headlands down coast and the north end of Isla San José.

35

05′

"The best water in Baja"–Rancho Dolores well

25° 00′

SM
NM
Km

25° 22′ 31″, 110° 59′ 24″

28 San Mateo. A beach I'm not familiar with. In between San Mateo and Punta San Telmo there are a few other nice but exposed beaches. South of San Mateo, there is a high crenellated wall of many colors that tops-out in turrets and a small peak. It comes straight out of the water. The shore here in general is abruptly cliffed with a long escarpment. Towards the end of the escarpment you'll see a break in the walls where a small, steep, exposed beach backed by a bunch of palm trees appears. On a plain behind this area is El Carrizalito, a scattering of a few houses behind beheaded palms. In the Punta San Telmo vicinity is San Carlos, a small ranch with a well that has good water.

25°20′

25° 19′ 20″, 110° 57′ 26″

Isla Santa Cruz

29 Punta San Telmo ✳✳✳ A long, low, sand and gravel beach forms the outside corner of the point. South of the point there is a good-sized white sand beach with an east-northeast exposure that gets small surf on a wind day. There are a few rocks to watch out for when landing at low tide. The best camping is on the south corner of the beach, up an arroyo where a bluff of red rock undulates gently down to the sand. The views from on top the bluff are magnificent.

Nestled between cliff walls there is an even larger—though less protected—beach further to the south; the landing is on smooth rocks at low tide.

15′

25° 18′ 19″, 110° 56′ 48″

30 Puerto Gato ✳✳✳ A large beach sits inside a very red cliff that offers excellent protection from the north. The eastern end of the beach is the most protected and has shade trees; unfortunately, it also has some trash. Sloping fins of sandstone cascade down to the beach from the cliffs above. The views of Islas Santa Cruz, San Diego, and San José are enchanting. The waters in front of this beach are also a common yacht anchorage. Farther into the bay, the beach broadens; this part of the beach is popular with commercial kayak groups. There is a slot canyon behind here offering a rewarding hike.

The bay also has a beach in its far southern corner, should you be experiencing weather from that direction.

10′

25° 17′ 19″, 110° 56′ 17″

31 Inside Punta Botella. A very nice beach with good fishing and snorkeling nearby. It doesn't have the reputation (or crowds) that Puerto Gato has.

Entering Ensenada Timbabichi, the northernmost beach has a fish camp with a few shacks. Near the fish camp you'll encounter a small entrance to a large lagoon that was once one of Baja's more remarkable fishing spots.

25° 15′ 36″, 110° 56′ 54″

32 Timbabichi. Below a set of towering mountains in the background, a distinctive white building rises above the shrubs of the coast and serves as a landmark to a small community. The building is an abandoned mission. Timbabichi has an estuary in front of it that can be paddled inland. When you run out of water on which to float, get out and hike along the road into town on the south side of the estuary. The people of the community are friendly, and most houses have *fresh water* available.

Timbabichi mission

05′

Isla San José

45′

25° 04′ 40″, 110° 51′ 34″

36 Rancho Dolores. This is the north half of the Dolores area. This landing is on a large but unprotected beach. The southern landing, around Punta Blanca, is protected. There is *fresh water* at both sites. Rancho Dolores is basically one house with a few smaller buildings nearby. The people are friendly, and will instruct you on how to get to the well. It is situated inland from the house, and is said by some to hold the best water in Baja. Passing irrigated fields, you come to a large concrete holding tank. Take water from the pipe feeding the pool. The water comes from a stream higher up in the valley. There are supposed to be waterfalls there, as well as an old mission. The southern half of Dolores is a verdant, palm filled arroyo coming down to a sand beach. A modern, country-style house sits in the back. Behind that is the caretaker's house; he is a good man. There is fresh water coming down pipes or hoses right at the beach. Please ask first before filling—the Rottweiler did not attack, but had me a little worried.

25° 10′

05′

36

Los Dolores

Isla San José

Punta los Burros

37

38

Punta el Cerro

Punta Alta

Nopolo

39

25°00′

Rounding **Punta Alta**, the islands of San Francisco and Espíritu Santo come into view. Just behind the point are two small coves backed by rock with developments in each; this makes up part of the community of Nopolo. There is no road access. There is protected beach in front of the houses, but camping would be a bit crowded here.

Punta Roja

40

41

Canal de San José

Punta Evaristo

24°55′

42

San Evaristo

50′

Canal de San José

Leaving Dolores heading south, the coast starts getting rugged again. Large, steep headlands jut into the sea. The communities of Los Burros, Nopolo, and San Evaristo hide in bays behind these headlands.

25° 02´ 56˝, 110° 49´ 38˝

37 Los Burros is a small community tucked under a rugged cliff in a valley between rising mountains. The beach is more or less protected but it is rocky. There is a cleared area for panga launching. The people are friendly but shy, and not used to outsiders in their village, which is a long distance from any highway. Fresh water flows out of a cave on the hillside to the south of the pueblito. The easiest place to re-supply water is in the northeast corner of the community, at a house past the small school. Locals can direct you there.

05´

25° 01´ 52˝, 110° 48´ 32˝

38 A dark sand beach nestled under soaring cliffs of volcanic rock. Thick leaved yucca plants cling to the hillside. The landing is sand/gravel and north-exposed, but in calm weather or weather from the south this would make a good camp for a mid-sized group.

24° 59´ 46˝, 110° 45´ 30˝

39 Nopolo. The southern half of the Nopolo community, with only a couple of houses near shore. Other houses are inland. Nopolo has fresh but brackish water. The locals get their water from Rancho Dolores via panga. The beach is camp worthy, but low and thin, as there is an estuary behind it. There are mangroves in the estuary, so it may be buggy at times. Sneaking into the estuary offers a protected landing. On a windy day, waves would probably wash over the beach. The word NOPOLO is spelled out in fading letters on the rock face above the south end of the beach. There is a big arch to the south that you can paddle under at high tide.

25°00´

24° 58´ 25˝, 110° 45´ 01˝

40 Arroyo Evaristo. A large valley that has a north-protected gravel beach with sand sleeping spots above. The camping area could hold a mid-sized group, but it is sometimes used as a fish camp. The hike up valley looks promising.

24° 56´ 05˝, 110° 43´ 20˝

41 A small point with a large rock at its end that sees a lot of osprey activity. There are landings on the north and south sides on a mixture of cobble and gravel. Camping for a mid-sized group is possible on dirt behind the beach in a clearing among some brush. This is the northernmost point of the coast road from La Paz.

24°55´

San Evaristo is built on the north and south sides of the rocky headland of Punta San Evaristo. There is a north-facing beach that is backed by a large evaporative salt flat, which is harvested commercially. Behind the salt flat, which is often flooded, is the northern half of the community. Here among a few palm trees is a tiny store, good people, and mildly brackish well water. This part of town is separated from its southern half by a low saddle that is easily traversed via dirt road.

24° 54´ 39˝, 110° 42´ 28˝

42 San Evaristo. A natural harbor with superb north protection. There are often yachts at anchor in the bay. The beach is sand, but it is pretty much occupied with small houses, pangas, and such. The less protected southern end of the beach might have room for campers, but it's kind of duny and there are a still a few houses scattered about. There is a desalinization plant on the main beach. My gut reaction is that these types of plants will be the death of coastal Baja as we know it, as they provide an opportunity for large-scale development to prosper in otherwise arid regions. I'll admit, however, that we did fill up on fresh water there. If no one is at the plant and you want water, climb the hill behind the beach and look for a small house near a large white cross; the plant proprietor lives here. There is also a small store a couple of buildings behind the desalinization plant. They don't sell beer.

50´

Cactus

Isla Catalina cacti

The serene desert scenery of Baja is surprisingly full of plant life, but it is a different form of life compared to that of more temperate and rainy climes. Though there are a number of almost moon-like landscapes in the peninsula and islands where vegetation is sparse, often there is a variety of plant life around. And it is primarily in the austerely beautiful, bare sculpted form of cacti.

Cacti make up the largest portion of the flora you will see in Baja. In fact, cacti are a modern, unique, and ingenious genera of plants that evolved in the Central Americas to accommodate the prevailing dry climates that followed the last ice age 10,000 years ago. There are 110 species of cacti found in Baja, and 80 of those are endemic to the peninsula. Other continents have similar drought-tolerant plants, but these are not related to cacti because they have different flower anatomy. Cacti and other succulents are adapted to long periods of drought with their thick, waxy, waterproof skins that prevent water loss and contain water-storing tissues that swell with moisture during rain events. Indians and animals have long known that cacti provide a good source of food and water, though it is tricky getting past all those prickers. The spines evolved from leaves and usually act as a good deterrent to herbivores.

One cactus to avoid is the "jumping cactus" or "attack cactus." If you pass close to one, a small section will jump out at you, sticking into your clothes or skin. And they are very stubborn to remove. These cacti are members of the Cholla cacti family. There are many species in many shapes, but they all grow in branching segments or lobes. Their seeds are often sterile so they propagate when sections are dislodged by passing animals. Often the section is carried a ways until it is dropped on new ground where it waits for the next rainfall. With just a small amount of moisture, it sprouts roots and grows a new plant. Some Cholla have spines up to three inches long and look like some kind of medieval torture device. And their daggers can even penetrate shoes, so step lightly. (There is a good picture of a Cholla on page 154.)

The tall and graceful Cardón cactus can reach ages of greater than 300 years. The long ribs that make up its skeleton act like an accordion during precipitation events, and are able to spread apart to accommodate an intake of moisture.

The giant Barrel Cactus pictured here is one of a group found only on Isla Catalina in the Loreto Marine Park. They are the largest species of Barrel Cactus in the world, growing to six feet.

– Lori Russell

Cactus flower, Photo by: Tom Merrill

Giant Barrel

Boojum Tree (not a cactus)

Isla Santa Cruz, Photo by: Tom Merrill

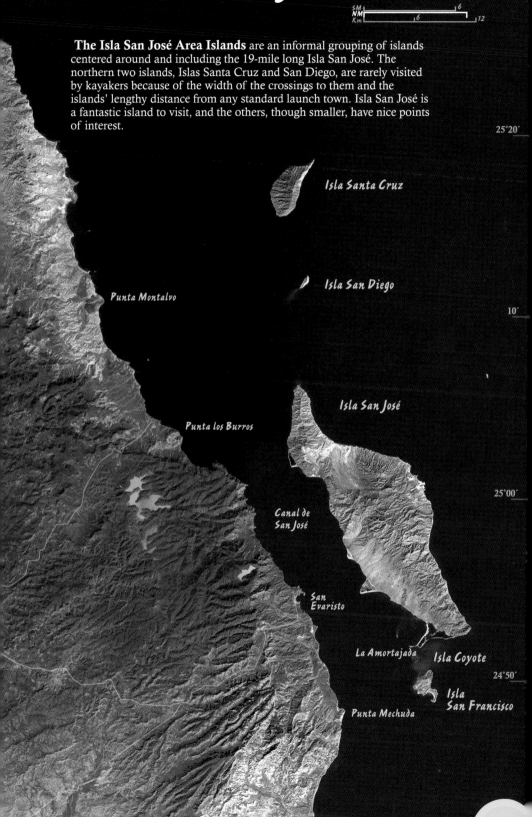

SM
NM
Km

The Isla San José Area Islands are an informal grouping of islands centered around and including the 19-mile long Isla San José. The northern two islands, Islas Santa Cruz and San Diego, are rarely visited by kayakers because of the width of the crossings to them and the islands' lengthy distance from any standard launch town. Isla San José is a fantastic island to visit, and the others, though smaller, have nice points of interest.

25°20′

Isla Santa Cruz

Isla San Diego

Punta Montalvo

10′

Isla San José

Punta los Burros

25°00′

Canal de San José

San Evaristo

La Amortajada *Isla Coyote*

24°50′

Isla San Francisco

Punta Mechuda

111°00′   110′   40′

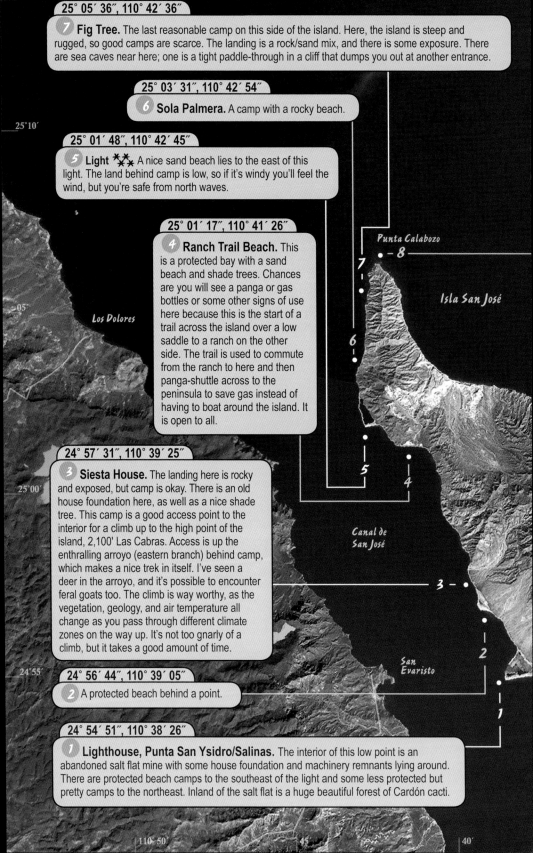

25° 05′ 36″, 110° 42′ 36″

7 **Fig Tree.** The last reasonable camp on this side of the island. Here, the island is steep and rugged, so good camps are scarce. The landing is a rock/sand mix, and there is some exposure. There are sea caves near here; one is a tight paddle-through in a cliff that dumps you out at another entrance.

25° 03′ 31″, 110° 42′ 54″

6 **Sola Palmera.** A camp with a rocky beach.

25°10′

25° 01′ 48″, 110° 42′ 45″

5 **Light ✳✳** A nice sand beach lies to the east of this light. The land behind camp is low, so if it's windy you'll feel the wind, but you're safe from north waves.

25° 01′ 17″, 110° 41′ 26″

4 **Ranch Trail Beach.** This is a protected bay with a sand beach and shade trees. Chances are you will see a panga or gas bottles or some other signs of use here because this is the start of a trail across the island over a low saddle to a ranch on the other side. The trail is used to commute from the ranch to here and then panga-shuttle across to the peninsula to save gas instead of having to boat around the island. It is open to all.

Punta Calabozo
– **8**

7

Isla San José

Los Dolores

–05′

6

24° 57′ 31″, 110° 39′ 25″

3 **Siesta House.** The landing here is rocky and exposed, but camp is okay. There is an old house foundation here, as well as a nice shade tree. This camp is a good access point to the interior for a climb up to the high point of the island, 2,100′ Las Cabras. Access is up the enthralling arroyo (eastern branch) behind camp, which makes a nice trek in itself. I've seen a deer in the arroyo, and it's possible to encounter feral goats too. The climb is way worthy, as the vegetation, geology, and air temperature all change as you pass through different climate zones on the way up. It's not too gnarly of a climb, but it takes a good amount of time.

25°00′

5

4

Canal de San José

3 –

24° 56′ 44″, 110° 39′ 05″

2 A protected beach behind a point.

24°55′

2

San Evaristo

24° 54′ 51″, 110° 38′ 26″

1 **Lighthouse, Punta San Ysidro/Salinas.** The interior of this low point is an abandoned salt flat mine with some house foundation and machinery remnants lying around. There are protected beach camps to the southeast of the light and some less protected but pretty camps to the northeast. Inland of the salt flat is a huge beautiful forest of Cardón cacti.

1

110–50′   45′   40′

SM
NM
Km

Isla San José is possibly the most diverse island in the Sea of Cortez. On the island's north end, there are dramatic rock pinnacles, sea caves, and a number of large arches. There are white sand beaches scattered around the island, and beautiful red cliffs along the outside. A magnificent Cardón cacti forest fills a plain on the island's southwest corner, and rising beyond it in the interior are high, rugged mountains. The bottom of the island has the largest mangrove estuary of any island in the sea. The estuary is a unique little world unto itself. San José is one of my favorite islands, and I can't wait to go back.

The tiny village and the protected natural harbor of San Evaristo is a convenient spot to launch from for an Isla San José trip, and is additionally described in the "Loreto to La Paz" chapter. Though not having any real shopping facilities, there is fresh water available here (which you will need because San José has no reliable source of fresh water), and it should not be too hard to find someone reliable to leave a car with.

All roads leading to San Evaristo are dirt and have possible difficult sections within them. A high clearance car, preferably 4-wheel drive, is best used to get to San Evaristo.

25°10'

25° 06′ 24″, 110° 42′ 16″

8 Punta Calabozo. Things are very rugged and dramatically beautiful up here—though if a north wind were up, this end of the island would be a daunting place. There are randomly spaced rocks offshore and a submerged reef starting a thousand yards to the northwest and extending in a northerly direction. On calm days, the diving here is classic. There are a couple exposed lunch-beach possibilities on shore. Boating around the tip of the island and starting to head south, you'll see rock pinnacles in the water and one pointed islet that is in fact a large arch.

05'

Photo by: Tom Merrill

Weary hikers, wary rattler. Same tree, same time. Photo by: Suzanne Clarke

25°00'

24°55'

la
yo

35'
30'
25'

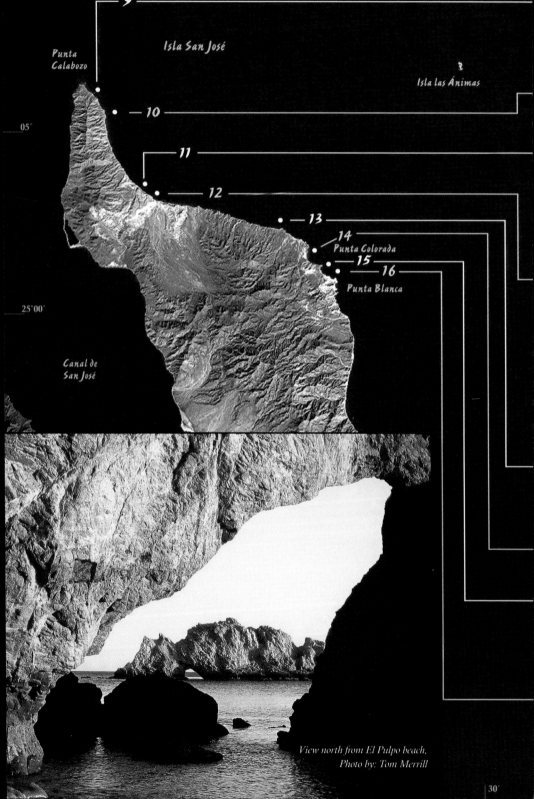

Punta
Calabozo

Isla San José

Isla las Ánimas

05′

— 10 —

— 11 —

— 12 —

— 13 —

14

Punta Colorada

— 15 —

— 16 —

Punta Blanca

25°00′

Canal de
San José

*View north from El Pulpo beach,
Photo by: Tom Merrill*

30′

25° 05′ 56″, 110° 41′ 53″

9 **El Pulpo.** Boating along the steep granite shore, you'll come to a monolithic double arch. Paddle through the arch and you'll come upon a small cobble beach backed by a 50-foot high vertical cliff. Off the south end of the beach is another massive arch. Small rocks trundle off the lip of the cliff on occasion, making the beach an undesirable camp. But oh, what a location!

25° 05′ 34″, 110° 41′ 34″

10 A fish camp with a protected landing.

25° 03′ 18″, 110° 40′ 24″

11 **Quatro Palmeras.** This is a lovely but slightly exposed camp with a rocky landing. It is easily discernible by an abrupt group of palms under a sheer cliff. Camping is on sand among large rocks composed of petrified seashells. Peregrine falcons roost on the giant cliff above.

25° 03′ 06″, 110° 40′ 02″

12 **Ranch.** This is a working ranch with a loose cluster of shacks, homes, chickens, people, and goats. The landing at the ranch is on an unprotected but large sand beach, which extends for more than a mile further down coast. The well water at the ranch is slightly salty most of the time, so the ranchers live off bottled water. If you have an emergency need for good drinking water you'll have to pay for it. If you're into fresh goat or chicken, the rancher will kill and butcher one for you. BBQ tonight?

Punta Blanca camp. Photo by: Tom Merrill

25° 02′ 30″, 110° 36′ 55″

13 A point visible from a ways off. Just before this point, there is a nice camp with sand landing and south-protection. The camp is at the east end of a long beach, which is perfect for beachcombing. The diving and fishing are worthy off the point, and an absorbing area of sloping rock shelves farther down coast offers good snorkeling opportunities.

24°55'

25° 01′ 29″, 110° 35′ 21″

14 **Hot Springs Cove.** A beach with a low tide hot spring in a quiet cove. It is a possible, small camp. A tarp is needed to make a pool of the spring to sit in.

25° 01′ 05″, 110° 34′ 56″

15 **Punta Colorada** ✲✲✲ This is a classic white sand beach in a cove protected by arms of red sandstone. It is the best camp on San José, and accordingly gets well used by commercial groups and is also occasionally used as a fish camp. There is an outfitter's camp on the beach just up coast from here. Be advised that there is confusion as to which is the actual Punta Colorada. INEGI calls it the bulge of land north of here; another map calls it the point of land to the south. At either location, there is nice slickrock hiking.

50'

25° 00′ 57″, 110° 34′ 31″

16 ✲✲This beach is just north of a headland with a **light**. Considered Punta Colorada on some maps, it is a whiter colored rock than the point to the north, and is known by us as **Punta Blanca**. It is beautiful but is not protected from north swell, though the landing is soft. Behind camp is a pyramid-shaped hill that turns vibrantly multi-colored at sunset.

195

25'   20'   15'

Punta Calabozo

Isla las Ánimas

Isla San José

25°05′

Punta Colorada

Nopolo
25°00′

Canal de
San José

— 17

24°55′

San
Evaristo

Punta San Ysidro

21

— 18

Isla Cayo

20

— 19

Isla Coyote

50

Isla San Francisco

110° 40′   35′   30′

35′   30

Paddling amongst the mangroves in the southern estuary

Isla San José

SM
NM
Km

Shore break layover day at Stonehead

24° 56′ 00″, 110° 33′ 30″

17 A semi-protected arroyo camp with a rocky landing. The sections of coast north and south of here a few miles in each direction are generally too rugged for camping, except at the mouths of a few arroyos.

24° 53′ 08″, 110° 31′ 47″

18 Stonehead. A remarkably beautiful camp if the landing conditions are right. The beach is steep, unprotected cobble. There is a shore break here if the sea is up. Camp is in a valley wedged between giant red and black rock headlands. The hike above the north headland is airy and the views are stunning.

24° 52′ 23″, 110° 34′ 06″

19 The Mangrove Lagoon, south entrance. This is a different paddling experience from other Baja areas. It is basically a giant estero with small entrances on the south and west sides. There are narrow watercourses twisting through the interior where one can almost get lost exploring. The fishing is excellent, and the peacefulness (during daylight hours) enthralling—I have fallen asleep in my boat here. The main watercourse runs north-to-south through mangroves to the island's west coast. It then drops you into a beautiful half-moon shaped bay with a sand beach.
 Just before you reach the southwest tip of the island, you'll notice a fair-looking, protected beach. Unfortunately, no-see-um flees tend to come out of the mangroves at night, so I avoid this beach like the plague now because of one mean no-tent experience when I had to sleep in the water at shoreline to escape the evil bugs.

24° 53′ 08″, 110° 34′ 22″

20 The north entrance to the mangrove swamp. Located in a pretty bay with a sand beach. It's still too close to the mangroves to take a chance with the nighttime bugs.

24° 54′ 26″, 110° 36′ 09″

21 A well with bitter water at an old ranch site. Near here you'll find a nice camp on a beach littered with much dried out coral. It is far enough away from the mangroves to be bug free.

Isla Santa Cruz is mostly a rugged island, but there are hiking opportunities on the west side. In the center of the west coast, above the shore, you'll see an arch where a cross has been erected. This area offers exploration potential, though the landing is rocky.

25° 15′ 39″, 110° 43′ 43″

1sc A fish camp on a small spit of land. This is the most protected landing on the island.

25° 16′ 57″, 110° 42′ 15″

2sc A camp with some protection. The landing is cobble and the sleeping area is cobble also. Watch out for aggressive mice.

Isla Santa Cruz

— 2sc

1sc —

25° 11′ 45″, 110° 41′ 58″

1sd The camp on the tiny **Isla San Diego** has a cobble landing and the sleeping area is cobble also. The island is pretty abrupt in its rise from the sea, but the beach is not steep, and is safe when the sea comes up.

Isla San Diego

— 1sd

20′
15′
10′
05′

The view south from the east coast of Isla Santa Cruz, Photo by: Tom Merrill

110° 50′   45′ *Isla San José*   40′

Contrasting rock, Photo by: Suzanne Clarke

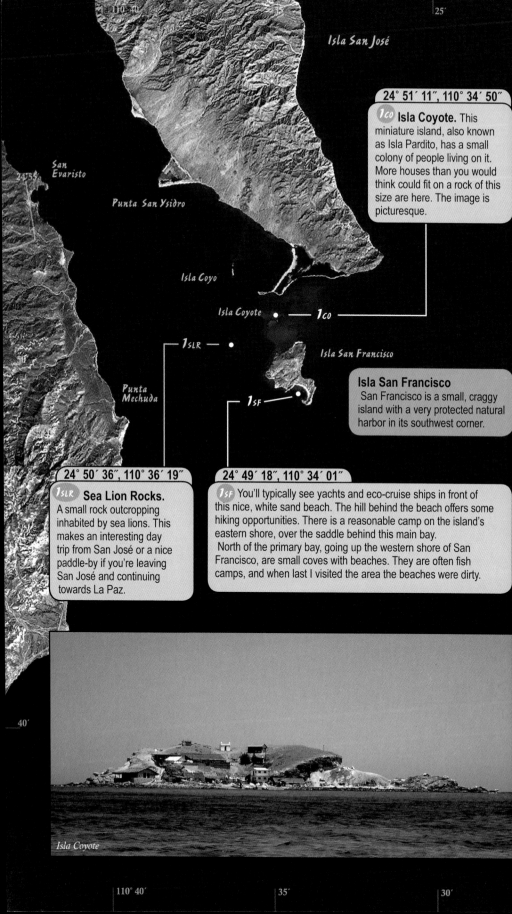

Isla San José

San
Evaristo

24°55′

Punta San Ysidro

24° 51′ 11″, 110° 34′ 50″

1co **Isla Coyote.** This miniature island, also known as Isla Pardito, has a small colony of people living on it. More houses than you would think could fit on a rock of this size are here. The image is picturesque.

Isla Coyo

Isla Coyote ● — *1co*

1slr — ●

Isla San Francisco

Punta
Mechuda

1sf — ●

Isla San Francisco
San Francisco is a small, craggy island with a very protected natural harbor in its southwest corner.

24° 50′ 36″, 110° 36′ 19″

1slr **Sea Lion Rocks.**
A small rock outcropping inhabited by sea lions. This makes an interesting day trip from San José or a nice paddle-by if you're leaving San José and continuing towards La Paz.

24° 49′ 18″, 110° 34′ 01″

1sf You'll typically see yachts and eco-cruise ships in front of this nice, white sand beach. The hill behind the beach offers some hiking opportunities. There is a reasonable camp on the island's eastern shore, over the saddle behind this main bay.
North of the primary bay, going up the western shore of San Francisco, are small coves with beaches. They are often fish camps, and when last I visited the area the beaches were dirty.

40′

Isla Coyote

Isla San Francisco viewed from Isla San José

24°55´

50´

45´

Sea Lion Rocks

40´

Dolphin Parades

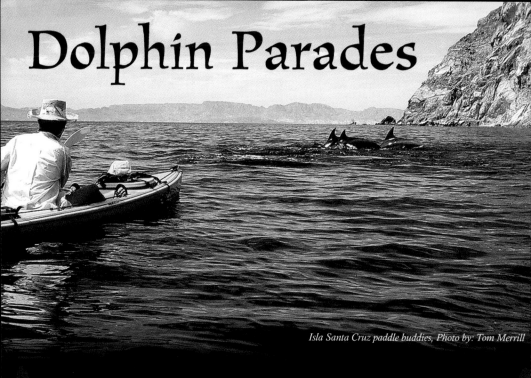

Few moments are as entertaining while paddling along as when a school of dolphin cruises close by. They are usually shy and keep a distance, but even from a ways, their pulsing, rhythmic, group-swimming style is captivating. You can see them swimming in pods of a few to a few hundred, like a parade in formation, arching their dorsal fins in the air. Sometimes, they will get frisky and leap out of the water to show off. Once while surfing my kayak in some large swells after a windstorm, a school of dolphin joined me in my glee, cresting the waves just beside my boat, probably critiquing my technique.

Dolphin are actually a species of small toothed whale, a mammal. There are about 50 species of dolphin, which include the popular killer whale or orca.

Some researchers think dolphin intelligence may rival human intelligence in its ability to analyze and solve problems. Dolphins may even have a complex language. They can make two different kinds of sounds. Under their blowholes is a specialized mechanism which produces rapid clicks and works like sonar or echolocation, reflecting off objects or other dolphins. They also produce a high-pitched whistle from the larynx used to communicate their emotional state to other dolphins in hunting, play, and courtship.

Dolphin are efficient predators, hunting in well-organized groups. They feed on tuna and schools of squid in the Sea of Cortez, but have never been known to attack humans. In fact there are numerous stories and legends of dolphin helping drowning sailors.

Recently, dolphin are at the heart of an international political strife between the United States and several South American countries. The conflict is referred to as the "Tuna-Dolphin Issue" and you can find many articles about it on the Web. The issue concerns a dolphin species that is often found swimming in close contact with large schools of tuna which they feed on. In fact, tuna fishermen use the easily identified dolphin on the surface of the water to locate the desired schools of tuna that may be swimming with them. But in scooping up the tuna with their huge seine nets, many—in fact millions of—dolphin have been killed and are discarded in the process. It is estimated that over 80% of the dolphin have been slaughtered in the Eastern Tropical Pacific Ocean, which includes Baja. The U.S. has tried to impose sanctions, and even a trade embargo on countries like Mexico and Ecuador, which use these fishing practices, but with only some success. The slaughter continues in the name of kitty food and tuna sandwiches.

– Lori Russell

Quatro Palmeras, Isla San José

203

110° 50′   45′   40′   30′   25′   20′

24°55′

Leaving San Evaristo, the coast becomes lower and the mountains recede inland. The views are still nice—some of the mountains have bands of multi-colored cliffs running across them. There are nice beaches here (some with road access), but most are not surf-protected.

San Evaristo

Isla San José

43

50′

44

Isla San Francisco

Punta Mechuda

45

45′

46

47

40′

Punta Coyote

48

35′

49

Punta el Guano

Isla Partida

Las Ánimas

30′

Isla Espíritu Santo

Punta Trabillas

50

51

25′

Desert turrets

La Paz

20′

SM
NM
Km

24°55′

24° 52′ 57″, 110° 41′ 07″

43 Punta Arena. A dark sand beach with a gravel landing. It is somewhat sheltered from north swell, but camp is low and can get windy.

24° 50′ 01″, 110° 40′ 20″

50′

44 An unprotected, dune-filled beach near an arroyo.

Punta Mechuda is a red rock headland that breaks up the lowland repetitiveness of the coast. There is a small south-protected beach on its north side.

24° 47′ 38″, 110° 39′ 42″

45′

45 Arroyo Verde ✕✕✕ A southeast-facing beach with fair protection. Landing is on sand/gravel and sleeping is on sand. This is a beautiful small arroyo that has sides made of cliffs that are banded in green rock. The level area extends deeply into the arroyo providing camping room for a large group, as well as sheltered cooking should there be a north or south breeze. Camp has a wilderness feel to it, as the nearby road is slightly removed and not noticed.

24° 44′ 48″, 110° 40′ 34″

40′

46 A slightly protected fish camp.

24° 42′ 30″, 110° 41′ 24″

47 A nice beach on the north shore of **Punta Coyote**; there is good rod fishing off the point.

24° 41′ 53″, 110° 42′ 26″

35′

48 This protected side of Punta Coyote is a major fish camp. The fishermen are friendly. There is a cleared landing among rocks for pangas in front of the camp. This is the takeout for some commercial sea kayaking trips doing the "Loreto to La Paz" run.
This reading is slightly down coast from the fish camp. Here you'll find a sand landing and privacy, as well as adequate camping spots among cacti and brush behind the narrow beach. This is the last protected landing for about 18 miles.

30′

24° 34′ 13″, 110° 44′ 03″

49 Fish Factory. There is a duny, unprotected beach below and to the side of this farm. A man-made inlet with a noisy pump in it supplies water to the farm. The sides to the inlet are steep so landing here isn't good, and the noisy pump makes for a miserable camp.

25′

At the fish camp of **Las Ánimas** there is supposed to be a protected landing, but I got this beta from fishermen at Punta Coyote and am not sure if they fully understood my question and I fully understood their answer. From offshore, the landing doesn't look too worthy, though there might be something behind the south end of a cliff.

24° 27′ 44″, 110° 41′ 10″

20′

50 Punta Trabillas. This point is mostly a bluff, but there are a couple of emergency landing beaches here. On a windy day it should be given wide clearance because waves back up off the point and create turbulence offshore. There is a nice but unprotected beach just south of the point.

24° 26′ 32″, 110° 41′ 16″

15′

51 El Saladito. A somewhat protected fish camp on a very low point. There are sand spots to sleep on near the fish camp.

Isla Cerralvo

205

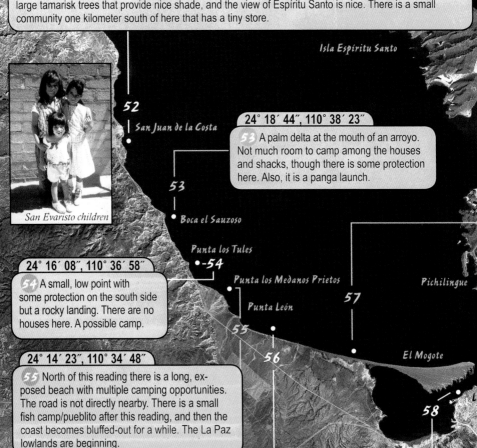

Paddling into La Paz

San Juan de la Costa. A recently abandoned phosphorus mine. The remains of a ruined pier sit out in the water off a large rock jetty. The mine was abandoned after a hurricane struck and dragged a tanker out to sea—the tanker had been tied up to the pier. With the expensive pier wasted, the owners decided to call it good and cut their losses, closing up the large mine. There is a mine employee ghost town up the hill above the jetty. Behind the jetty you'll find a small, scraggly, wave-protected beach that doesn't make a pretty camp. The road, paved from here south, is very near the beach.

24° 22′ 50″, 110° 41′ 07″

52 A bit farther south of the jetty. This is a nice enough beach considering the nearness of the road and the decayed industrial look and feel of the place. There is some surf but a sand landing. There are large tamarisk trees that provide nice shade, and the view of Espíritu Santo is nice. There is a small community one kilometer south of here that has a tiny store.

Isla Espíritu Santo

52

San Juan de la Costa

24° 18′ 44″, 110° 38′ 23″

53 A palm delta at the mouth of an arroyo. Not much room to camp among the houses and shacks, though there is some protection here. Also, it is a panga launch.

San Evaristo children

53

Boca el Sauzoso

Punta los Tules

•-54

24° 16′ 08″, 110° 36′ 58″

54 A small, low point with some protection on the south side but a rocky landing. There are no houses here. A possible camp.

Punta los Medanos Prietos

Pichilingue

Punta León

57

55

24° 14′ 23″, 110° 34′ 48″

55 North of this reading there is a long, exposed beach with multiple camping opportunities. The road is not directly nearby. There is a small fish camp/pueblito after this reading, and then the coast becomes bluffed-out for a while. The La Paz lowlands are beginning.

56

El Mogote

La P

58

24° 11′ 59″, 110° 32′ 00″

56 **El Pozo de Rodriquez.** An arroyo with a couple of shade palapas. It is sometimes a fish camp and panga launch, as well as a common place for La Pazians to access this part of the coast.

110° 50′   45′   40′   35′   30′   25′   20′

An Elephant Tree

24° 10′ 56″, 110° 27′ 07″

57 A possible camp coming into **El Mogote**. El Mogote is a low peninsula just before La Paz. Most of it is beach, and camping is possible and pleasant in many places. The beach is exposed, but it doesn't look like there would be a shore break if the wind were up. El Mogote is currently being developed towards the tip across from downtown La Paz. A very large condo project and home sites are in the works, as well as a new marina on the inside shore.

Isla Cerralvo

Rounding the corner of El Mogote puts you just offshore of downtown La Paz. On the east of town is the upscale Marina Palmira. In the center is the malecón, the seaside road and pedestrian boardwalk that is more or less the tourist center of La Paz. Near the middle of the malecón there is a small beach area where you can land if you wish, but it does not make a good takeout. Farther west is the Marina La Paz where it is possible to take out for a nominal fee, and taxis are always available at the gate. Past the marina, west another nick, you'll come across a small takeout beach/panga launch.

24° 08′ 42″, 110° 20′ 33″

58 A beach near the La Paz RV Park. If you wish to camp with your boat in town, the La Paz RV Park is probably the best place to do it. The RV park is one block in from the water. This reading is for a beach one block west of the RV park. The beach and RV park are west of a 13-story orange condo complex and a new 8-story building. The Park is on the corner of Calle Del Tesoro and Brecha California. There are showers, a pool, and they do offer car storage. The 2007 cost was $16 U.S./two person tent. Note: Don't swim in the inner portion of La Paz Bay, it is hepatitis central.

Paddling near Bahía Balandra, north of La Paz

La Paz is a Mexican city but its gringo tourism is growing. The countryside on the perimeter of town is being pushed toward second home development and golf course status. La Paz itself is growing too, and fast. Though a sign on the city's border lists the population as 170,000 inhabitants, reasonable estimates are that the town has almost doubled in size in the last 10 years and is now past the 300,000 mark.

There is an international airport in La Paz, making it a good town from which to stage a kayaking trip. La Paz has many buses running to and from it, and a ferry hooks it up to mainland Mexico.

The heart of La Paz is the malecón, the seaside street and boardwalk that is on the north side of central downtown. Off the malecón are numerous restaurants and hotels with pleasant views of the harbor. This is where the gringos congregate. South of the malecón and spreading out around it is the majority of town, a cityscape of mid-sized buildings housing stores of all kinds that line a grid-pattern of mostly one-way streets. On the outskirts of this are the dense but lower profile residential communities. There is also a university on the edge of town.

La Paz can be a bit difficult to navigate at first, but give yourself some time and experience and the traffic patterns will become more understandable. Despite its busyness, I enjoy La Paz more than say, Cabo San Lucas, which is a mess of traffic and poorly planned over-development. When you go to La Paz, you know you're going to a city; there's still a touch of authenticity to La Paz.

La Paz offers all amenities and shopping opportunities you'll need including hotels, large stores for one-stop shopping, and myriad restaurants. I have stayed at La Perla off the malecón a couple of times and found it clean and convenient, and they offer secure parking; but it is getting a little pricier as time goes by. The kayak outfitter, Mar Y Aventuras, has a hotel attached to it that caters to kayakers and adventurous types and looks cozy; they also run a kayak shuttle service and sell permits for Isla Espírítu Santo. The Hotel el Morro, off the northeast end of the malecón, is also a good place to stay; the friendly outfitter, Baja Outdoor Adventures (B.O.A.), is just behind it. B.O.A. runs shuttles for private trips, and also offers guided tours and gear rentals.

La Paz

Bahia de La Paz

Marina de La Paz

Military yard

La Paz RV Park

Airport/Points North

Todos Santos/Los Cabos
Blvd Forjadores

1	CCC (store)
2	Bus Station
3	Soriana (store)
4	Internet
5	La Costa (rest.)
6	Mar y Aventuras
7	Immigration
8	Auto Repair
9	Fish Tacos
10	Fishing Shop
11	Bank
12	Baja Outdoor Activities
13	Baja Expeditions

There are many restaurants in La Paz, but I like to eat at the Marina La Paz restaurant because it's on the water, affordable, quiet, and away from the hubbub of the malecón. Another good restaurant with a palapa setting, quiet waterfront, and sand floor is La Costa, west of the marina a little bit. There are plenty of other restaurants to choose from on and around the malecón, as well as a great fish taco stand on a side street off Ocampo two or three blocks in from the seaside. A good seafood restaurant off the malecón tourist path is the Bismark II, at Degollado and Altamirano.

Shopping is easy at the CCC on B. Dominquez and Jalisco; it is a big store and has most soft items needed for any kayak trip. For an even bigger store, Soriana's at the "Y" intersection in south central La Paz will fill the void of the mall starved. For anglers and spear fishermen alike, there is a great fishing shop, the FerreMar, on 16 de Septiembre north of Altimirano.

Outside the malecón, downtown La Paz

Espiritu Santo arch

24°50'

```
SM |_____|_____| 12
NM |        6                12
Km |_____|_____|_____
         6              12
```

Isla Espíritu Santo is the most popular island to kayak to in the Sea of Cortez. Just about a mid-sized island, Espíritu Santo is very beautiful and very accessible to La Paz. It offers the perfect week-long trip for kayakers flying to Baja on a tight schedule. Unique to Espíritu Santo are long fjord-like inlets, deeply recessed into the west coast of the island. There are some very pretty beaches within these inlets (so many that they are not "starred" as they are in other chapters). The volcanic terrain of the island is sparsely vegetated and easily hiked for the most part. There is also a sea lion colony on Los Islotes off the northern end of the island.

Because of its popularity, Espíritu Santo became the first island in the Sea to institute a permit system regulating camping activities. Permits are available from the SEMARNAT office in La Paz at: 5 de Mayo No. 1035 Interior I, e/Primo Verdad y Marcelo Rubio. Some of the commercial kayak outfitters in La Paz also offer permits for sale. The permits do not assign camps for groups, but rules stipulate that if you come upon an occupied beach that you continue on to the next camp. (This might not pertain to Playa Bonanza, the long beach on the southeast shore.) Normal camping rules apply on Espíritu Santo, particularly the "stoves only, no fires" rule for cooking. Additionally, groups are asked to use a portable toilet system to pack out solid human waste. If you don't own such a toilet, they are available for rent at Mar Y Aventuras in La Paz.

40'

- Los Islotes

Isla Partida

Playa Tecolote is the most common launch point for an Espíritu Santo trip. The crossing to the island is about five miles to the north. If northerly winds come up, you can get pinned down at Tecolote if you are not a strong paddler or are out of practice. If the waves are small and the breeze favorable, the crossing shouldn't cause too much consternation. However, many kayakers opt for a motorized panga ride out to the island to avoid wind delays. There are usually pangas at Tecolote, but you can also get a guide service in La Paz to organize a shuttle for you. If you paddle, there are a couple of buoys delineating the channel roughly into thirds to help guide you. These mark the deep-water center of the channel where the ferry and other large ships pass through. A large reef with good fishing lies north of the second buoy.

30'

Isla Espíritu Santo

Note: Though most of the sea experiences northerlies as the dominant wind during the paddling season, the area outside of La Paz sees a good share of southerly breezes. While they mostly occur in summer, these winds can kick up well into fall and start in early spring. These southerly breezes are known as Coromuel, an off-pronunciation of the name Cromwell, an English pirate who used these unusual southerlies to his advantage to sack and plunder Spanish ships carrying shwag from the new world to the old.

Tecolote

20'

La Paz

110° 40'   30   20

24° 28′ 57″, 110° 24′ 14″

8 **Isla Ballena.** There is no camping on Isla Ballena, though it makes an interesting paddleround. The southeast side features good swimming and snorkeling, though you would have to dive from your boat as landing is not permitted on Isla Ballena due to the presence of seagull and pelican nesting areas. There is a light on the southern tip. The northwest side of Ballena is an untamed wilderness with high cliffs looming over deep clear waters and submerged boulders fallen from the precipices above.

24° 28′ 36″, 110° 23′ 06″

7 A small, very pretty beach comprised of coarse sand and broken coral. There are rocks rimming this beach, so glass boaters should beware, particularly at low tide. However, a channel cleared by fishermen provides a sufficient landing ramp. The beach has sloping rock shelves on each short arm that would be good for a brief stroll or angling. The shelves also make great sand-free cooking platforms. The geology here is dramatic, as red rock near the beach transforms abruptly into black rock and merges into the water.

24° 27′ 40″, 110° 22′ 26″

6 **El Gallo.** Though this is a small beach, it is attractive and can hold a good-sized group. It is nestled into the southern arm of a larger bay and just across from the islet, Isla Gallina.

24° 26′ 47″, 110° 22′ 19″

5 **Coralito.** Though the beach is mid-sized, it could hold a large group. It is located in an inlet bay. (These little inlets are a distinctive feature of Espíritu Santo.) There are fish camps on each arm of the bay. Snorkeling is a possibility near both north and south points, with the north sporting a small coral reef.

24° 26′ 26″, 110° 22′ 20″

4 The entrance to a mangrove-lined estuary, which you can only enter at high tide.

24° 26′ 08″, 110° 21′ 53″

3 **San Gabriel.** The main beach in this large bay is not great for camping due to its narrowness, mangroves, and a huge tidal flat; however, there is a small, slightly elevated beach that makes a nice camp located in a mini bay within the larger bay. The sleeping spots are back in the flora behind the beach. Though somewhat buggy, sunset views of high pink cliffs nearby are sweet.

In spring, there can be heavy algae deposits on these southern beaches creating an unpleasant squishy sensation under foot and a less than desirable odor.

24° 24′ 34″, 110° 20′ 54″

2 **Dispensa.** There is a fish camp here, but the white sand beach makes a nice protected camp if fishermen are not present. There is another beach farther back into this bay, but you'll have to cross over a long tidal flat and there is a mangrove lagoon in the eastern corner. It will be a long, unpleasant slog across the flat at low tide to the higher camp-worthy portions of the beach, and the mangroves make for a buggy camp both here and at Dispensa (except in the winter months).

24° 20′ 16″, 110° 18′ 39″

1 **Tecolote,** though a naturally attractive beach, can get busy and a bit trashed because of its proximity to La Paz, particularly on weekends and especially on Mexican holidays. At these times, cookouts, volleyball games, four-wheelers tearing up the dunes, pangas in the bay pulling screaming kids on giant inflatable bananas, and just about everything in between may assail you. On weekdays, it is generally peaceful.

There are four or five restaurants at Tecolote, all toward the west end of the beach. At the restaurant formed by the prow of an old ship we found someone to look after our car one trip. (However, it is a good idea not to leave anything in the car while you are out paddling.) If you wish, there is camping without facilities on the east end of the Tecolote beach.

Isla Espíritu Santo

NMI   1.5 2   3

24°30′

8

Isla
Ballena

7

Isla Gallo

6

Isla Gallina

5

4′

Punta
Prieta

3

Bahía
San Gabriel

Punta Colorado

2′

Punta
Dispensa

Punta Lobos

Punta Bonanza

25′

Isla Espíritu Santo

Punta Lupona

1

24° 24′ 10″, 110° 19′ 33″

1 **Punta Lupona.** A charming, white sand beach towards the spit. It is mildly long, and a good place to celebrate your crossing, but it is somewhat prone to winds.

Canal de San Lorenzo

A small camp near Isla Ballena

T

Tecolote

Bahía
Balandra

213

The paddle north of Ensenada Grande gets more promising as you approach the increasingly dramatic north coast, but there is some current here. It is about here that seas hit the island with force when weather comes in from the north. There is a magnificent arch halfway up to El Embudo. The granite edifice juts out perpendicularly from its adjoining cliff. For something so large, you can almost paddle past it without distinguishing it from its mother cliff if you happen to be a little too far out. Unless you have a sea, hug the coast here so you get the pleasure of passing underneath this monolith.

24° 33′ 55″, 110° 24′ 21″

17 **Ensenada Grande North.** The southern and nicest beach here is reserved for day trips; camping is not permitted, though our group stayed here once in a storm. From the landings in Ensenada Grande there is access to the sloping volcanic bench of the interior where you can hike painlessly to the back of the island and take in the dramatic views of the east coast.

24° 33′ 36″, 110° 23′ 49″

16 **Ensenada Grande South.** The wide Ensenada Grande is roughly divided into two parts by a point in its center. In this southern half, there is an intimate beach on the south arm and a large beach farther in. Commercial groups often occupy it.

24° 33′ 18″, 110° 22′ 52″

15 **El Cardonal,** a two-mile long inlet with a big beach in the back. Mangroves to the south of it create bug problems after rainy spells.

24° 32′ 19″, 110° 23′ 20″

14 **El Cardoncito.** Another narrow, steeply walled inlet. I don't have first hand experience with the mid-sized beach, though it is supposed to be rocky. There is another well here but the water is not for drinking.

24° 31′ 52″, 110° 22′ 31″

13 **Caleta Partida West.** This is a long channel, and is a world unto its own in some degree because of how protected it is. It separates Isla la Partida from Espíritu Santo, but just barely. Halfway into the channel, you'll see a large harbor on the southern shore of Partida. The harbor is a mooring ground for a good number of yachts. The top of the harbor is a nice camp, but be prepared for beachcombing visitors from the yachts who sometimes arrive on jet skis.

To the east, the channel gets shallower and shallower, and comes up to a spit of dunes that appears from the naked eye to join the two islands together. But there is a twisting canal to the south of this spit that provides access to the east side of the islands. Fishermen's huts line the spit on both sides of the shallow channel, but the vibe is tranquilo and friendly and it is possible to camp north of the shacks.

24° 30′ 56″, 110° 23′ 15″

12 **El Mesteño.** A fjord-like bay with a nice beach set back into it.

24° 30′ 27″, 110° 23′ 04″

11 **El Candelero.** This large bay with islets has a prominent rock prow dividing the beach in two. The southern beach is uninhabited, but the northern beach is a kayak outfitter's camp. The outfitters are friendly, and might allow small groups to camp on the perimeter of their beach if they are not busy. There is a brackish well behind camp.

24° 29′ 37″, 110° 23′ 13″

10 **El Manglito.** A narrow inlet, with a tiny beach at its head. An interesting spot for a small group, with an arroyo hike behind.

24° 29′ 24″, 110° 22′ 59″

9 **Playa Ballena.** A beautiful beach designated "No Camping" to preserve archeological sites nearby. These are fish traps built into the rocks at shoreline by the Pericue Indians, some of North America's earliest inhabitants.

24°35′

30′

Isla Espíritu Santo

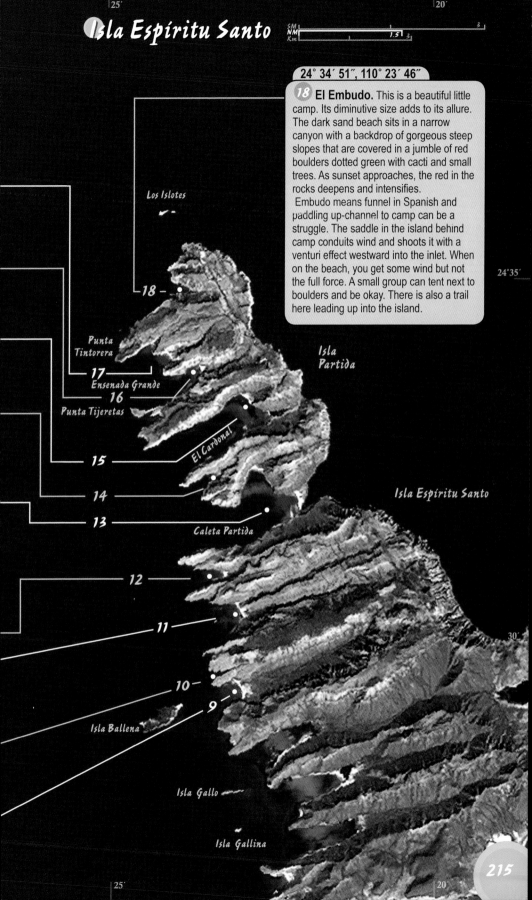

24° 34′ 51″, 110° 23′ 46″

18 **El Embudo.** This is a beautiful little camp. Its diminutive size adds to its allure. The dark sand beach sits in a narrow canyon with a backdrop of gorgeous steep slopes that are covered in a jumble of red boulders dotted green with cacti and small trees. As sunset approaches, the red in the rocks deepens and intensifies.

Embudo means funnel in Spanish and paddling up-channel to camp can be a struggle. The saddle in the island behind camp conduits wind and shoots it with a venturi effect westward into the inlet. When on the beach, you get some wind but not the full force. A small group can tent next to boulders and be okay. There is also a trail here leading up into the island.

25′

20′

Los Islotes

18 –

24°35′

Punta
Tintorera

Isla
Partida

17
Ensenada Grande
16
Punta Tijeretas

El Cardonal

Isla Espíritu Santo

15

14

13

Caleta Partida

12

11

30′

10 –

9

Isla Ballena

Isla Gallo

Isla Gallina

215

25′

20′

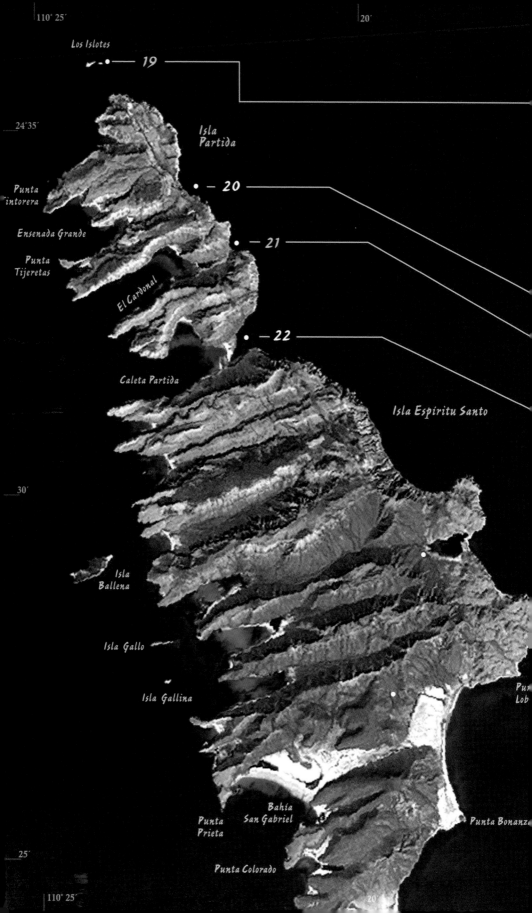

110° 25′   20′

Los Islotes

— 19

24°35′

Isla Partida

Punta Pintorera

— 20

Ensenada Grande

— 21

Punta Tijeretas

El Cardonal

— 22

Caleta Partida

Isla Espiritu Santo

30′

Isla Ballena

Isla Gallo

Isla Gallina

Pur
Lob

Bahía
San Gabriel

Punta Bonanz

Punta Prieta

25′

Punta Colorado

110° 25′   20′

Isla Espíritu Santo

SM
NM
Km
1.5 | 3

24° 35′ 54″, 110° 24′ 09″

19 Los Isoltes. Though in no way a camp, a visit here is often the climax of a trip to Espíritu Santo. These are two rock islets a half mile off the north tip of Partida that serve as a home to a sea lion colony (and a strong contingent of boobies).
I love sea lion pups, but one time diving off Los Isoltes I got too close and playful with some pups underwater for too long and mom shot down from the surface at warp speed, came right at me, and bared her fangs directly in front of my face. "HOLY *#&%!" I deferred to mom quickly and now swim a bit more mindful of these creatures than before. I know people have patted pups and have even seen a picture of a pup lying across someone's kayak while they were floating, but don't take these animals for granted. Look and enjoy. Dive, but don't dive too close.

Down the Outside. This side of the island can cause kayakers to be a little apprehensive. You may encounter north winds with big waves sometimes and there is a minimal selection of quality campsites. But if conditions are right, go. The northeastern coastline is where the scenery gets intense. There are huge bluffs of black rock latticed with pink intrusions, topped by a layer of rich red rock, all dropping directly into the ocean. And it gets better as you proceed south.

24° 34′ 06″, 110° 22′ 38″

20 An exposed cobble lunch beach or camp for the hardcore wilderness kayak fisherman.

24° 33′ 25″, 110° 22′ 03″

21 A wet suit changing beach or hard-luck camp near a pretty spire.

24° 32′ 01″, 110° 21′ 51″

22 Caleta Partida East. The first beach from the east is rocky, though the paddle into the channel provides a break from travels down coast. You can continue to a weather-safe sand camp on the west side of the strait, or use the channel to bail out of the east coast altogether if the weather is gnarly.

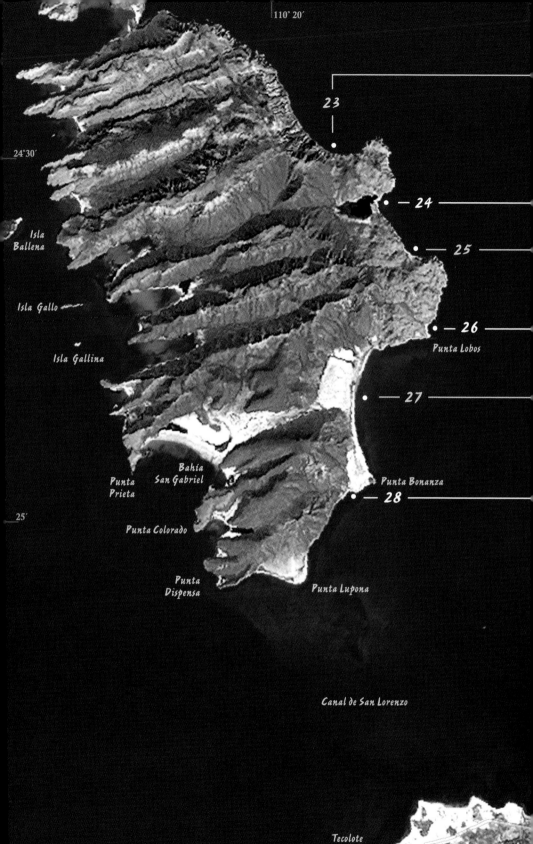

110° 20′

23

24°30′

Isla
Ballena

24

25

Isla Gallo

26

Punta Lobos

Isla Gallina

27

Bahía
San Gabriel

Punta Bonanza

Punta
Prieta

28

25′

Punta Colorado

Punta
Dispensa

Punta Lupona

Canal de San Lorenzo

Tecolote

20′

110° 20′

Isla Espiritu Santo

SM
NM
Km

1.5

3

3

24° 30´ 04˝, 110° 19´ 02˝

23 **El Pailebote.** This is a large camping area, but it is cobblestone and you must deal with sleeping on small roundish rocks. There is a good campsite near a cave/arch. There is shade, a good kitchen area, an easy carry, but minimal sleeping options. Other parts of the surrounding beach have more sleeping room.

24° 29´ 22˝, 110° 18´ 24˝

24 A rock beach with a lagoon behind it. The lagoon has camp-worthy beaches, but getting to them is the problem.

24° 28´ 40˝, 110° 17´ 56˝

25 This is an interesting camp. The beach is north-exposed, but what looks to be a cobble/small boulder beach with inadequate sleeping potential has behind it a hard, flat arroyo of coarse red sand with many sleeping opportunities. There are beautiful cacti and other vegetation in the arroyo, but they are spaced along the perimeter of the tenting zone.

24° 27´ 36˝, 110° 17´ 36˝

26 A beach above a **light**. A reef offshore of the point is tricky to navigate at low tide—with waves it should be boated wide. On calm days this is a great place to snorkel.

24° 26´ 47˝, 110° 18´ 38˝

27 **Playa Bonanza.** For those who have come down the east coast of the island and passed mainly cliffs, rocky points, and cobble beaches, rounding the corner of Punta Bonanza will reveal an almost hallucinogenic site of a gloriously long beach of white sand backed by dunes. The landing up north is the most protected, while the landing down south gets surf on north wind days.

24° 25´ 23˝, 110° 18´ 52˝

28 **Los Morritos.** A protected cove with a stone beach. It is an oft-used fish camp.

East coast gravel camp

The Suicide March of the Squid

At certain times in the spring, you may paddle along a shore of Baja and see schools of two foot long squid, swimming close to the surface, and gathering at water's edge. As you arrive at a lovely cove to make camp, you are suddenly engulfed in a horrendous stench of rotting flesh and realize that the tide line is littered with carcasses of dead squid, baking in the hot sun. Many are being vandalized by scavenging seagulls and vultures only too pleased with this bountiful harvest—on to another camp. But in the next harbor you are horrified by hoards—hundreds, maybe thousands of bloated, floating dead squid carried in by the tide. But this time the wind has warned you by carrying the aroma from a half mile away. You know you'd have a hard time relaxing here. Don't get discouraged. Keep paddling and hope it's better at the next beach. Either that, or in another couple weeks, the beaches will all be clean again after the carcasses have been fully composted, devoured by sea maggots and recycled into the food chain. In the meantime, be resourceful. Reach out and scoop up one that has just landed, is still fresh and wriggling, and grill him up for dinner.

Recently beached squid display marvelous chameleon colors, changing their bodies from pale orange to deep purple, to stripes and spots, and many variations in between. Here their bodies throb and choke on the air as they gasp their last breath, the gulls already pulling their limbs apart. If you try to save one by throwing him back in the water, he just turns right around and thrusts himself back onto the beach in a defiant suicide leap.

Once you get over this macabre parade, however, they taste quite fine grilled in a pan with olive oil, onions and garlic. We recommend eating the outer body flesh, about a half-inch thick. It separates from the core with a few easy slices of the knife. Work around a few areas of cartilage, then remove the thin, outer skin. Tenderize the steak by beating it between two smooth rocks, pounding until it is almost in pieces. Grill over medium heat, but do not overcook. The frayed piece comes back together under heat and tastes like firm chicken.

What are those Squid up to Anyway?

Squid are like weeds. They are opportunistic. They reproduce and grow rapidly, moving into any open niche in the ocean ecosystem. They are ravenous carnivores and in turn, serve as principle diet to many of the large predator fish, like dolphins, whales, tuna and shark. They are a very important part of the ocean food chain, perhaps comprising some of the largest biomass (the largest amount of critters by weight) on the planet.

Squid are in a class called Cephalopods along with octopus, cuttlefish and nautilus, which belong to an ancient group of invertebrates (critters without a backbone) called mollusks. They have fossils that date back five or six hundred million years (very old, long before mammals were around), yet are considered the most complex and intelligent of their family—other family members being clams, scallops and other brainless shellfish. The Cephalopods have the distinction of being free-swimming and have large, complex eyes, a great advancement from their clam cousins in the mud.

Squid also have cells in their skin called cromatophores, which produce different colors as needed, presumably to visually communicate their intentions.

Squid live a very short and fast life, with many of the common species growing to adult size of two feet in just a few weeks. Most species live only a few months or a year. Along the way, they are efficient and voracious predators, eating everything including smaller squid. They travel in schools, using safety in numbers, but also providing a large, dense source of food for the larger fish. At their zenith, they mate in big groups, flashing their bright colors and patterns in a complex mating dance before the males

Photo by: Lori Russell

inject the females with sperm. Shortly after laying thousands of eggs on the sea bottom and reefs, their body tissues change and deteriorate rapidly. Many die in the water. It is not known if the end of the mating cycle is what causes others to commit suicide on the beaches, or if they are just traveling and responding to some irresistible electromagnetic homing impulse that says "the beach is the right direction."

Recent studies have shown a dramatic increase in the numbers of squid worldwide, even as most other fish are showing a sharp decline. In fact, it is believed that as the oceans are being fished out of most large predators (whales, sharks, tunas), the space is open for the squid to expand their populations due to less predation.

– Lori Russell

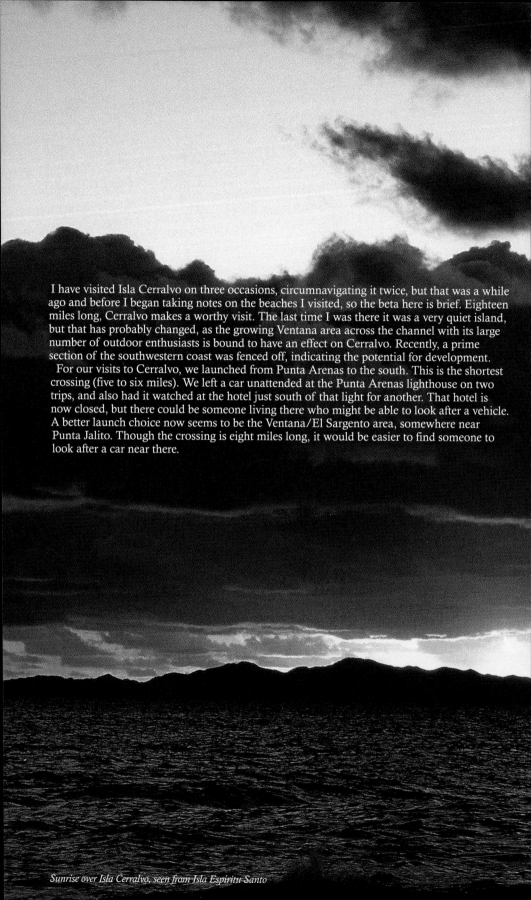

I have visited Isla Cerralvo on three occasions, circumnavigating it twice, but that was a while ago and before I began taking notes on the beaches I visited, so the beta here is brief. Eighteen miles long, Cerralvo makes a worthy visit. The last time I was there it was a very quiet island, but that has probably changed, as the growing Ventana area across the channel with its large number of outdoor enthusiasts is bound to have an effect on Cerralvo. Recently, a prime section of the southwestern coast was fenced off, indicating the potential for development.

For our visits to Cerralvo, we launched from Punta Arenas to the south. This is the shortest crossing (five to six miles). We left a car unattended at the Punta Arenas lighthouse on two trips, and also had it watched at the hotel just south of that light for another. That hotel is now closed, but there could be someone living there who might be able to look after a vehicle. A better launch choice now seems to be the Ventana/El Sargento area, somewhere near Punta Jalito. Though the crossing is eight miles long, it would be easier to find someone to look after a car near there.

Sunrise over Isla Cerralvo, seen from Isla Espíritu Santo

Isla Cerralvo

SM
NM
Km
12
12
24

Punta Norte

Punta Limón

Punta el Mostrador

Punta Sur
Punta Jalito

Punta Montaña

La Ventana

Punta Arenas

Bahía de los Muertos

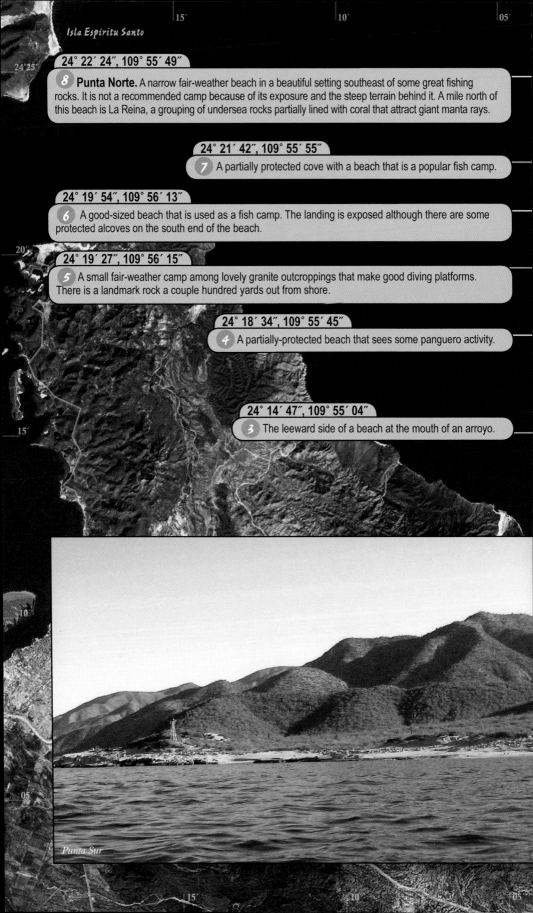

24° 22′ 24″, 109° 55′ 49″

8 **Punta Norte.** A narrow fair-weather beach in a beautiful setting southeast of some great fishing rocks. It is not a recommended camp because of its exposure and the steep terrain behind it. A mile north of this beach is La Reina, a grouping of undersea rocks partially lined with coral that attract giant manta rays.

24° 21′ 42″, 109° 55′ 55″

7 A partially protected cove with a beach that is a popular fish camp.

24° 19′ 54″, 109° 56′ 13″

6 A good-sized beach that is used as a fish camp. The landing is exposed although there are some protected alcoves on the south end of the beach.

24° 19′ 27″, 109° 56′ 15″

5 A small fair-weather camp among lovely granite outcroppings that make good diving platforms. There is a landmark rock a couple hundred yards out from shore.

24° 18′ 34″, 109° 55′ 45″

4 A partially-protected beach that sees some panguero activity.

24° 14′ 47″, 109° 55′ 04″

3 The leeward side of a beach at the mouth of an arroyo.

Punta Sur

SM
NM
Km

110° 00′   109° 55′   50′   24°25′

Punta Norte

8 — •

7 — •

Isla Cerralvo   20′

6 — •
5 — •

Punta Limón

4 — •

Punta el Mostrador

3 — •   15′

Canal Cerralvo

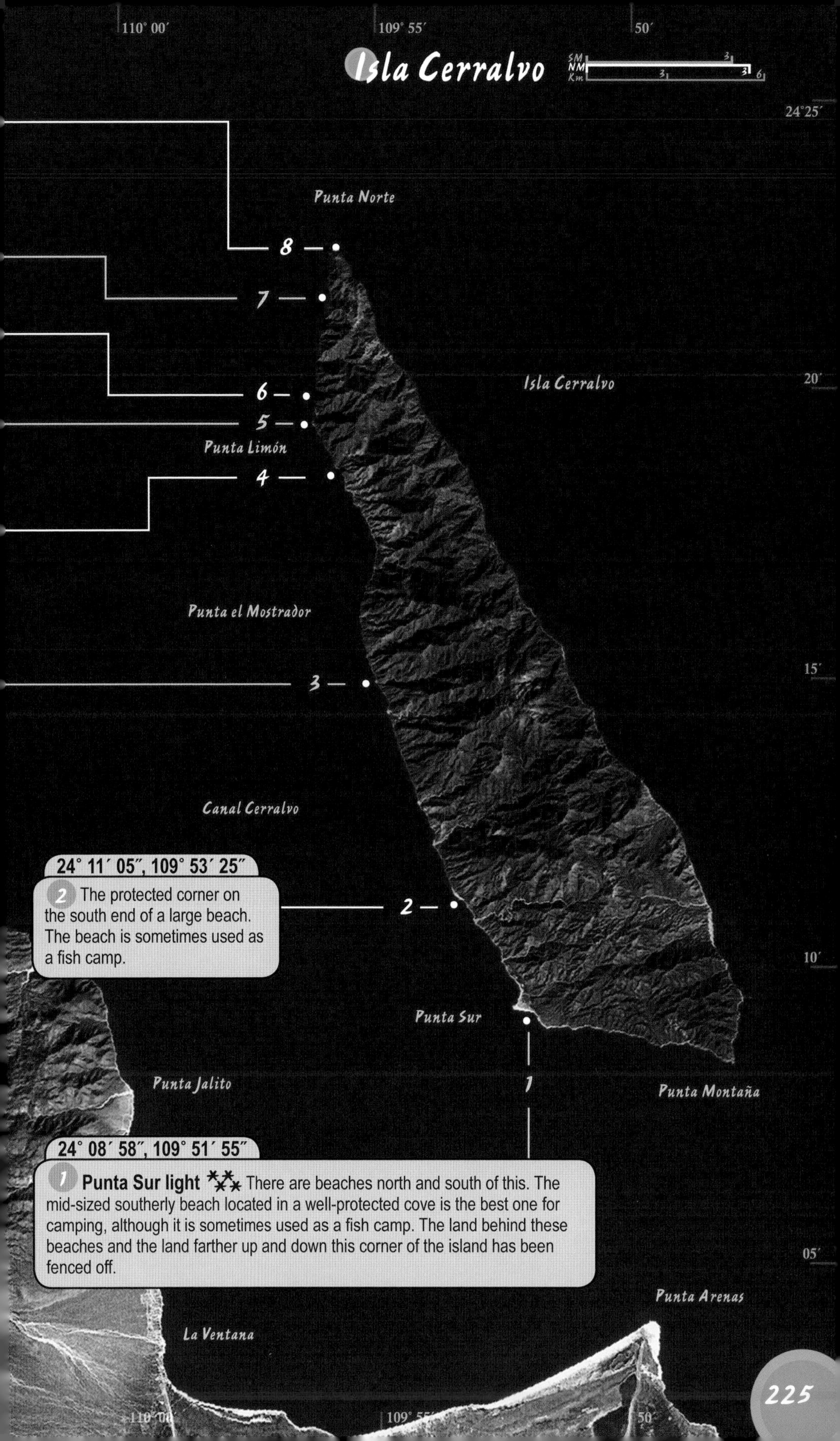

24° 11′ 05″, 109° 53′ 25″

2 The protected corner on the south end of a large beach. The beach is sometimes used as a fish camp.

2 — •

10′

Punta Sur

1

Punta Jalito   Punta Montaña

24° 08′ 58″, 109° 51′ 55″

1 **Punta Sur light** ✶✶✶ There are beaches north and south of this. The mid-sized southerly beach located in a well-protected cove is the best one for camping, although it is sometimes used as a fish camp. The land behind these beaches and the land farther up and down this corner of the island has been fenced off.

05′

Punta Arenas

La Ventana

110° 00′   109° 55′   50′

Two pelicans hoping for a handout

Punta Jalito

24° 08′ 52″, 109° 51′ 23″

15 A medium-sized beach with shade.

24° 08′ 45″, 109° 50′ 28″

14 A small sand beach.

24° 08′ 12″, 109° 48′ 11″

13 **Punta Montaña. Light.** There is a beach east of this light that you can access through a narrow channel between rocks.

The northeast corner of Cerralvo is rugged and abrupt, and there are numerous offshore rocks.

Punta Norte

24° 17′ 17″, 109° 52′ 44″

9 A cove with some protection. The beach has a rocky landing and is sometimes used as a fish camp. Just around the corner to the north is a less protected beach that is home to some palm trees and a shack.

9

24° 15′ 15″, 109° 51′ 22″

10 A large gravel spit with some north-pro on its south side.

20′

10

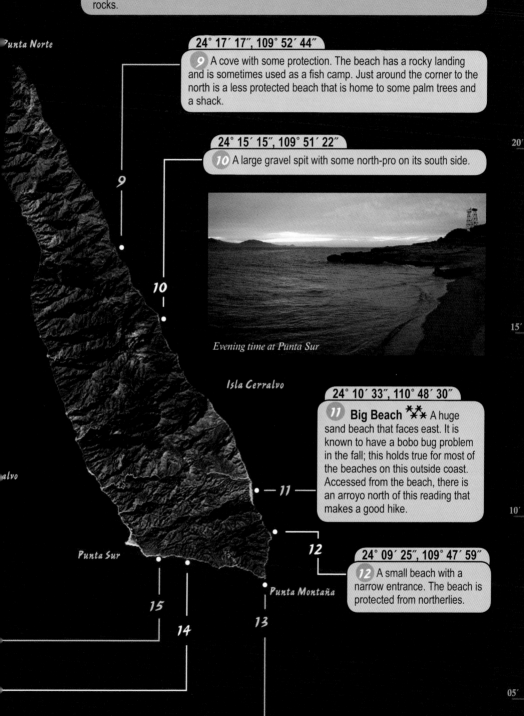

Evening time at Punta Sur

15′

Isla Cerralvo

24° 10′ 33″, 110° 48′ 30″

11 **Big Beach** ✶✶ A huge sand beach that faces east. It is known to have a bobo bug problem in the fall; this holds true for most of the beaches on this outside coast. Accessed from the beach, there is an arroyo north of this reading that makes a good hike.

11

10′

12

24° 09′ 25″, 109° 47′ 59″

12 A small beach with a narrow entrance. The beach is protected from northerlies.

Punta Sur

Punta Montaña

15

13

14

Punta Arenas

05′

alvo

109° 55′   50′   45′

Cerralvo Crossing

My third trip to Isla Cerralvo was a fishing expedition back in my younger days. The goal was to kayak out to the south end of the island, spear as many fish as possible in a couple of days, then get them back to Cardo's house in Cabo where we could freeze them and then fly them back to our homes in the United States at some later date. So the fish would not go bad on the island in the desert heat, we decided to tie ice coolers to the top of our boats.

Because of normal gear-loading confusion, morning café social obligations, and the general pre-trip procrastinations of which we specialize in, we didn't make it to the launch beach at Punta Arenas until late afternoon. We unloaded the boats and the gear in a pile on the beach. We decided Cardo would drive the car down to the hotel a mile or so south of the launch site and store it in a safe place while I loaded the boats. So he drove off and left me with the stack of gear.

I got most things in the boats, but when it came to loading the coolers, I was perplexed. We hadn't brought straps, and the rope work to tie them down so they were sea-worthy was proving to be more complex than I had anticipated. As I fumbled at this problem, a souped-up pickup truck came swerving down the beach and stopped not too far away from me. Two hefty beer-drinking Mexican men got out of the truck. They stood and talked quietly among themselves for a bit, looking my way occasionally. They then seemed to agree on something and started walking over toward me. Being a bit of a paranoid guy, bad thoughts started going through my head. I was alone in the middle of nowhere with only a knife to defend myself against two larger and probably more capable hombres. And if I reached for the knife on the boat it would start things off on a decidedly bad note.

Without hesitation the men came right up to me. "¿Necessitas ayuda?" "Do you need help?" one of them asked in Spanish. "Here, let me show you how it is done," he said. Together they knelt over a kayak and proceeded to tie a cooler with the rope in a very professional way that I have not been able to duplicate since. The knots were clean and perfectly spaced. The cooler didn't budge an inch. They then lashed the other cooler to the other boat. I went from fear of being mugged to a state of major appreciation in a matter of minutes, hating myself for having those initial negative thoughts.

When they were done, I thanked them heartily. They smiled and said "No problema," and wished me a good trip, then walked back to their truck, got in, and left.

With the approach of dusk, the clouds were beginning to change color when Cardo came trudging back up the beach. We both knew it was past time to push off, but the sea was relatively calm and it was a beautiful evening. We knew the island fairly well, and knew our landing beach and that it was at the base of the southwest light. We decided to go for it and have the flashing light guide us in when nightfall descended. I had thought about doing nighttime crossings for years, but it never happened—it was never the right moment. Now here we were about to start one on a moonless night with no forethought to it at all. We were packed, the landing beach was just across the six-mile wide channel, and it was simply time to go.

Photo by: Doug Driskell

We pulled the kayaks into the water and immediately felt a top-heavy swaying of them from the weight of the coolers filled with ice. "This won't work," Cardo said. But he knew what to do: Since it would be night and the temperature would be dropping during the short crossing, the ice would not likely melt if we took it out and put it in the boats just for the crossing. Cardo is the boss on our trips, and the idea made partial sense to my smaller brain, so that is what we did.

Things felt good as we paddled away from the endless white beach of Punta Arenas and headed out to the mountainous Isla Cerralvo. The remains of daylight only lasted the first couple of miles, and then there was a nice sunset. The small pulse of the beating light was already visible, so confidence was up and there were little worries about the impending darkness. And dark it got. Though the stars were out, the darkness was deep when it came upon us. The sea became larger and the Cerralvo light seemed farther away than earlier. Cardo disappeared from my side and became only an occasional voice out in the black. I enjoyed the stargazing while I quietly paddled.

For that trip we had old sit-on-top kayaks each with a hull that had one large, undivided chamber inside. The seat was a hollowed-out depression over the inner chamber. About halfway through the crossing I noticed my butt feeling somewhat colder than the waters of the warm sea should be making it. There was no denying what it was. "Cardo, I think my ice is melting," I said off into the dark. "Yea, mine is too," was the reply from the invisible fisherman. Okay, so no ice, a cold butt, and a boat partially full of melt-water. Unpleasant, but not bad, I thought. In any case, nothing to do about it now—you can't pump out a sit-on-top with gear tied over the hatches, especially if you aren't carrying a pump. So we paddled on, and I went back into my reverie, fixated toward the beat of the light and zenning on the mantra of paddle strokes. I was doing well, but after a while Cardo grunted from out in the darkness, "Dave, I'm sinking." What? The master going under? Impossible. "Are you sure?" I asked. "There shouldn't be enough water from the ice to sink you." "Yep," was his reply, "it lowered my hull line to where I think it leaks through a bad hatch. It's getting pretty hard to paddle this thing." Well, isn't this going to be exciting, I thought. Glad it's not me. "Can you make it to the island?" A couple of grunts from him and then a, "Well, we'll see."

As we got closer to the island, another glow became visible near the lighthouse. After another mile it became apparent it was from a campfire. Strangers, what kind of strangers? Somebody was camped on our landing beach. It had to be fishermen. Apprehension was starting to run a little high with the announcement that Cardo's boat was going under. And now this. When on fishing jaunts, we always tried to avoid Mexican fishermen so they wouldn't be jealous of our catch and start getting territorial on us. We were getting close enough to the island to vaguely discern their forms around the fire. Though the landing beach was right in front of us, Cardo vetoed landing at it, even though it was the one beach we were familiar with. We knew there was another smaller, less protected beach around a short corner to the north, but we were less familiar with it, and it was pitch black at that part of the island.

Just call us dumb and stubborn. We veered course for the north beach. As we approached the point separating the two coves, a new noise greeted us—the sound of waves on rocks. Surf always sounds bigger at night—it couldn't be that big based on the swell we experienced during the crossing, but it sounded big enough. I was worried. Knowing this bay was just north of the light, we paddled into where it should be. The shoreline was invisible. We went deeper into the cove and hovered outside the break. "Cardo, we can't land here, I think it's rocks!" "We have to, I'm sinking, I've only got a few minutes left!" I told him to wait while I checked out more of the cove first. I paddled to the side and made the best attempt I could to discern what was beach and what was rock by the sound of the waves hitting the shore. As I'm deaf in one ear this was tricky—I was turning my head and cocking my good ear toward the shore like a silly parrot. It was impossible to see the detail of the land. I sensed a softening of the surf in one place. It could be the little beach, but I wasn't sure. It was too late to think too much about it. I called Cardo over and we decided to go for it. I went first because at least I had back-paddling capability. The surf had to be small even if I was landing on rocks, but it was scary gliding into the black coast. At the last second, as a wave pushed me into shore, I glimpsed a gravel landing. An instant later, my bow skidded into the soft beach. I got off my boat and secured it, then called Cardo in.

Tropical Pacific sunrise east of Cabo San José

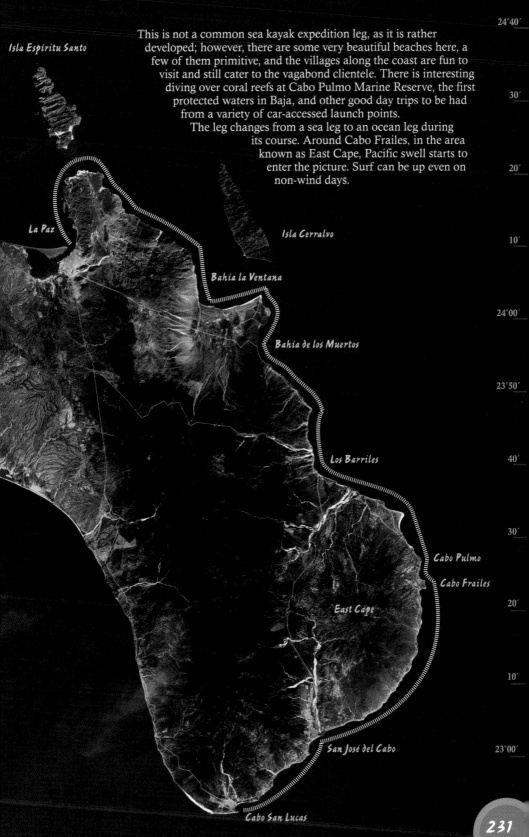

SM
NM
Km

15

15

15

30

24°40′

Isla Espíritu Santo

This is not a common sea kayak expedition leg, as it is rather developed; however, there are some very beautiful beaches here, a few of them primitive, and the villages along the coast are fun to visit and still cater to the vagabond clientele. There is interesting diving over coral reefs at Cabo Pulmo Marine Reserve, the first protected waters in Baja, and other good day trips to be had from a variety of car-accessed launch points.

The leg changes from a sea leg to an ocean leg during its course. Around Cabo Frailes, in the area known as East Cape, Pacific swell starts to enter the picture. Surf can be up even on non-wind days.

30′

20′

La Paz

Isla Cerralvo

10′

Bahía la Ventana

24°00′

Bahía de los Muertos

23°50′

Los Barriles

40′

30′

Cabo Pulmo

Cabo Frailes

20′

East Cape

10′

San José del Cabo

23°00′

Cabo San Lucas

110° 30′ 20′ 10′ 110° 00′ 109° 50′ 40′ 30′ 20′

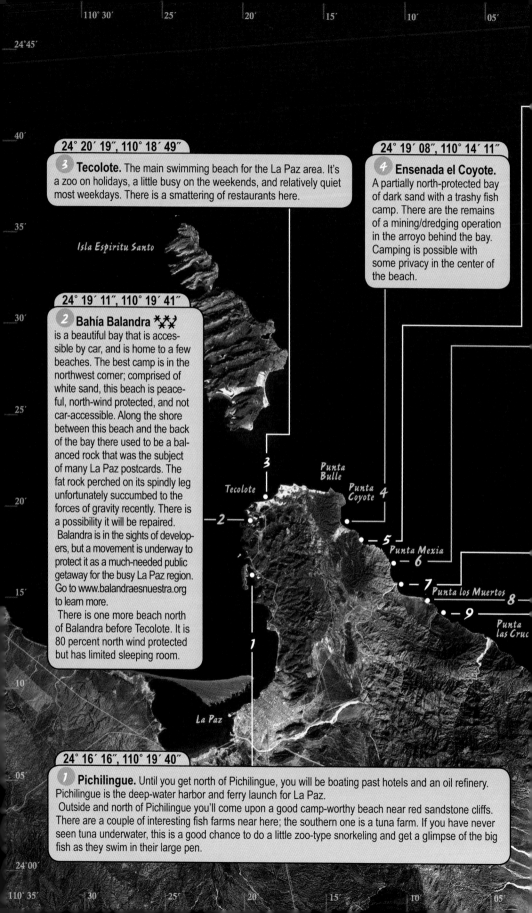

110° 30′ 25′ 20′ 15′ 10′ 05′

24°45′

40′

35′

30′

25′

20′

15′

10′

05′

24°00′

110° 35′ 30′ 25′ 20′ 15′ 10′ 05′

24° 20′ 19″, 110° 18′ 49″

3 **Tecolote.** The main swimming beach for the La Paz area. It's a zoo on holidays, a little busy on the weekends, and relatively quiet most weekdays. There is a smattering of restaurants here.

24° 19′ 08″, 110° 14′ 11″

4 **Ensenada el Coyote.** A partially north-protected bay of dark sand with a trashy fish camp. There are the remains of a mining/dredging operation in the arroyo behind the bay. Camping is possible with some privacy in the center of the beach.

Isla Espiritu Santo

24° 19′ 11″, 110° 19′ 41″

2 **Bahía Balandra** ✳✳⸮ is a beautiful bay that is accessible by car, and is home to a few beaches. The best camp is in the northwest corner; comprised of white sand, this beach is peaceful, north-wind protected, and not car-accessible. Along the shore between this beach and the back of the bay there used to be a balanced rock that was the subject of many La Paz postcards. The fat rock perched on its spindly leg unfortunately succumbed to the forces of gravity recently. There is a possibility it will be repaired. Balandra is in the sights of developers, but a movement is underway to protect it as a much-needed public getaway for the busy La Paz region. Go to www.balandraesnuestra.org to learn more.

There is one more beach north of Balandra before Tecolote. It is 80 percent north wind protected but has limited sleeping room.

Punta Bulle

Tecolote **3**

Punta Coyote **4**

2

5 *Punta Mexia*

6

7 *Punta los Muertos* **8**

9

Punta las Cruc

1

La Paz

24° 16′ 16″, 110° 19′ 40″

1 **Pichilingue.** Until you get north of Pichilingue, you will be boating past hotels and an oil refinery. Pichilingue is the deep-water harbor and ferry launch for La Paz.

Outside and north of Pichilingue you'll come upon a good camp-worthy beach near red sandstone cliffs. There are a couple of interesting fish farms near here; the southern one is a tuna farm. If you have never seen tuna underwater, this is a good chance to do a little zoo-type snorkeling and get a glimpse of the big fish as they swim in their large pen.

24° 18′ 11″, 110° 13′ 01″

5 **Playa el Bote.** An east-northeast facing beach of dark gravel and some sand. There is a little surf protection. It is road accessed and a little trashy.

24° 16′ 51″, 110° 11′ 08″

6 ✱✱✱ A beach in a little inlet that has seen no development (as of '05). It is very lovely but has limited surf protection. The inlet is fringed by cliffs that offer shade in the early and late hours of the day. Though the beach is small, there is plenty of camping room behind it in a sandy arroyo.

Tecolote at Easter

24° 15′ 41″, 110° 10′ 42″

7 **Punta Rosario.** A settlement of houses with palm trees and other cultivated greenery lying north of a large arroyo. The large beach to the south, Playa la Sopresa, is pretty but exposed.

24° 14′ 46″, 110° 08′ 53″

8 ✱✱✱ Inside **Punta los Muertos.** For the time being, this is an undeveloped big beach. There are two small islands to the northeast of it. A coral reef extends between the north end of the beach and the islotes. In general, the scenery along this coast is very pleasant and hilly.

Isla Cerralvo

24° 14′ 10″, 110° 08′ 15″

9 **El Saltito.** Though developed, this is a very cute beach that allows camping ('05). The owners are not home much, and the caretakers that live behind the main house don't mind campers.There is fresh water available from a spigot behind the house, but please ask the caretaker, José, first before filling up or camping.

Heading farther down coast you will encounter a long but unprotected beach with a dirt road directly behind it. There is one potential semi-protected camp on the north corner of this beach in an arroyo. The landing is on smooth rocks. After this long beach you'll see a small point with three crosses on it. Vampires swing wide.

Bahía la Ventana

Punta Arenas

24°20′ *Punta Coyote*

24° 12′ 49″, 110° 05′ 21″

10 The handsome **Las Cruces hotel** and development with its white stucco buildings and red-tiled roofs, all surrounded by palms. There is a breakwater here that affords a surf-free landing on a white sand beach. Camping is not allowed but it is a nice lunch spot and one of the only safe havens in this area for a wave-weary paddler.

Punta las Cruces

Isla Cerralvo

10

15′

Punta las Cruces

11

Canal Cerralvo

10′

Punta Gorda

12

Punta Jalito   *Punta Montaña*

13

05′

14

El Sargento   *Bahia la Ventana*   *Punta Arenas*

La Ventana   **15**

Punta Perico

24°00′

24° 03′ 45″, 109° 49′ 41″

15 **Punta Arenas.** The low point (there is a **light** just inside of it) gets surf a short ways offshore due to shallows, so swing wide if the wind is up. Rounding it, things quiet down enough to land. This is a huge beach with a closed hotel at its southern end. The beach does see car traffic.

Bahia de los Muertos

23°55′

50′

45′

40′

Wilderness beach south of Las Cruces

Below Las Cruces you'll encounter a primitive and rugged section of coast that hasn't seen the encroachment of roads yet. Hilly terrain with thick vegetation limits hikers to short ridge-hikes or arroyos for the next few miles, but the beaches that nest between the ridges are nice and there is privacy.

24° 11´ 08″, 110° 02´ 56″

11 A large arroyo with a massive flat zone for camping. There are palm trees in the arroyo. The landing is on smooth small rocks at low tide and sand at high tide.

These two miles are a succession of small points, all with a similar look—a small, peaked promontory jutting out from a hill or a ridge, then a beach in the cove behind it. There are three possible and pretty camps in this area.

24° 08´ 10″, 110° 00´ 10″

12 A somewhat protected beach and nice camp in an arroyo. Landing is on smooth rocks. This is the last private beach before heading into Ventana.

24° 07´ 44″, 109° 59´ 52″

13 **Punta Jalito.** This rather indistinct point marks the beginning of a broad coastal plain and the turn into Bahía la Ventana. It also brings the road back into play, which gets wider as it approaches El Sargento. There are car-accessible campsites here.

El Sargento is a small community with a panga launch beach. This area of the coast is getting built up, primarily by gringo windsport people making second homes. On the west side of town there is a small store, and *fresh water* is available at the house nearby.

24° 03´ 24″, 109° 59´ 19″

14 The community and beaches of **La Ventana** comprise the windsport capital of the Sea of Cortez. So what does that mean for the kayaker? It means, "Watch out, slow poke!" There is a long beach here, but no protected landing, and the waves hit shore at an angle. It's a funny feeling to have your boat swamp as you land, and then break your back pulling the damn thing out of the drink while a bunch of windsurfers look on assuming what you're doing is normal kayak procedure, so why bother to lend a hand? There is an RV park at this reading that will be full of windsporters, many staying all winter. When the weather is calm they mountain bike—there are some good single tracks in the area. A few of them kayak. There are showers and bathrooms and water in the park, and the cost is reasonable. There is an okay small restaurant behind the west corner of the park and a store with Internet next to it. There are some other restaurants around. All in all, it's a fun place to hang if you can adjust to the wind.

Not kayaking

Punta Arenas

Punta
Perico

Though rocky and cliffy, **Punta Perico** doesn't see the surf offshore that Punta Arena does. There is a fair amount of coral on low reefs around the south end of the point. This is a developed area of vacation homes with one protected landing.

24°00′

— 16 —

Bahía de los Muertos

23°55′ — 17 —

Quality camp time

50′ — 18 —

Punta Pescadero

— 19 —

45′

Bahía las Palmas

40′

Barriles — 20 —

La Ribera

Punta Colorada

35′ — 21 —

Punta
Arena

22

Barriles

1 Mercado
2 Taco Stand
3 Hotel Palmas de Cortez
4 Tio Pablo's
5 Verdugo's RV and Motel
6 Hotel los Barriles
7 Internet/Mercadito
8 Casa Pequena
9 The Office
10 Merado Faila
11 Otra Vez
12 Haircutter
13 Rest. Barrilito

Playa Norte
RV Park
1 1/2 Miles

13
12

11
10
9
8 7
6
4 5

To
Car Storage
(Allejandro +
Guadalupe)

1   2

3

N

W   E

S

MEX
1

30′

25′

20′

Cabo
Fraile

15′   10′   05′   109° 00′   108° 55′   50′

24°05′

SM
NM
Km

24°00′

23° 59′ 34″, 109° 49′ 44″

16 Muertos Beach. Developers are changing the name of this area to "Bay of Dreams." Whatever. There is camping on the sand beach down from a panga launch. The landing is very protected, but wind does blow into camp. There is *fresh water* at an expensive restaurant in the area. The bay is popular dorado fishing ground. It is possible to buy some live bait from the fishermen to aid in your hunt, if so desired.

Paddling across Bahía de los Muertos, you'll begin to see mountains along the coast. There is, however, a dirt road paralleling the shore.

23°55′

23° 54′ 39″, 109° 49′ 30″

17 This is the beginning of a long, white sand beach. It is surf-exposed, but the landing is soft. Below a small octagonal house sitting on an orange rock buttress is a camp that is out of the wind. Numerous other camping sites on the beach would be nice in calm weather.

23° 50′ 47″, 109° 44′ 49″

50′

18 El Cardonal. A community with a nice beach, though there is no protection or privacy here. The mountains begin to recede again.

23° 47′ 56″, 109° 41′ 55″

45′

19 Punta Pescadero. Jagged rock outcroppings off the point and around the inside of the bay to the south demand care as you round. After the corner is a white sand beach with a house above it. The safest landing is behind the third or fourth rock group into the bay, where there is also some camping potential.

23° 40′ 58″, 109° 41′ 43″

40′

20 Barriles. A fun town and beach popular with windsport folk—but watch that landing! Barril means barrel in Spanish, and it refers to the shape of the waves here. A sloping sea bottom and a down-coast wind combine to create large, curling, deep waves. These waves angle into shore, have considerable suck after they hit, and there is no protected zone. A clean landing here on a windy day is a work of art. Showers and margaritas await the successful paddler!
This reading is near Verdugo's Hotel and RV Park, which is right in town but a bit pricey. Besides all the amenities of a nice RV park, Verdugo's has a bar and a pool overlooking the water, and a restaurant upstairs that serves a good breakfast. Another good camp option is the Playa Norte RV Park, and just above that there is free camping in either of the large twin arroyos. In town, Tio Pablo's is a fun place to eat and sort of a central meeting ground, and Otra Vez is another good spot to get a full meal.

35′

The coast south of Barriles is largely developed, fronted by an unprotected sand beach. Around the town of La Ribera there is room to camp, but the landing is still exposed. There is also an RV park there. La Ribera looks cute and interesting, but I haven't visited.

30′

23° 35′ 08″, 109° 31′ 11″

21 Punta Colorada is a little jut of red rocks. The bay south of it has a hotel in it. After the hotel, there is a long beach with a few houses scattered about.

25′

23° 33′ 21″, 109° 28′ 06″

22 Punta Arena is a low point with a concrete **light** on it. Inside of the point, the north swell mellows out and there is good camping on a large-grain white sand beach.

0′   15′   10′   05′   109° 00′   108° 55′

23° 26′ 37″, 109° 25′ 36″

23 Cabo Pulmo is a small, palm-filled community with a mixed population of gringos and Mexicans. It is a chill place with a protected landing. This reading is from a cobble bank north of the center of town. Camping here is okay. There are a couple of restaurants and a small store in town. Behind town, across the road and slightly to the north, is Tito's, the funky roadhouse restaurant of choice.

The waters between Cabo Pulmo and Cabo Frailes are a national marine reserve, and fishing is prohibited. There are coral reefs in front of the village of Pulmo that provide convenient snorkeling and the chance to see many fish, including some very large ones farther out.

23° 22′ 44″, 109° 25′ 50″

24 Cabo Frailes is a beautiful granite buttress coming out of a lone hill. There is a sea lion colony at the base of it. The beach at Los Frailes provides protected landing. Camping is in an arroyo between a collection of RV never-say-winter gringo fisherman-types and Mexican pangueros, with a little more privacy at the north end of the beach. Avoid camping at the turtle hatch sanctuary located at the center/south section of the beach.

There are a number of houses scattered about and a restaurant/hotel. The patio dining at the hotel is nice, but not cheap. There is *fresh water* at the hotel. Quito's, an appealing restaurant located in a quiet ranch setting among verdant desert features, is inland and just south of the main part of the community.

23° 14′ 34″, 109° 25′ 50″

25 Punta Peruchera. A landmark of sorts with a light and a small cluster of houses nearby. From about here and continuing on down to Cabo, the shoreline waters are dotted with patches of rocks. These create navigational hazards if the surf is up.

23° 06′ 20″, 109° 32′ 31″

26 A camp at an arroyo mouth. There can be car-campers here. It is a good launch point for kayak fishing in this area.

23° 05′ 10″, 109° 34′ 22″

27 Punta Gorda, with some conical hills in the background, is a small hill with a line of rocks extending out into the ocean. West of Gorda is a long, undeveloped beach with a large arroyo behind it. This is the last "wild" beach before the major development, Los Cabos, begins.

23° 03′ 30″, 109° 40′ 12″

28 La Playita. A long beach and the panga launch for San José del Cabo. Just east of this is a red- and white-striped **light**. Though unprotected from south swell, this is a major landing zone for small craft. A phone and taxis are nearby.

Cabo San Lucas

Cabo San Lucas. Home of the Giggling Marlin.

Cabo San Lucas

Punta
Arena

Cabo Frailes

23

Cabo Pulmo

Cabo Frailes

24

30´

25´

20´

South of Frailes, development increases as you get closer to Cabo, but there still are some good camping spots between houses, as well as at arroyo mouths. The beaches are lovely white sand set among low granite bluffs and small rock formations. Even without wind there can be waves, sometimes large. The ocean swell can come from the south, so you have lost your protection. Also, most areas of this lower coast have a bit of a shore break, so a timely landing with a quick exit from the boat is prudent.

25

Punta
Peruchera

15´

10´

26

27   Punta Gorda

28

San José del Cabo

05´

Punta
Palmilla

San José del Cabo. The first of the two Cabos. There is now a new marina at the mouth of the San José River. San José was a quaint town but has been tainted by over-tourism, over-building, and over-population. There is an old mission off the town square with numerous restaurants and stores surrounding it. The Los Cabos airport, with major flights back to the real world, is just north of town.

23°00´

A lot of huge hotels, frenetic traffic, and limited public beach access.

22°55´

Trigger fish and puffer fish, Photo by: Suzanne Clarke

Beware the Bobos

A paddler who left his bug net in the car. Photo by: Lori Russell

The dreaded Bobos! It sounds like a joke, but you won't be laughing if you forget your mosquito netting. Bobos are the dreaded gnats of Baja. They, and other insects such as no-see-ums, mosquitoes, and flies hatch in swarms shortly after a major rain event or seasonal birth cycle. Mangrove swamps sometimes see a lot of insect activity, as well. Strangely, bobos don't bite, but they make it their business to investigate every nook and cranny and orifice on your body, driving you absolutely nuts. Long sleeves and pants are your best protection. Bug juice is sometimes effective, as well as a good, smoky campfire. Wind keeps them away and they disappear at night. Otherwise, a mosquito net over a hat is the best way to keep them out of your face. Luckily, they don't stay long after a rain event, and you don't find them often in the desert or on many beaches. But be prepared anyway.

– Lori Russell

Bahía Magdalena is the commonly referred-to name for a 130-mile long area of protected water that is actually three separate bays and a number of natural canals. The bays and canals are protected from ocean swell by four islands, the largest and central of which are Isla Magdalena and Isla Margarita. The overall area, if you include the outside of the islands, offers the most diverse sea kayaking territory in Baja. You can paddle for miles in the peaceful closeness of a mangrove-lined canal and then come out onto a huge bay of mellow waves where the opposite shore is barely visible. You can paddle through a channel between islands, and then out onto the Pacific where the waters are cool and the waves are for real. The Pacific side of the Bahía Magdalena area is not necessarily unfriendly. There are some amazing beaches out there, as well as magnificent headlands to paddle by. But the outside is wild if nothing else because of surf.

Magadelena Bay is famous for being the principal calving area for the California grey whale, which migrates from Alaska down to Baja and then back in a yearly cycle. The large animals are so abundant inside the protected waters that you can easily approach them during the calving months between January and April. Private kayaking groups are discouraged from launching during this time. If you are allowed to launch in whale season, you will be told to paddle directly across from the launch area to the opposite shore on one of the islands, and you will be told to stay along shore and not explore the middle of the bay. This is to keep kayakers from sneaking up on whales. They can't hear the quiet boats, and they sometimes freak when they are suddenly approached. Guided trips are also a big source of revenue for the locals, and getting commercial business keeps them happy. If you want an unfettered chance to explore the bays and canals, it is best to go before or after whale season.

Isla Magdalena eastern coast

Whales are not the only animals found here. The mangroves, though inhospitable for hiking, offer sanctuary for numerous bird species. Hornbills, osprey, falcons, egrets, herons, and finches are commonly seen. Fishing for broomtail grouper in among the mangrove roots can be excellent, and there are clams, scallops, and crabs in shallower parts of the bays. Large game fish patrol the Pacific waters outside the bay.

The weather at Bahía Magdalena and other parts of the Pacific coast can be quite a bit different than the other side of the peninsula at the Sea of Cortez. In the second half of winter, as water and air cool down, the days can be foggy. By early summer it is usually overcast around the bays evening to morning but breaking up into sunny skies before noon and staying clear most of the day. Later in the summer, when the waters have warmed up, there is less fog, increased sun, and hot temperatures. Fall tapers off to pleasant days that last into winter. For kayakers wishing to do an extended trip, the predominant winds are out of the northwest arising mid-morning, and though the bays and canals do not see big seas, going against the wind in these protected waters can be a real chore.

Besides wind, parts of Mag Bay (its gringo nickname) experience significant tidal current. This is especially true of the canals and bocas (mouths) between islands. Also, when the tide floods or ebbs near a boca, the canals among the mangroves in that area become rivers that fill and drain with the current. Some of the tributary canals, or esteros (estuaries), empty completely at low tide, leaving long but temporary sand flats.

For terrain, Mag Bay has a variety, with both mountains and plains along its shores. The east shore is the huge Llano de la Magdalena, a vast plain rolling down from the spine of the Baja peninsula. To the west, Islas Magdalena and Margarita both have some mountainous terrain. However, if one had to quickly pick the two dominant shore features of the bay, they would be: miles of tangled mangrove forests, and endless white sand dune beaches—polar opposites when it comes to locating camps.

Adolfo Lopez Mateos

Isla Magdalena

Puerto San Carlos

Bahía Magdalena

Pacific Ocean

Bahía Almejas

Isla Margarita

SM
NM
Km   34   68

Grey whale breach. Photo by: Dave Becker

25° 05′ 30″, 112° 09′ 58″

4 About here and continuing south a ways, the dunes and sand camping of the inside coast of northern Isla Magdalena give way to mangroves. Camping is possible south of here until the San Carlos vicinity only at interspersed sections of sand found between mangrove forests. In the main canal, large ships sometimes make their way between Lopez Mateos and the deep water channel to the Pacific between Islas Magdalena and Margarita.

25° 01′ 47″, 112° 10′ 16″

5 An area of sand between sections of mangroves.

24° 58′ 13″, 112° 09′ 07″

6 **Curva del Diablo.** A large twist in the canal. You may end up paddling against the wind in the lower half of the twist.

24° 52′ 13″, 112° 10′ 44″

7 **La Libertad.** A large tongue of sand with camping possible north and south. There is a large tributary canal, Estero el Garrotazo, north of here.

24° 49′ 46″, 112° 12′ 34″

8 A zone of sand and scrub vegetation. Low tide creates shallows.

24° 47′ 45″, 112° 18′ 23″

9 **Cabo San Lázaro**. If a group were adventurous enough to come down the outside of Isla Magdalena, this rugged headland is the end of the long northern beach and the top of a 5-mile leg around steep, mountainous terrain.

24° 44′ 56″, 112° 15′ 37″

10 **Punta Hughes**. There is a commercial surf camp near here. Surfers come for a point break fed off the south swell in summer. Fresh water may be available in an emergency.

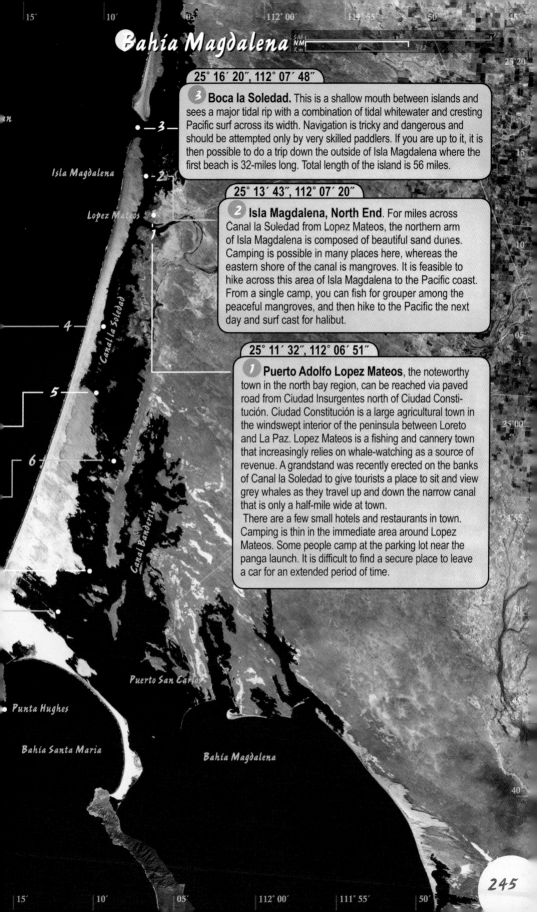

Bahía Magdalena

25° 16′ 20″, 112° 07′ 48″

3 Boca la Soledad. This is a shallow mouth between islands and sees a major tidal rip with a combination of tidal whitewater and cresting Pacific surf across its width. Navigation is tricky and dangerous and should be attempted only by very skilled paddlers. If you are up to it, it is then possible to do a trip down the outside of Isla Magdalena where the first beach is 32-miles long. Total length of the island is 56 miles.

25° 13′ 43″, 112° 07′ 20″

2 Isla Magdalena, North End. For miles across Canal la Soledad from Lopez Mateos, the northern arm of Isla Magdalena is composed of beautiful sand dunes. Camping is possible in many places here, whereas the eastern shore of the canal is mangroves. It is feasible to hike across this area of Isla Magdalena to the Pacific coast. From a single camp, you can fish for grouper among the peaceful mangroves, and then hike to the Pacific the next day and surf cast for halibut.

25° 11′ 32″, 112° 06′ 51″

1 Puerto Adolfo Lopez Mateos, the noteworthy town in the north bay region, can be reached via paved road from Ciudad Insurgentes north of Ciudad Constitución. Ciudad Constitución is a large agricultural town in the windswept interior of the peninsula between Loreto and La Paz. Lopez Mateos is a fishing and cannery town that increasingly relies on whale-watching as a source of revenue. A grandstand was recently erected on the banks of Canal la Soledad to give tourists a place to sit and view grey whales as they travel up and down the narrow canal that is only a half-mile wide at town.

There are a few small hotels and restaurants in town. Camping is thin in the immediate area around Lopez Mateos. Some people camp at the parking lot near the panga launch. It is difficult to find a secure place to leave a car for an extended period of time.

Isla Magdalena

Lopez Mateos

Canal la Soledad

Canal Banderita

Puerto San Carlos

Punta Hughes

Bahía Santa Maria

Bahía Magdalena

245

24° 46′ 51″, 112° 06′ 17″

11   Built on an island, **Puerto San Carlos** is a pleasant enough fishing town that has all the amenities you'll need to see a kayak trip off. Tourism is increasing every year as the whale-watching business picks up. Town has a more authentic feel to it before and after whale-watching season. There is a marine biology institute here, a cannery, a large modern pier, and a fuel storage facility/power plant north of town.

Coming into town on the paved road from Ciudad Constitución, there are a few car-camp spots available north of the road just before things get busy. The heart of downtown has one primary street and a couple of secondary streets, and the eastern side is a cluster of small homes. Nice hotels are the Brennan and the Alcatraz. More affordable but sufficient is the Palmar. Secure car storage is available at the Hotel Brennan if you stay there. The Palmar can also store a car. There is a great little supermarket in town, Falayma, which is full of staples and has a good selection of fresh fruit and veggies. There is purified water in town, though the artesian water from hoses seems to be fine.

There is a small assortment of restaurants: Loncheria La Pasadita is good and cheap for breakfast or lunch, Los Arcos has a variety of seafood at dinner, and the Hotel Alcatraz has an eclectic patio/courtyard with a happening dinner restaurant adjoining it.

For shuttle purposes, hitching is relatively easy in this part of the world, though it seems there are more undesirable types cruising around every year. There is also a scheduled bus twice daily between San Carlos and Ciudad Constitución.

24° 44′ 17″, 112° 08′ 23″

12   This thin south-central arm of Isla Magdalena is an easily-landed beach backed by white sand dunes stretching north and south. It is a short hike over to the Pacific and Bahía Santa Maria. Though the dunes are a lovely place to camp, when the wind blows, sand in the air becomes a major nuisance. Low tide presents a wide sand flat and loading complications.

24° 38′ 08″, 112° 08′ 19″

13   **Puerto Magdalena.** This fishing village is a temporary anchorage for yachts cruising the west coast of Baja and seeking respite from traveling the exposed Pacific leg between San Diego and Cabo San Lucas. There is fresh water available here.

This is a mountainous part of the island, but just before the hills rise up, north of the village and south of a corner of mangroves, there is a road that crosses the island. There is a shuttle run across this road to ferry fishermen and pangas to Bahía Santa Maria. It is possible to have kayaks driven across here, making boating the Pacific and a partial circumnavigation of the island a realistic and worthy trip to consider.

24° 35′ 10″, 112° 04′ 23″

14   **Punta Belcher.** South of Puerto Magdalena, there are a couple of gravel camp possibilities leading up to this point. They aren't great but they don't have the low tide issues of the sand dune camps. Unfortunately, trash washes up on almost all of these inside beaches; mostly in the form of brightly colored oil containers that the fishermen use while out on the water and then promptly discard overboard. This point has an old pier on it and also a permanent fish camp. There is camping on the south side of the point down from the fish camp.

24° 32′ 20″, 112° 03′ 20″

15   **Punta Estrada.** Inside of this point there is a cove with a small beach with three houses on the hillside above it. Pacific swell is starting to be an issue here.

Canal de Navegación. This is the deepwater entrance into Bahía Magdalena. It is also a fish magnet. The 3 ½ -mile wide canal is abundant with wildlife. You'll see fish, sea lions chasing fish, porpoises chasing fish, and pelicans and sea gulls chasing fish all at the same time. With the added dimension of being on the Pacific, this an invigorating place.

Bahía Magdalena

SM
NM
Km

Canal Banderitas

11 — Puerto San Carlos

12

ria

13 — Puerto Magdalena

Bahía Magdalena

14 — Punta Belcher

Punta Estrada

15 — Canal de Navigación

Punta Redonda

Pacific Ocean

Isla Margarita

Bahía las Almejas

Punta Tosca

Map inset

1. Hotel Alcatraz
2. Hotel Brennan
3. Rest. La Pasadita
4. Rest. Los Arcos
5. Hardware store
6. Mini Super Falayma
7. Agua Purificada
8. Hotel Palmar
9. School
10. Cannery
11. Marine Biology School

La Paz
Chametla
Mexico
Pier
Juarez
Morelos

Puerto San Carlos

Panga Launch

Paddling among the mangroves, Photo by: Gordon Taylor

Isla Margarita is a hilly island on its north and south ends but there is a lowland area in the middle. The outside of the lowland is a long, heavenly beach with a graduated surf break in front of it. There is a marine (military) base on the inside of this lowland at Puerto Cortés. I camped on the Pacific beach west of Puerto Cortés and was woken up in the middle of the night by a marine patrol. They were concerned about drug running, and questioned me for a while. Letting me off the hook for that, they told me the whole island is reserved for the military. Fishermen have told me that is not so. In any case, to avoid running into a patrol, camping at the southern end of the large beach on the outside affords you greater privacy.

24° 30´ 57˝, 112° 00´ 25˝

16 Punta Redonda. Light nearby. There are small landing beaches on each side of this magnificent, steep point, though these are swell-dependant and should be looked at carefully before you make an attempt on either one of them.

24° 31´ 19˝, 111° 58´ 52˝

17 A gravel beach safely inside of the point. Camp is small and partially wind-protected, and would be nice except for trash. There is another small beach with a camp one mile south of from here.

24° 28´ 51˝, 111° 56´ 10˝

18 A nice ocean beach enclosed by tall hills. The break is manageable if the swell is coming from the south.

24° 28´ 16˝, 111° 55´ 26˝

19 A cove protected from winter north swell, but not summer south swell.

24° 26´ 13˝, 111° 52´ 08˝

20 Big Beach. This is the north end of an 11-mile long beach. It is 1 ½ miles wide for much of it. The break is gradual. It is a magnificent place with a stunning backdrop of twin peaks to the south. Unfortunately, it is road-accessed to the marine base at Puerto Cortés on the east coast, and occasionally there are people in military uniforms with guns walking around.

24° 21´ 47˝, 111° 46´ 03˝

21 South End, Big Beach. This end of the beach sees no military activity because of some hills that separate it from its greater northern half. There is a sea lion colony living not far south of here, and some of them come up to feed and surf on the waves of this beach.

24° 18´ 10˝, 111° 42´ 38˝

22 Punta Tosca. Lighthouse. With south swell, rounding this point is straightforward. There is a shipwreck in 50 feet of water just off the point.

Having fun on the Pacific on a layover day

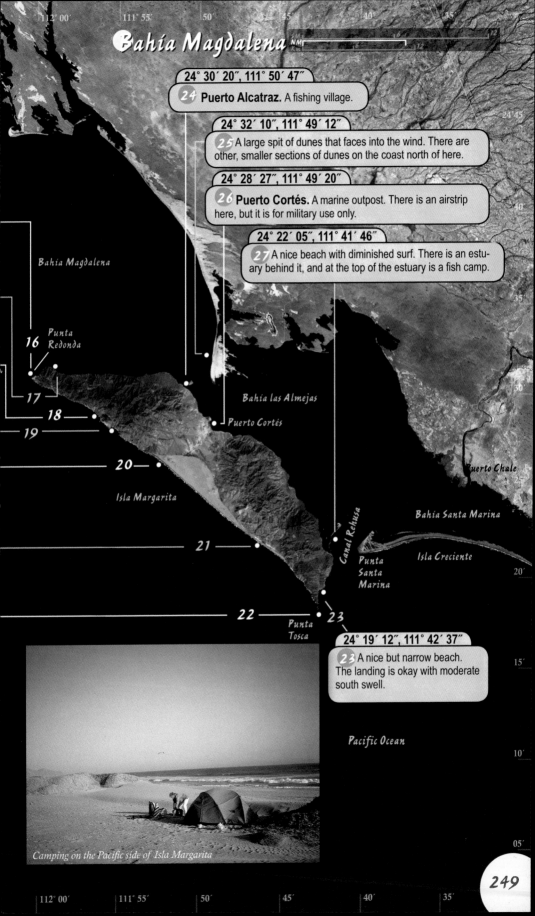

24° 30′ 20″, 111° 50′ 47″

24 **Puerto Alcatraz.** A fishing village.

24° 32′ 10″, 111° 49′ 12″

25 A large spit of dunes that faces into the wind. There are other, smaller sections of dunes on the coast north of here.

24° 28′ 27″, 111° 49′ 20″

26 **Puerto Cortés.** A marine outpost. There is an airstrip here, but it is for military use only.

24° 22′ 05″, 111° 41′ 46″

27 A nice beach with diminished surf. There is an estuary behind it, and at the top of the estuary is a fish camp.

24° 19′ 12″, 111° 42′ 37″

23 A nice but narrow beach. The landing is okay with moderate south swell.

Bahía Magdalena

Punta Redonda

16

17

18

19

20

21

22

23

Isla Margarita

Bahía las Almejas

Puerto Cortés

Canal Rehusa

Punta Santa Marina

Bahía Santa Marina

Isla Creciente

Puerto Chale

Punta Tosca

Pacific Ocean

Camping on the Pacific side of Isla Margarita

249

112° 20′   15′   10′   05′   112° 00′   111° 55′

24°45′

40′

35′

30′

25′

20′

15′

10′

05′

24° 00′

Northwest coast of Isla Margarita

Canal Rehusa. This is a hallucinogenic place. The canal is shallow, as it is basically an extension of the low Isla Creciente to the south. This causes south swell to break miles out from shore. When the break and the tidal currents collide, there are large standing waves appearing in random locations, coming from seemingly nowhere but lasting for quite some time. There is often a circular race of whitewater in the middle of all this. A channel of calm water between this outer break and the shore break hitting Isla Margarita creates a route of navigation between Punta Tosca and Bahía las Almejas. A paddle in or out of the canal should be timed to the tides, as they really flow here.

Big Beach, Isla Margarita

Big Beach sand dunes

Bahía las Almejas is a very shallow bay loaded with scallops, clams (almejas), and a tasty blue-gray crab.

rtés

Bahía las Almejas

Puerto Chale

30

Bahía Santa Marina

Canal Rehusa

Punta Santa Marina **28**

Isla Creciente **29**

Punta Tosca

Pacific Ocean

24° 22′ 30″, 111° 39′ 05″

28 A camp on the inside of the low-lying Isla Creciente. It is the only camp in the area from which you can get out of the north wind, and that is done by tucking in close to mangroves, which cover much of this inside coast. Among the island's mangroves there are a few canals you can explore.

24° 24′ 17″, 111° 33′ 34″

29 The entrance to the canal that leads to Puerto Chale. From out on the bay it is easy to choose the wrong canal and get dead-ended.

24° 25′ 16″, 111° 33′ 08″

30 Puerto Chale. This is a dusty little fishing village of good people. There is a large shrimp farm across from it. There are a couple of stores, both very small but with enough commodities to get by. There is water for sale, and cold beer. The ride in from the highway is on dirt and not too long, but there can be washboards, making it seem longer. There are a couple of super-pangas in town—one owned by a good go-to guy named Jesús—that have shuttle capability. Jesús' casa is under the one pine tree in town. It is possible to camp at the south end of town.

Fishing in

Southwest coast of Isla Ángel de la Guarda, Photo by: Lori Russell

Baja

It's world famous. If you want to supply your camp with fresh food, the selection of edible fish offshore of Baja is incredible: tuna, dorado, wahoo, yellowtail, grouper, snapper, corvina, triggerfish… just to name a few. Non-Mexicans cannot take mollusks, or crustaceans (read: lobsters). If you are fishing from land in Baja, you do not need a license, if you are fishing from your kayak or spearfishing, you do need one. Additionally, if you fish from a kayak in Mexico, your boat must be permitted, which is a form of registration. If you do not fish from your kayak, it does not have to be permitted. These are the rules, but how they are enforced and where is a somewhat different story.

Kayak permitting for fishermen in the Sea of Cortez among private boaters in Baja seems to be a southern thing as opposed to a northern thing. Areas around La Paz and to the south are starting to see some enforcement of the registration rule, though most privately owned kayaks you see down there are still not registered. The farther north you go, the less registered kayaks there are, unless you are talking about the north Pacific Coast above Ensenada, where fishing the kelp beds for calico bass has gotten quite popular. So enforcement of the registration rules is spotty as far as kayaks go, but… if you ran into the wrong situation, if you met a really stubborn and pissed-off official that you couldn't bribe, technically your boat could be confiscated if it had fishing gear or fish on it and it wasn't permitted.

To play by the rules, licenses and boat permits can be obtained in Baja sea towns at government (oficina de pesca) harbor offices or near a migración office. An easy way to get the proper paperwork if you are not in Mexico is to do it before your trip via the Mexican government's CONAPESCA (Comisión Nacional de Acuacultura y Pesca) office in San Diego, CA. You can download an application form from their website at www.conapescasandiego.org or write, call, or fax them at:

CONAPESCA
Oficina de Pesca
2550 Fifth Ave. Suite 15
San Diego, CA 92103

Tel: 619-233-4324
Fax: 619-233-0344

Pricing is about $25 to $45 for a fishing license and a permit for a kayak costs $33. Mexican fishing licenses and boat permits can also be obtained from some San Diego area tackle shops.

Isla San José arroyo hike

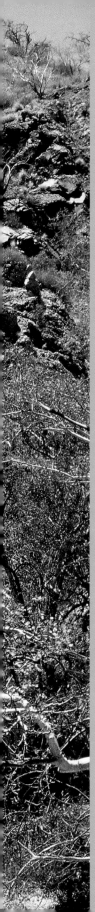

Hiking In Baja

If you have planned some layover time in your trip, or you are laid over by winds, you will certainly enjoy a hike from many of the camps, and a chance to stretch your boat-bound legs. Some hikes are easy and could be managed with flip flops on well traveled trails, but many are fairly rugged, with steep, loose scree and rough lava rock with no marked trail and always the threat of thorny cactus. A decent pair of shoes is advised for the stouter hikes.

Some of the terrain of Baja is easy-going, like the sandy floors of long, twisting arroyos. But much of the land is rugged and harsh, with a feeling of "other-planetness" about it. You will see a desert landscape with plants and geology unlike any other; an ecosystem that has evolved on less than four inches of rain a year, and yet supports a vast variety of animals and plants. You will see mountain ranges that rise 4000 feet out of the ocean with pinnacles and sheer cliffs of interlaced colors of desert sandstone and granite, broken open by flows of basaltic lava, frozen in its tracks where it meets the sea.

If you arrive in Baja following a rain event, like a tropical storm, you will see the desert bloom into a velvety carpet of green. Every patch of earth, even the rocks themselves, seem to sprout a variety of herbs that lend a green hue to the otherwise barren, sun-baked rocks. You may even call it lush. The variety of vegetation is astounding and marvelous, with hundreds of species of cactus and drought-tolerant trees and shrubs. It is often too dense and too prickly to hike through. A virtual cactus jungle. Bring a good plant guide ("Baja Calilfornia Plant Field Guide"). And the sun in winter months is often pleasant, but closer to summer, it is unforgiving. Hike in the mornings or evenings, wear sun protection, and bring water.

The views from any high point that you reach will amply reward your efforts. You will see sculpted mountainscapes receding into layers of blue overlapping blue, falling into the sea; swirls of wind and current on the water's surface across an infinite horizon. And you may see some whales offshore, passing by. Bring a pair of binoculars. And, oh! don't forget the camera.

– Lori Russell

Driving in Baja

A long road trip is often a burden, particularly when you're driving through strange and massive urban areas (Los Angeles and San Diego) and then accessing the zone of the world's busiest border crossing (Tijuana) and, completing that crossing, entering what by many people's standards is a disorganized country (Mexico). And yet as many times as I have made this journey, which is often, the trip has been enjoyable more times than not. If you've got the time, driving to Baja can be quite pleasurable.

This is not to say I have not encountered problems, but most of them can be blamed on the vintage cars I used for the trip—a lost engine, a lost transmission, a blown radiator fan, a dislodging of the exhaust system, to name my memorable breakdowns. Even in the event of a mishap, somehow it all works out. Enjoy the views of fascinating landscapes, the taste of a cold Pacifico beer (if you're the passenger), and the sounds of great music that seems enhanced in such a distant environment while you feel the peace of the wheels rolling underneath. To me, the vacation starts as soon as I am past Tijuana driving on the bluffs high above the glorious Pacific Ocean. I am in a different world, and it is exciting. Soon to come is the Sea of Cortez, where I feel comfortable and can be myself.

But let's get practical here. Driving in Baja can be as much of an adventure as the kayaking that you're getting down there to do. Of all the crossing towns at the top of the peninsula, the story will focus on going south through Tijuana. But first let me give a quick mention to some of the other towns: If I had to choose one at which to cross, if it

weren't out of the way, it would be Tecate. This small town is mellow, the guards at the border are personable, and it hooks up to Mexico Highway 1 with a modern road. I have crossed at Mexicali a number of times, and it is always easy; the only problems I've encountered were on the return trip north, as it is easy to miss the exits to the border on the highway. Soon there will be a new through-road in Mexicali that will make the north crossing easier. Mexicali is a mid-sized city compared to Tijuana. Yuma, Arizona, is a small crossing where generally you get across easily. Finding your way through the Colorado River delta towns to get to the peninsula takes a little bit of navigation, but works. A word of note to travelers heading down Mexico Highway 5 to access the coast road at San Felipe: that road is fast traveling until about 30 kilometers south of San Felipe, and after that it has a lot of small vados (washes) across it that will send your car flying if you are speeding. From Puertecitos to Mexico Hwy 1 via Bahía Gonzaga, the road is dirt with washboards and sharp rocks. People who choose to drive this road at high speeds should be stocked with multiple spare tires.

Now back to the San Diego-Tijuana route. You might want to camp somewhere around San Diego the night before you cross the border. There are a number of nice California State Parks along the coast leading up to the Border; however, these are inland from the Interstates, and will take extra time to deviate to. The most practical place to camp before a San Diego area border crossing is at Campland on the Bay on the north end of Mission Bay in north

San Diego. Unfortunately, it is not cheap. The community of Mission Beach has a low rise skyline and has good and funky restaurants; kayak, fishing, and dive shops; and a promenade in front of the ocean beaches. Campland on the Bay's website is www.campland.com.

Attempting to drive through San Diego, it is best to avoid rush hours. Southern California metro traffic is not pretty. Below San Diego, the U.S. Interstates end at the small town of San Ysidro. There is a chance to avoid the San Ysidro/Tijuana main crossing and deflect to an alternate crossing east at Otay Mesa if there is traffic at the main border. It is not as convenient, but it is less crowded. Its hours of operation are 6 a.m. to 10 p.m. The hotline number to check on border wait times at San Ysidro is 619-690-8999; and for Otay Mesa 619-671-8999. Locals who cross the border frequently slightly prefer the San Ysidro crossing, all things considered.

To buy pesos and get Mexican car insurance, you want to exit the highway in San Ysidro (even if you have decided to go to Otay Mesa). To exchange dollars for pesos, shop for the best rate on the billboards in front of the shops and look for one that does not charge commission. San Ysidro almost always has the best dollar/peso exchange rate of anywhere on the peninsula. Mexican car insurance is a must. Your U.S. policy won't cover you in Mexico and if you are in an accident, you may be arrested if you cannot provide proof of insurance or pay the damages on the spot. Mexican car insurance costs about the same wherever you buy it. You can get car insurance at a drive up window in San Ysidro, or you can get it in advance via websites such as www. Mexbound.com or www.Bajabound.com.

Hitting the Border

I still get a little nervous when I approach this thing, even though I have it down good enough now where the crossing is relatively painless. Know this: if you are going further south than Ensenada, you will need a tourist card, which is a visa of sorts. I am rarely asked for mine when in Baja, but if you don't have one, you might have a more complicated time leaving Mexico. To get a tourist card, you want to be in the far right hand lane as you approach the border. This is the lane for declaring items, and it's not that you want to declare anything or get your car looked over by the Mexican police, it's just that this is the lane that leads to where you get a tourist card. By coincidence, it has the least traffic and you will not get searched if you pull over, park, and walk straight to the Migración office, which is located in a low building to the right of the Declarations parking area. You will need a passport, and $20 U.S. The officer will have you fill out a simple form and direct you to a bank next door that handles the money; you will then go back to Migración to get your card stamped. Going to the bank and not being able to give money directly to Mexican government officials is a quirk you'll encounter when you try to purchase things like fishing licenses, Marine Park permits in Loreto, and other "official" types of purchases. It is to prevent graft.

Once you cross over the border into Tijuana, I don't recommend taking time out to explore the city. Tijuana is riddled with crime, particularly at dark. For normal, apprehensive, I-feel-safer-in-the-country kayaker types, get the heck out of that place directly by following the signs to Ensenada. Follow the signs closely. There are a few

quick exits to make that come immediately after the border, and traffic is of the typical big city, me-first rush variety. Do not take the Libre (free) road south. Take the Cuota (toll) road, as it is much faster. Obey the speed laws in Tijuana and remember that speed limits are in kilometers. If you stay near the limit, you will be the slowest car on the road and an embarrassment to yourself. But if you go over the limit, you are a target for corrupt traffic cops, who may pull you over and ask for cash to get you off the hook, which doesn't happen a lot, but can happen. Don't give the Tijuana cops an excuse to pull you over. You can start breathing easier and increase your speed when you are outside the city limits.

A word about Baja police: I have encountered a few, and find them to be reasonable people for the most part, but there are some bad apples. Things are different in Mexico than in the United States. If you are caught in Mexico breaking a law (such as speeding, running a stop sign, or going the wrong way on a one way street) and you are pulled over, payment in cash is expected on the spot. If you think the price is too high, bargain. But you should pay the cop. You broke the law, so don't cry about what a corrupt system it is. At least your

name doesn't go into a computer, and your insurance company will never find out. But if you didn't break the law, and feel the bust is bogus, challenge the guy. This bad bust is called "La Mordita," the snakebite. If you know you are being targeted unfairly, start to put pressure on the cop. Ask him what his name is; write it down. If he says you'll have to go to the station if you refuse to pay, call his bluff. It is doubtful he will take you in.

South of Tijuana is the beautiful ocean. You can enjoy the views until Ensenada. If you crossed the border late in the day, there is a good, oceanside campground on the bluffs before Ensenada at km 94 called Playa Saldamunda. There is a quick turn into the campground, which is rimmed by small white stones.

Ensenada is getting to be a big town. There are two ways through it. One is to bear left on approach to town and go around the backside of downtown on a bypass route. This route is really not any faster than turning right at the north of town and going closer to the water and into downtown. Central Ensenada is modern, and the roads are good. If you stop to eat in Ensenada, make sure you can see your car from the restaurant. Don't leave it and all your gear out on the street while you go into Husong's

narrow one. Your biggest causes for concern are tractor trailers cutting corners on hilly curves. The truck drivers are skilled, though they are overworked and their trucks are too long for some of the turn radiuses.

It is wise to be cautious about them, but I think livestock and animals on the road are an overrated danger. I find there is a greater problem in the western United States with deer and elk on the road. Though I do not recommend it, I have driven many miles in Baja at night. The only mishap occurred when I was riding in the front seat of a bus, drinking rotgut tequila with the off-duty driver (they pair up for long routes), when we hit a cow square on. It was there in the headlights one instant, then there were a couple of bumps, and then it was smooth sailing again.

With the pressure off after getting through the border and past the two big towns, you can settle back into the heart of the drive and start to ruminate as you gaze across the vast horizons. Hopefully, there won't be too much trash littering the landscape to disturb your thoughts. A plastic bag stuck on a cactus is the Mexican national flower. The country south of Ensenada is hilly. It is wine and olive country. There is a good campground in Santo Tomas. Camping is under olive trees. There is a restaurant across the street where you can sample some of the local wines.

The next stretch of road to San Quintin sometimes experiences heavy fog due to its proximity to the Pacific. San Quintin is busier every year but is still of manageable size. Somewhere about halfway through town on the east side of the main street you'll see a big green colored building that's a supermarket. I start to stock up here if I am boating up north. For my trips, I tend not to buy much food in the United States except specialty items. I like to shop Mexican for the atmosphere, the price, and the availability of cheap produce, of which I stuff my boat with a hearty dose. If you're hungry when you get to San Quintin, the roadside stands that sell seafood cocktails are to die for. Don't let the appearance of the beat up, dusty town fool you. The seafood cocktails here are as fresh and hearty as they get anywhere.

South of San Quintin, turning west at km 16 or 17 there is a great, though sometimes windy, campground on the Pacific called El Pabellon. You camp on an endless beach, and could take your boat out into the crashing waves if you're feeling up to the challenge of a surf launch in the ocean. The proprietor of the campground can procure you lobsters at a reasonable price if you tell him in advance.

Some 10 kilometers or so north of El Rosario you can pull off the road at free camp spots

Cantina to do shots. If your car is still there when you return, there won't be anything left in it or on it. If you get a motel in Ensenada, make sure it has gated parking. (If you didn't get your tourist card in Tijuana, there is a Migración office near the harbormaster at the downtown waterfront.)

On the south end of Ensenada there are many stalls along the highway that sell tamales. These are good places to store up on snacks. There is also locally grown olives and olive oil sold here, though these products are not as cheap as you might expect. If you are heading east from Ensenada, the road across the peninsula to San Felipe is good.

Continuing south on Highway 1, you will soon encounter either your first or second military checkpoint. You don't have to hide the beer, but you do have to hide the drugs. Just kidding. These checkpoints are strange. There are five or six if you go all the way to Cabo. They disturb some people but rarely present problems. Many times you are flagged through, but if you are stopped, do what they say. Do not try to bribe military people. They are looking for guns going south (it is illegal for a gringo to have a firearm in Mexico) and drugs going north.

From here south, the journey becomes more relaxing. Highway 1 is a good road, albeit a overlooking the Pacific; this is a good place to get that sunset fix. Though it is beautiful ocean, I have seen some nasty current pools off this shore. I would think twice about boating or swimming here. Coming down the hill into El Rosario, there is a Pemex station, as well as a great restaurant, Mama Espinosa's, just before the turn east. In the second half of town there is a small but okay store on the north side of the road to restock on beer, ice, avocados, and tortillas. You're all set for the next leg.

Leaving El Rosario, there is a bridge over a vast wash. In the fall, the floor of this wash is sometimes covered with the area's huge crop of red chilies drying in the sun. From here, Highway 1 heads up into the interior of the peninsula. A long climb puts you into beautiful desert country. Cacti and plants of many varieties, including the very tall Boojum Tree, grow alongside the road. Hills and ancient volcanoes spread out on the horizon, and piles and formations of pink granite rocks are everywhere. The outpost of Cataviña is in the center of this zone and is home to the somewhat-pricey Hotel La Pinta, a state run hotel with clean rooms and good food. They installed gas pumps near La Pinta a few years ago, but they were closed down almost as soon as they opened because the operators were running away with the cash. Because of the lack of gas in Cataviña, it is a good idea to have a full tank of gas before leaving El Rosario. Just down the road from La Pinta you can turn to the east to Rancho Santa Ynez, an interesting place to stay with bunk rooms and a restaurant. Camping in the area north and south of Cataviña is possible on dirt side roads. If you do camp, it is a good idea to get away from the road so the sound of trucks at night don't keep you up, and also so no undesirable strangers happen into your camp.

Below Cataviña is the dry lake of Laguna Chapala. Once in my travels, after a tropical storm had moved through, there was enough water in the lake to kayak. At the north end of Chapala there is a dirt road to Coco's Corner and Bahía Gonzaga. If you are ever traveling down that way, pull into Coco's and sign his visitor register. The beer-can architecture along the fences and wires around his compound can't be missed. The fridge is always stocked with Pacifico, and Coco is always welcoming. He is gruff and gregarious and hopefully will be around longer, though his health problems were mounting last I visited. If you are a girl, or have a girlfriend along, bring a set of wild panties to donate to his collection that hang from the roof of the shack. My girlfriend once asked him if there was anything that we could bring him from the north the next time we came down, and his grizzled reply was, "Well, I'm partial to white meat, if you know what I mean…"

South of Chapala and then some is the turn to Bahía de los Ángeles. The road down there is excellent and fast. A billboard of a girl in a bikini swimming marks it. I've been tempted to get up there and paint a shark fin in the water behind the girl á la "Jaws." If you are driving to L.A. Bay and have extra time, there is a turn in the desert (28 59 05, 113 44 20) up a wash and then another left turn that leads to an area of prehistoric cave paintings (28 54 44, 113 43 14). The road is not bad, but is sandy in places. The area is also a great one to camp in if you want a night of desert silence before you hit the sea.

Next stop is the border crossing between Baja Norte and Baja Sur, marked by one of the largest flags you'll ever see. You may

Coco's Corner

be asked for your tourist card here, and the undercarriage of your car will likely be sprayed with pesticide so you don't carry any invasive species into the agricultural area farther south. Just past the border is Guerrero Negro.

Guerrero is a town built up because of the massive evaporative salt mining operation there. It took me the longest time to feel comfortable in this flat and bland looking town. It is often chilly and foggy with a cloudbank coming in off the Pacific. But after finding some good restaurants and getting to know the people better, I now feel at ease stopping there. For finer, inside dining, try the Malarrimo on the east end of town, north side. It is a motel and also allows camping behind it. Our favorite place, if it is open and the weather is nice, is Mariscos Tony's, a little blue stand on the north side of the road two blocks west of the orange water tower. Tony's ceviche cannot be beat, anywhere. The waters offshore of Guerrero Negro are harvested for the largest and most tender scallops in the world. The Loncheria el Pasajero, a small red and white building 1½ blocks west of the Malarrimo, offers very simple but hearty breakfasts and lunches. They make their own corn tortillas to order and have fresh stew daily.

The highway leaves the Pacific coast at Guerrero Negro and cuts across the peninsula to the Sea of Cortez. Not too farther east is a turn to San Francisquito, the launch point for trips in the Midriff area of the sea. The washboards on this side road bring up the nagging Baja back road question, "Do I drive slow, to avoid flat tires or breaking my car; or do I speed up, because speed smooths out the washboards and I can't handle driving at a snail's pace?" It is the constant dilemma. I've done it both ways—driving fast like an obsessed Baja 1000'er, and going slow while slowly going mad. Do you feel good about the strength of your car or your roof rack? Do you

have the fortitude to handle a breakdown in the desert where it might take a couple of days to get help and do the repair? Or, conversely, can you handle the mental challenge of driving at an 18th century pace in a 21st century vehicle? I can only say that more times than not, I take the slow approach. "Pass me over another cerveza now, please."

Back on the highway, before you hit the coast and get your first view of the Sea of Cortez at Santa Rosalia, there is one more town that makes a nice stop. This is San Ignacio. San Ignacio is a small village in the heart of the volcanic desert set in a cleft in the desert floor amidst an unlikely oasis of palm trees. A spring starting west of town and flowing east a short ways before it disappears back underground creates a lagoon surrounded by thick groves of date palms. Crossing the lagoon and winding through the palms puts you at the downtown plaza of San Ignacio. The preeminent building on the west side of the shady plaza is a mission constructed in the 1600's. Should you be hungry, there is a good restaurant off the southeast corner of the plaza called Rene's. Before the plaza is Restaurante El Padrino, behind which is a campground. There is also a La Pinta hotel across from El Padrino.

The last leg of the drive before reaching the sea takes you past the Tres Virgenes, a series of dormant volcanoes. The one closest to the highway is a steep, towering cone of 6,500' in height. It is a magnificent view.

Most of the other towns encountered in the drive to Los Cabos are described in the body of the book where they fall in a north to south journey along the shore. Each has its own, distinct personality. Between them are periods of coast and awesome sea views, or hilly desert, where a sense of vastness humbles the traveler.

261

Flying into Baja

Colorado delta area, Photo by: Charles Jackson

It is often not convenient or possible to drive into Baja; work, family schedules, or distance preclude the possibility of taking the time to drive. For those needing to get to the peninsula quicker than a car will take them, there are a number of airports in key sea kayaking locations that are accessible by commercial airlines and other carriers. (If you had access to a small private aircraft that could carry boats, then you'd really be golden, as there are a multitude of dirt airstrips in Baja.) The commercial airports favor the southern half of the peninsula. Unfortunately or fortunately (depending on how you look at it), the wild north is still difficult to get to.

The biggest airport near sea kayaking country in Baja is at Los Cabos. Situated north of Cabo San José, the Los Cabos airport is also less than three hours drive from La Paz. Cabo has more international flights and more direct connections to U.S. cities than any of the other sea kayaking airports. Because of the high volume of vacationers that seek out the sun and beautiful beaches of the Los Cabos area, flights to there are less expensive than to other Baja airports. So it is easier and cheaper to get to Los Cabos, but Los Cabos is the southernmost access point in Baja, limiting its practicality for those wishing to boat in the central Sea of Cortez.

The next biggest airport and one that is closer to prime Baja sea kayaking country is the La Paz airport. La Paz is a town of 350,000 or so, and the airport is still relatively laid back. Though it is closer to the United States than Cabo, flights are more expensive to La Paz. Flights to La Paz often connect through larger Mexican cities on the mainland. But flying into La Paz is very convenient if you want to boat Isla San José, Isla Espíritu Santo, Isla Cerralvo, or "Loreto to La Paz," and it is also not too far from Bahía Magdalena.

Loreto, in south central Baja, has an airport with international service, but the only direct flights to the United States are through Los Angeles or San Diego, and these are on a limited schedule. However, there are connections to other western U.S. cities via Hermosillo on the mainland. Loreto is an access point to many of the south central Baja legs and islands described in this book, and is about three hours from Bahía Magdalena on the Pacific.

Another town that bears mention as a Baja sea kayaking air portal is Guerrero Negro, which is located on the border of north and south Baja. Guerrero is on the west coast, but it is not too long of a drive from there to Bahía de los Ángeles. It is also just above Laguna San Ignacio, a famous grey whale haven.

Ground Transportation

After landing in Mexico and going through customs, the next step is getting to your launch town from the airport. Many commercial outfitters pick you up at the airport if it is near their operation, so that makes that easy. If you're not getting picked up with an arranged ride, you can either rent a car; take a hotel shuttle service; take a taxi; or hire a *collectivo*, which is a limousine taxi that offers flat rates per customer but makes multiple stops along the way (it's a lot cheaper than a regular taxi if you are traveling with a very small group). Collectivos are usually vans or mini-vans. If you land at Los Cabos, taxi people and other car services trying to hustle your business before you get out the door of the airport will assault you. Other Baja airports are mellower in this respect. If you're going the taxi/collectivo route, brush past the hustlers and go outside the airport and see if you can hire a collectivo or a taxi with the right configuration for your gear. Talk to the driver and ask him his rates. You might be able to hire the ride you want right off the curb, or you might have to go through a middle man to call up the car for you, but try to get him to call up the car and driver that you prefer.

Taxis and collectivos in general are great ways to get around. You can use taxis for shopping trips if you're boating from town to town, or you can set up your own shuttle with one. Getting a taxi to drive you from town to your launch site should be no problem, but setting a future date to be picked up is sketchy unless you really trust your driver. They just forget, or get busy doing something else, or might not properly understand you when you try to set a specific time and day for the pick-up.

The most affordable way to get to La Paz from Los Cabos is by bus. There are buses about every three hours between the two towns. Take a taxi or collectivo to the bus station. Also, if you are a private group, you can use buses for other legs mentioned in this book, particularly "Mulegé to Loreto" and "Loreto to La Paz." Though there are no buses to Bahía de los Ángeles, you can easily hitch in or out of that town, connecting to the bus route at the intersection out on Highway 1. There are two or three buses a day up north. Buses cannot handle full length kayaks.

Freshman class arrivals at Los Cabos Airport

Baja is user-friendly for the non-Spanish speaking gringo. In most areas of the peninsula English is spoken at least a little and usually understood. If you are from the United States, chances are that you know some Spanish already. It is hard not to have picked up some of the language even if you have never been south of the border. "Yo quiero Taco Bell!" If not, well then it's "Hasta la vista, baby." Also, many Baja Mexicans have spent time in the U.S. and learned some English.

Americans coming down to Mexico and requiring services have given reason for many Mexicans to learn English. English is the language of money. In Los Cabos, people do not get hired for a job on the front lines of the tourist industry without being able to speak English. As well, most restaurants throughout the peninsula have menus printed in both languages.

However, English is not understood universally in Baja, and there are times you will need some command of the Spanish language. Chances are, the more rural you go, the less English will be spoken. If you need to arrange a shuttle with a fisherman, if you are shopping in a small town, or if you need directions, it is good to know some Spanish. What's more, if you start a conversation in Spanish, the person you are speaking to will feel more respect for you trying to speak in his tongue. Anything's better than barging into a restaurant, stamping your feet on the ground, and bellowing so the whole room can hear, "Y'all got bacon and eggs in this place?"

A quirk about knowing just a little bit of Spanish is that often, if you start a dialogue in Spanish with a Mexican, and do an okay job at it because those are the few words you know and you've been practicing them a lot, the Mexican's reply might be in rapid fire Spanish because he thinks you understand the language. How those people can speak so fast is a wonder. Of all the key Spanish phrases to know, "Habla mas despacio, por favor" (speak more slowly, please) might be the most important.

An irony about sea kayaking in Baja is that it can be an immersion into true Mexico, but once you are out in the wild places, you don't need any Spanish. The majority of a sea kayaker's time in Mexico will be spent away from Mexicans.

All things considered, it is best to arm yourself with a little knowledge of the Spanish language. Carry and study a pocket phrase book that has a concise dictionary in it. Learn how to conjugate a few of the basic verbs in a tense or two and then substitute some key recurring nouns that you know.

Spanish Lexicon

This is a list of Spanish words that appear frequently in this book:

arena – sand
arroyo – a canyon wash
blanco – white
boca – mouth, as in an inlet
cabaña – a small beach house or hut
candelero – candlestick, usually referring to rock spire formations
Cardón – tall cactus prevalent in Baja
casa – house
casita – small house
ensenada – an inlet, cove, or bay
estero – estuary
faro – light, lighthouse
gasolina blanca – white gas for camp stoves
gringo – "green go" (Marines leave), catchword for "American"
isla – island

islote – small island
lobo – wolf (also sea lion)
malecón – seaside avenue in a town
mar – sea
mercado – store, grocery store
palapa – a palm-thatched, open-sided beach hut
panga – open fishing boat
panguero – fisherman who uses a panga
pila – an elevated water storage container
playa – beach
punta – point
tienda – store
tranquilo – tranquil, peaceful, chill
ventana – window, usually in reference to an arch
viento – wind

Bibliography

Baja Almanac
© Baja Almanac Publishers, Inc
Las Vegas, NV

INEGI topographic maps
Instituto Nacional de
Estadística Geographía e Informática
Mexico City, Mexico
www.inegi.gob.mx

Sea of Cortez Paddle Charts
Ed Gillete and Gerry Cunningham
© 1996 by Cortez Designs, Inc.
Patagonia, AZ

Baja California Plant Field Guide
Norman C. Roberts
© 1989 by Natural History Publishing Co.
La Jolla, CA

*The Complete Cruising Guide to the Middle Gulf
Sea of Cortez*
Gerry Cunningham
© 1994 by Cortez Designs, Inc.
Sahuaro Press
Tucson, AZ

The Baja Catch, 3rd edition
Neil Kelly and Gene Kira
© 1997 by Apples & Oranges Publishers
Valley Center, CA

Google Earth

*Fundamentals of
Kayak Navigation, 3rd edition*
David Burch
© 1999 by The Globe Pequot Press
Guilford, CT

Best Places Baja
Edited by Lori Makabe
© 2003 by Sasquatch Books
Seattle, WA

The Baja Adventure Book
Walt Petersen
© 1992 by Wilderness Press
Berkeley, CA

Adventure Kayaking Baja
Andromeda Romano-Lax
© 2001 by Wilderness Press
Berkeley, CA

*National Audubon Society
The Sibley Guide to Birds*
David Allen Sibley
© 2000 by Chanticleer Press, Inc.
New York, New York

Computer Programs:
 Ozzie Explorer
 Adobe Photoshop, Illustrator, InDesign
 Jasc Paint Shop Pro
 Microsoft Word

La Paz Outfitters and Guide Services

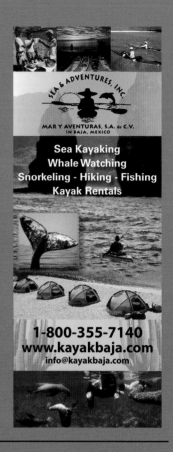
Loreto Outfitters and Guide Services

Also

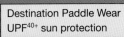

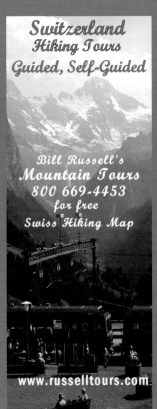

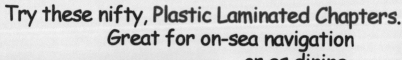

Crossing from the Midriffs, Photo by: Lori Russell

Suggested Trips

Expert Level Trips

(Any trip can become expert when the wrong weather sets in, but these trips require competent self-reliance in wilderness settings and certain skills, such as a roll, before they should be attempted regardless of the conditions.)

Boojum Tree